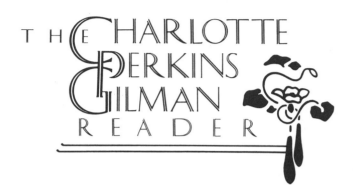

THE **CHARLOTTE PERKINS GILMAN** READER

THE CHARLOTTE PERKINS GILMAN READER

Edited and introduced by

ANN J. LANE

University Press of Virginia
Charlottesville and London

THE UNIVERSITY PRESS OF VIRGINIA

Originally published in 1980 by Pantheon Books, a division of
Random House, Inc., New York.
© 1999 by the Rector and Visitors of the University of Virginia
All rights reserved
Printed in the United States of America

First University Press of Virginia edition published 1999

ISBN 0-8139-1876-6 (paper)

∞The paper used in this publication meets the minimum require-
ments of the American National Standard for Information Sciences—
Permanence of Paper for Printed Library Materials, ANSI
Z39.48-1984.

Library of Congress Cataloging-in-Publication Data

Gilman, Charlotte Perkins, 1860–1935.
The Charlotte Perkins Gilman reader / edited and introduced by
Ann J. Lane.—1st University Press of Virginia ed.
    p. cm.
ISBN 0-8139-1876-6 (pbk. : alk. paper)
    1. Women—Social life and customs—Fiction. I. Lane, Ann J., 1931– .
II. Title.
PS 1744.G57A15 1999
813′.4—dc21   98-53475
                                                            CIP

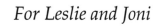

For Leslie and Joni

CONTENTS

Preface to the New Edition

IN 1898 when *Women and Economics: A Study of the Economic Relation between Men and Women as a Factor in Social Evolution* appeared, Charlotte Perkins Gilman achieved instant acclaim and international recognition. Although none of Gilman's subsequent work achieved as much attention as this first book, she enjoyed substantial success for many years as a lecturer, essayist, and critic-at-large. (For an idea of the enormous range of subjects Gilman embraced, the various kinds of publications in which she placed her work, and the assorted genres she used, read Gary Scharnhorst's *Charlotte Perkins Gilman: A Bibliography.*) But as America became increasingly conservative in the post–World War I period, Gilman, along with most radical critics, fell into obscurity.

In 1966 *Women and Economics,* long out of print, suddenly reappeared, in retrospect a harbinger of changes soon to come, with a splendid introduction by the well-known historian, Carl Degler, thus legitimating her return. (Degler's original version of his introduction had appeared as an article in the *American Quarterly* in 1956 under the title "Charlotte Perkins Gilman on the Theory and Practice of Feminism," and in 1960 William Doyle had written his dissertation at the University of California, Berkeley, on the subject "Charlotte Gilman and the Cycle of Feminist Reform," but neither of these works on Gilman created any noticeable response because there was yet no cultural echo.)

In 1970 the women's movement was emerging and that was to make the critical difference, because a new, large, and feminist audience was in the process of creation. In that year Gilman's little-known books *The Home: Its Work and Influence* and *The Man-Made World: or, Our Androcentric Culture* were republished (in the case of the latter, for the first time in book form) by Source Book Press, and while it was good to have them available, they, too, made little impact. Gilman's autobiography, *The Living of Charlotte Perkins Gilman: An Autobiography*, which first appeared in 1935 and sold few copies, was reissued in 1972. In the late 1970s Carol Ruth Berkin published an article, "Private Woman, Public Woman: The Contradictions of Charlotte Perkins Gilman"; Polly Wynn Allen-Robinson wrote a doctoral dissertation, later published in book form, examining Gilman's social ethics; Helen Jo Potts wrote her dissertation on Gilman's humanist approach to feminism; Dolores Hayden read a paper, later published, entitled "Charlotte Perkins Gilman: Domestic Revolution or Domestic Evolution"; and Susan Ware wrote a piece on Gilman's early lectures. Interest in Gilman was clearly developing.

But the current generation rediscovered Gilman not as she had been best known originally—through her essays, books, and articles from an economic-sociological-anthropological perspective—but through the Feminist Press's edition of her originally published 1892 short story "The Yellow Wallpaper," which appeared in 1973, has been in print ever since, and is the Feminist Press's best seller. In 1979 Gilman's now famous but then unknown utopian fantasy, *Herland*, appearing serially in 1915 in Gilman's magazine, the *Forerunner*, was published in book form for the first time with my introduction, and that too has been in print ever since. I was then at the Bunting Institute of

Radcliffe College, immersing myself in Gilman's massive body of work and just beginning to contemplate a future biography.

Gilman's reputation was in the process of taking off for the second time, only now it was for her fiction that she became known to a new generation. In 1980 this collection, a sampling of Gilman's varied fictional writings, was originally published. (This same year saw the publication of Mary A. Hill's biography, *Charlotte Perkins Gilman: The Making of a Radical Feminist, 1860–1896*.)

Would Gilman be perplexed, dismayed, or disappointed that her huge volume of nonfiction work is not the basis of her newly acquired reputation? Certainly not, and for at least two reasons. First, it is not entirely so. Several of her nonfiction works remain in print, including *Women and Economics*, her autobiography, and the seven-volume reprint of her monthly magazine, the *Forerunner*, which appeared first in the years from 1909 to 1916. There is also Larry Ceplair's 1991 edition, *Charlotte Perkins Gilman: A Nonfiction Reader*.

Much more significantly, Gilman wrote fiction for the same reason she wrote everything else and for the same reason she spent years on the lecture circuit. She wrote and she lectured in an effort to convert people to her ideas. She used fiction, for example, to illustrate her deeply held belief that the home and domestic life as currently constructed are the source of the oppression of women. She made gender the center of her analysis in a way that no one had ever before and thereby made the invisibility of gender oppression visible. She insisted that centuries of subordinating women produced an inferior product. We are not even good at our central task—mothering—she said in many ways and in many forms. How could we be? As inferior beings we cannot excel at society's most precious responsibility: educating and molding the next generation.

Gilman had no doubt what women were capable of achieving if given the chance, placing great hope in the rising women's movement of the late nineteenth century. Another fifty years, she said more than fifty years ago, will show more advance than the last five hundred.

She was not satisfied with the way the world was arranged, largely but not entirely because of its gender relations. She was also a socialist. She believed that the relationship between men and women is and has been for a long time not working to the advantage of men and women and children and animals and that it should and must be changed substantially. She believed that individualism, especially in its extreme version in the United States, was outmoded, making us one of the most backward nations in the world. She believed that institutionalized religion is, and has been for centuries, a major hindrance to human growth. She believed that the profit motive as the central force in human society must be eliminated.

Equality and justice, fairness and decency, can prevail, she was certain, if enough people can be persuaded of the importance of her message and those of others who share her perspective. Gilman looked to the power of ideas as the primary way to change thinking and therefore behavior. False ideas have shaped us throughout most of human history. She saw her role as participating in the ongoing and longstanding effort to persuade and convince all of us, or enough of us, that the way we run our world is not to the benefit of most of us.

Any vehicle that accomplished her task, any message that successfully persuaded, was therefore good and right. Carolyn Heilbrun describes feminist scholarship as "not merely museums for the display of culture," but as "theatres for its ongoing creation and re-creation." Gilman would agree, I am certain, and be delighted that her words are being read and her ideas are being explored in whatever form we today choose. Gilman could not help but be pleased and probably amused at the existence of the Charlotte Perkins Gilman Society, now in its eighth year; its publication, "The Charlotte Perkins Gilman Newsletter"; and the two international Charlotte Perkins Gilman conferences already held, the first at the University of Liverpool in 1995 and the second at Skidmore College in 1997.

As all work that we do, especially the work of writers, is ultimately autobiographical, please read about the major issues in her life, and you will see those questions appear in many forms in her fiction. Personal matters, yes, but ones that continue to confront us today, sixty-four years after her death.

Most of the intellectual work that women of the past have done is valued by us as retrieved voices, as expressions of a legacy from our foremothers. We pay homage to them but we do not use their ideas to build on. We read across disciplines but rarely back in them. Perhaps we do not, cannot, fully understand how severely we have been damaged by having been denied access to learning about ourselves. Now that we have learned in these last three decades what we were not allowed to know for centuries, we must move beyond just reclaiming that history and paying obeisance to its existence to incorporating and using that knowledge. Gilman is one of the few feminist writers who is read widely, who we do know, and whose concerns are as relevant in our time, alas, almost as much as they were in hers.

If many of Gilman's lapses—her ethnocentrism, antiSemitism, and racism—offend today's readers, as they should, let us understand that it is probably harder for us as well to be free of cultural biases we do not see in ourselves. She broke from many harmful and debilitating conventions, but not all.

In "The Yellow Wallpaper," the opening selection in this volume, the central figure says toward the end: "I've got out at last . . . , so you can't put me back." Gilman, too, is out at last, again, and this time here to stay.

> *Ann J. Lane*
> *Charlottesville, Virginia*
> *October 1998*

THE FICTIONAL WORLD OF CHARLOTTE PERKINS GILMAN

by Ann J. Lane

The way each of us comes to face our death ordinarily has little connection to the way we have lived, but Charlotte Perkins Gilman died in a manner that testified to the struggle and the triumph of her life. Her death was of her choice, though within the sharp limits set by her cancerous body. Still, it was an act of will, of rationality, of affirmation. As she had lived her life, so she used her death for its instructive value. In her last months she worked vigorously on a nearly finished manuscript; but when severe pain debilitated her, she preferred, as she explained in the note she left behind, "chloroform to cancer."

I begin with her death because her story often leans heavily on her loveless and lonely childhood, her repressed adolescence, and her anguished young womanhood, culminating after marriage and motherhood in a nervous breakdown, from which she never entirely recovered. What is really significant about Gilman—her ideas, her writing, her lectures, her example—is not where she began but where she ended.

Charlotte Anna Perkins, born in Hartford, Connecticut, on July 3, 1860, was raised by her mother, Mary A. Fitch. Her father, Frederick Beecher Perkins, grandson of the noted theologian Lyman Beecher, nephew of Henry Ward Beecher and

Harriet Beecher Stowe, was a well-known man of letters, one-time head of the Boston Public Library and later the San Francisco Public Library. Perkins left his wife and children soon after Charlotte's birth, and thereafter he provided little support in any way to his family, which included, in addition to Charlotte, an older son, Thomas. As a young girl and then a young woman, Charlotte Perkins made frequent overtures to her father, but he always remained a remote and ungiving figure in her life. Her mother, living in poverty and isolation, frequently moving from place to place, led a bitter and lonely life.

Charlotte Perkins studied art for a time at the Rhode Island School of Design, and later earned her living by designing greeting cards, teaching art, and, for a brief period, tutoring children. At the age of twenty-four, after a long period of uncertainty and vacillation, she married Charles Walter Stetson, an extraordinarily handsome and charming local artist. Their only child, Katharine Beecher, was born the following year. From the beginning of her marriage, Charlotte Stetson suffered from depression. After the birth of Katharine, she became so seriously depressed that her husband persuaded her to consult the well-known Philadelphia neurologist S. Weir Mitchell, a specialist in women's nervous disorders. Mitchell had propounded his famous rest cure in the 1870s. Treatment required extended bed rest as well as near total inactivity and isolation. This regimen had two goals. First, subjected to such severely enforced isolation and inactivity, the patient was, in Mitchell's own words, "surfeited with it and welcomed a firm order to do the things she once felt she could not do"—that is, return with unquestioning acceptance to the busy life of housekeeper, wife, and mother. Second, she was introduced to the "moral medication" of the physician, so that she would come to trust and depend on him for moral guidance. In Charlotte Stetson's case, Mitchell's treatment, which forbade her ever to write or paint and limited her reading time to two hours a day, almost drove her entirely mad.

Calling upon an inner sense of survival, she rejected both husband and physician and fled to the house of the Channings, friends in Pasadena, California, whose daughter, Grace Ellery Channing, was Charlotte's dearest friend. Ultimately Charlotte Stetson moved permanently to California, with her daughter.

She and Walter Stetson were divorced some time later. He immediately remarried—Grace Ellery Channing—and the three, remaining cordial thereafter, were jointly involved in the rearing of Katharine.

In her public writing, Charlotte Stetson assumes full blame for her broken marriage, insisting that she was unable to function as wife or mother, despite Walter's tender, loving patience. But there are hints of more complicated reasons for marital discord and tension between the exuberant and unconventional yearnings and appetites of Charlotte's restless spirit and Walter's own conflicting notions of propriety and desire. During their engagement, for example, Charlotte was offered a copy of *Leaves of Grass* by a mutual friend of hers and Walt Whitman's. Apparently Walter Stetson accepted, at least for his fiancée, the conventional view of his day that defined Whitman's poetry as unseemly and unsavory. Charlotte refused the book, saying that she had promised Walter she would never read any of Whitman's work.

Just days after their marriage, Charlotte complained twice in her diary about suffering Walter's displeasure for being, as she said, "too affectionately expressive." Charlotte Stetson's last words in her journal of 1887, written to her husband as they were about to separate, were bitter:

> No one can ever know what I have suffered in these last 5 years. . . . Can Love hurt thus? . . . learn to doubt your judgment—before it seeks to mould another life as it has mine. I asked you a few days before our marriage if you would take the responsibility entirely on yourself. You said yes. Bear it then.

Perhaps the young husband found Charlotte's romantic and passionate expectations distasteful or perplexing, not surprising given the sexual code of the time. Perhaps Walter communicated conflicting ideas to the innocent, but not naïve, bride. His marriage portrait—he looks like a combination of Byron and Brando—confirms the notion that Charlotte was intensely attracted to this very sexual- and romantic-looking man, who may then have found her response to him unsettling and forbidding.

Since matters of sexuality were not often acknowledged or

examined, the young couple were likely enveloped in a tangle of unexplored but terrifying emotions, which surely contributed to their ultimate estrangement.

In California, Charlotte Stetson supported her mother (who stayed with her until her death by cancer in 1892), her daughter, and herself by running a boardinghouse. In this period she launched her career. "The Yellow Wallpaper" appeared in 1892; a book of verse, *In This Our World*, was published in 1893. In 1894 she and Helen Campbell co-edited *The Impress, A Journal of the Pacific Coast Women's Association*. She was drawn increasingly to the political and social movements on the West Coast: woman suffrage, trade unions, Edward Bellamy and Nationalism. She began to earn a living on the lecture circuit.

Since her mother was away a good deal, young Katharine went to live with her father and stepmother, whom the child knew and loved. Charlotte Stetson, with a small reputation at this time, was promptly condemned by the press for "abandoning" her child and being "an unnatural mother." She had already affronted public opinion by divorcing a man for no apparent cause and, even more, by continuing a warm friendship with his new wife. However, placing her career above her responsibilities as a mother proved unforgivable, especially to a world that had locked women securely in their place—at home.

She was so unnerved by the scandal that she literally gave up her home. She left California and took to the road for five years of lecturing. In this rootless environment she wrote her most famous book, *Women and Economics*. In 1900 came *Concerning Children*; in 1903, *The Home: Its Work and Influence*; and in 1904, *Human Work*. From 1909 to 1916 she edited and wrote all the copy for *The Forerunner*, a monthly magazine. In 1911 she published *Man-Made World*; in 1923, *His Religion and Hers: A Study of the Faith of Our Fathers and the Work of Our Mothers*. In 1935, shortly after her death, her autobiography, *The Living of Charlotte Perkins Gilman*, appeared.

In the spring of 1900, after a long and demanding courtship, she married George Houghton Gilman, her first cousin, also a descendant of Lyman Beecher. If Charlotte Stetson had withheld her deepest thoughts and feelings from her husband, Walter, Charlotte Gilman withheld little from her husband, Houghton.

In the years before the marriage finally occurred, Charlotte Stetson, ceaselessly traveling and lecturing, wrote almost daily letters to Houghton. She revealed much in that extraordinary collection of intimate and self-examining correspondence: her fears, her passion, her doubts, her anxieties, her triumphs, and her feelings of dependence. Houghton Gilman could have no question about his wife's commitment to her career, her recurring anguish about her sanity or her abilities as a mother, her worries about their forthcoming marriage, her determination to achieve self-realization through her work, her need for his stability, love, and strength, and her resolve to conquer, or at least to co-exist with, her devastating and terrifying depressions.

They lived very happily for more than three decades, until Houghton Gilman died suddenly in 1934; two years earlier she had learned of her inoperable cancer. After her husband's death, Charlotte Gilman returned to Pasadena to live near and then with her daughter, who died in 1979. Grace Channing, also a widow, joined Gilman and remained with her until Gilman's suicide in 1935.

During most of her lifetime Charlotte Perkins Gilman was widely respected and internationally recognized. However, post-World War I audiences rejected her double commitment to the rights of women and to socialism. Demand for her lectures and her books had declined markedly by 1920 and continued downward thereafter, until new interest, sparked by the contemporary women's movement, rescued her from oblivion.[1]

Gilman believed that women's subordination started with the expropriation by men of the agricultural surplus women produced, limiting women's full expression and autonomy and therefore dehumanizing them. Beginning with recorded history, men appropriated women's work and, by forcing them to depend economically on male authority, demeaned them. By the nineteenth century it was assumed that one entire sex should function as the domestic servants of the other. Gilman felt that at one time the involuntary sacrifice of equality made by the female sex had been necessary for evolution, because male traits of assertiveness, combat, and display were essential for the growth of the social organism. Civilization, however, now required the restoration of the original balance to include female qualities of cooperation and nurturance. The subordination of women could only end when women led the struggle for their own autonomy and equality, thereby freeing men as well as themselves from the distortions that come with dominance.

Gilman's cosmic world view utilized history, sociology, philosophy, psychology, and ethics in an effort to understand the past and, more important, to project a vision of the future. Her sociological and historical works analyze the past from her peculiar humanist-socialist perspective. (Gilman insisted she was not a feminist; rather the world was "masculinist," and it was she who sought to introduce a truly humanized concept.) In her fiction she suggests the kind of world we could have if we worked at it; the kinds of choices we could make, if we insisted on them; the kinds of relationships we could achieve, if we went ahead and demanded them. The fiction illustrates the human drama inherent in the history and sociology, for, as she said, "Until we can see what we are, we cannot take steps to become what we should be."

Gilman's fiction is part of her ideological world view, and therein lies its interest and its power. We read her books today because the problems she addressed and the solutions she sought are, unhappily, as relevant to the present as they were to her time. Several themes appear persistently. Children are central to her fiction, and their needs are examined in a variety of ways. Children are best reared collectively. They are raised by women, but not usually by their biological mothers. It is through the thoughtful and lovingly planned socialization of children that humane and democratic values are to be achieved and permanent change thereby sustained. Gilman envisioned an ideal society in which the profit motive is removed from social life and where genuine community dominates, although she never challenged the value and supremacy of the nuclear family or monogamous marriage.

The prerequisite for genuine autonomy for all adults is economic independence, and all citizens ideally leave their homes each day to do "world-work" (her phrase). Children of all ages go to their world-work as well, that is, to child centers or to school, and the family reunites at the end of the day in a home that is a place of love and relaxation, not a place of work for any of its members. Household chores are accomplished as all work is accomplished—as a public activity, as a form of work for those who choose it. Housecleaning and cooking, laundry and sewing, are social activities no different from shoemaking or coal mining or shipbuilding. The distinction between women's work and men's work disappears, with the exception of child-rearing, as the category called women's work disappears. Gilman recognized that the home was the primary location of inequality for women.

Until we all decide to bring about an ideal state, which Gilman is persuaded we can do, she suggested we make other arrangements: baby-gardens, what we call day-care centers, which benefit the children in them and the mothers freed by them; flexible career adjustments to allow men and women to pursue their talents; unusual marital arrangements unfettered by traditional notions of who supports whom and who does what work in the home; liberation of children from oppressive parents, who ordinarily take the shape of tyrannical fathers and passive mothers.

In Gilman's stories, certain characters break out of limiting places with the help of intervening others. There is a formula and there are stock characters who work out the formula. The young girl-woman, restricted by her traditional view of parental obligation or social place, or endangered by an innocence that does not protect her from a cruel libertine, is offered the model of an older woman, frequently a doctor, who presents her with options she never knew existed and knowledge she did not have. Middle-aged and older women, having done their service to husband and children, often extract from their own previously unexamined experience possibilities for new opportunities that point out the pleasures and powers available in our last years. Support for the young does not usually come from within the immediate family, neither from parents nor from siblings. Indeed, the young frequently need to reject their immediate families to seek help from others, sometimes a grandfather or an aunt, more often not a relative at all. Men who are redeemable, and Gilman does offer many such examples, are decent, sensitive, and well-meaning, though conventional; but they are capable, when pressed, of changing, a quality of conversion without which they are lost.

Although Gilman was a socialist, and identified herself as

such, and although her utopian fiction creates an ideal socialist society, the strategies she offered in her realistic fiction were often strangely conservative. There were many cooperative ventures scattered throughout the nation; yet her short-term, immediate suggestions for individual or social reform took women out of the home and into capitalistic business activities, not into producer or consumer cooperatives. Gilman evaded the issue of class by examining women's issues alone and resolving women's problems without reference to class. Most of the employed women of her time were servants, and yet Gilman's solutions, for individuals or projected onto a larger social screen, very rarely addressed the concerns or needs of a servant class in a way that could be expected to win them over to her point of view.[2]

Gilman gave little attention to her writing as literature, and neither will the reader, I am afraid. She wrote quickly, carelessly, to make a point. She always wrote fiction to meet a deadline. Still, she had a good ear for dialogue, was adept at sketching within a few pages a familiar but complicated set of relationships, and knew well the whole range of worries and joys women shared. She wrote to engage an audience in her ideas, not in her literary accomplishments.

"The Yellow Wallpaper," initially published in 1892, is the first selection in this collection. It is easily the best of Gilman's fiction, and the single piece for which she is now most recognized—an odd situation because her once-formidable reputation did not in the past rest on her imaginative work. Her fame came from her studies in sociology and social theory, *Women and Economics* bringing her immediate international acclaim when it appeared in 1898. "The Yellow Wallpaper," a study of a young mother painstakingly and lovingly driven into madness by a well-meaning husband following S. Weir Mitchell's notions, is Gilman's retaliation against the psychiatric profession. It stands apart from her other fiction for two overriding reasons, which, when set out together, seem to be contradictory. It is the best crafted of her fiction: a genuine literary piece, unlike the rest of her creative writing. It is also the most directly, obviously, self-consciously autobiographical of all her stories. It was drawn from anguish and pain. In no other fictional writing did Gilman give so much of herself, expose her feelings so fully.

In the remaining stories in this collection, and in the entire body of published and unpublished fiction from which they were selected, Gilman examines, clearly and pointedly, a variety of problems women share and a variety of proposed ways of dealing with those problems. Although Gilman later ascribed a didactic reason for writing it, "The Yellow Wallpaper" came from a deep and private part of her that she ordinarily kept well protected from the public, and perhaps from herself. She may have taken the risk with the hope that writing "The Yellow Wallpaper" would purge her of the demons she so feared would one day claim her permanently. However, the debilitating depressions never did disappear entirely and for many years neither did the frightening specter of insanity. Never again did she publicly plumb her emotions with the intensity and honesty that permeate "The Yellow Wallpaper." Instead, she wrote to Houghton.

"The Yellow Wallpaper" has often been reprinted as a horror story; its most famous appearance in that genre is in William Dean Howells's *Great Modern American Stories*, in 1920, in which Howells described its chilling qualities. Horror writer H. P. Lovecraft called it one of the great "spectral tales" in American literature.[3] Not until 1973, in the Feminist Press edition introduced by Elaine R. Hedges, was it read from a feminist perspective.

In this volume one can see "The Yellow Wallpaper" for the first time in the context of a wide selection of Gilman's fiction in general, and it becomes of a piece with them, while remaining at the same time special and different. Gilman used fiction as a device to offer an answer to the question she always posed: "But what if . . . ?" What if she wants a family and a career, and her husband-to-be objects? What if her children are grown up and she is bored? What if her husband is abusive and she wants to leave him, but she does not know how? What if her vacuous life causes her to make impossible demands upon her caring husband? What if she does not have the patience to rear the child she loves? What if the work she desperately wants takes her away from the man she adores? What if her elderly mother is ill and she does not want to sacrifice years nursing her? Except in "The Yellow Wallpaper," there is always a feasible, positive alternative, and there is always a happy, or at least a moderately happy, ending. The questions, in one form or another, came from Gilman's own experience, either because she had herself come to a satisfactory resolution or, more often, because she had not and suffered the consequences, which she wished to spare subsequent generations. If there were not many models after which young women could fashion a new way of life, then Gilman would create them in fiction.

"The Yellow Wallpaper" must have haunted Gilman all her life because it answered the question: But what if she had not fled from her husband and renounced the most advanced psychiatric[4] advice of her time? The risks in both her actions were severe, and costly, but the alternative, as she posed it in "The Yellow Wallpaper," was worse; and she knew it. Rigidly enforced confinement and absolute passivity—elements significant in the lives of women of her time and carried to an extreme in Mitchell's treatment—contributed strongly to the madness in her short story, and needed to be discarded, as Gilman herself had discarded them, if women were to achieve sanity and strength. In "The Yellow Wallpaper" we see what happens to our lives if we let others run them for us. In the remaining stories, we learn which choices are truly ours.

Many Gilman enthusiasts do not much like her fiction. They consider it too ideological, too didactic. Gilman mischievously used the commonly shared forms and structures of her day—farces, domestic novels, mysteries, adventure stories—and infused them with her own brand of feminism and socialism. Her work is ideological, but she implies that all literature is ideological, only its familiarity, its "naturalness" to us, makes it appear to reflect all possible world views. Although she does not challenge all the conventions of her day, she introduces a new sense of intellectual play when she poses her "What if" questions in the arena of traditional male-female relations, thereby exposing the absurd pieties embedded in domestic life.

Nine of the ten short stories in this collection come from Gilman's magazine, *The Forerunner*. She published many short stories in other magazines, and many of her short stories were never published. When I completed my final selection of stories to be included in this volume, I discovered either that Gilman had indeed selected the best ones for her own magazine, or that she and I shared a similar judgment about her work. For whatever reason, without my planning it so, all but one of the stories I chose had appeared originally in *The Forerunner*.

Gilman was determined to package her social vision in ways persuasive to a general audience. These short stories are written in the style and with the simplicity common to women's magazines of the day. Each story is a lesson. Each focuses on a specific problem, usually but not always a problem shared primarily by women, and each has a happy resolution. The happy ending, however, comes about as a result of a good deal of intelligence, resourcefulness, and, most important, a willingness to defy convention, to look afresh at an old situation. What each story requires is the shaking off of traditional ways of doing things, especially as they relate to accepted male or female behavior. One can almost assume that as part of the formula some usual mode of thought or action will be replaced by a different, but possible, method of thinking about or doing things.

The first two stories after the grim "Yellow Wallpaper" employ a whimsical turnabout contrivance to advance ideas. "When I Was a Witch" has a wishes–come–true technique that is used, not to turn everything touched to gold, but to improve the quality of collective life. Gilman's gripes will sound familiar: crowded, foul-smelling public conveyances; rude public officials; lying newspapers; platitudinous ministers; dishonest boards of directors. But what do you imagine would happen to our cities if the homilies to which we pay lip-service were acted upon with sincerity: if people told only the truth in their pulpits, in their newspapers, in their stockholders' meetings? What would happen if the pain we inflict on others we felt in their place? The point she makes is droll, because we, in fact, would be astonished if truth, decency, courtesy, and generosity ruled our public life.

"If I Were a Man" applies the same sport to a husband-and-wife switch. When Mollie Mathewson, a "true woman," suddenly finds herself Gerald Mathewson, she discovers what it feels like to be a man: the quiet superiority; the pleasure of his large size; the comfort of his sensible clothing and shoes; the sense of power from controlling his own, earned money. In the body and mind of a man with the "memory of a whole lifetime," Mollie sees the world as a big place, a place of business and politics and action. Most startling of all, she learns what men really think about women.

Gilman felt strongly that innocence was a device through which girls and women were victimized, so innocence is the moral villain of "The Girl in the Pink Hat." An effort to seduce an innocent is foiled, partly because the young lady, though naïve, is not without courage and determination, and partly through the interference of a woman who is a combination of Nancy Drew and Miss Marple. Such interference by an older woman occurs often in Gilman's fiction. In this story the villain can be recognized by the smell of his breath and by his attempts to "assert a premature authority" over the woman he claims to love. Gilman frequently created a particular kind of man who is successful in winning women and then mistreating them. Trust, if not rooted in knowledge and experience, is dangerous, we learn.

In "The Cottagette" we see how to catch a man and how (almost) to lose one, if we accept without thinking the standard canons of female wiles. Malda follows the advice of her friend Lois because Lois, who is thirty-five and divorced, claims to know the real route to marital success. The two women live in a mountain cottage, part of a community of artists, and they eat in a central boardinghouse. This arrangement leaves Malda free to enjoy the beauty of the countryside and do her work, which is embroidery. To win her man, she follows Lois's counsel and turns the cottage, where no obligations oppress her, into a home, where she bakes and cooks and cleans. Once she begins cooking, however, she finds she no longer has time to roam. The baking distracts her; people begin to drop in; delivery people interrrupt her; the house is noisy. She has a home. She is prepared, nevertheless, to sacrifice her time, her pleasures, her work, to make that home for the man she loves, who, fortunately, wants her the way she was, "wild and sweet . . . truly an artist," not a household drudge. We discover that gratifying and beautiful work need not be esoteric; that there are men who value women as individuals, not as domestic servants; that "older" women of thirty-five need not have the right answers; that the traditional way is often the wrong way.

"The Unnatural Mother" comes out of Gilman's private pain, for it was a phrase often used against her in the press. In this story the mother is considered unnatural because she willingly sacrifices her own child to save the community. Ironically, the child survives, the town inhabitants survive, and only she and her husband perish. Even after death she is still condemned as an unnatural mother by the townspeople she saved because, they say, "a mother's duty is to her own child . . . the Lord never gave her them other children to care for!"

The tension between career and family, a problem in Gilman's time as in ours, is a frequent theme in her fiction. "Making a Change" is a typical piece on the subject. Julia, a wonderful musician and an exalted beauty, has neither the patience for unrelieved mothering nor the abilities for household management. She tries only because it is her duty. Everybody is miserable: the baby cries, the wife is distraught, the husband sulks, and the mother-in-law wrings her hands. Then the women conspire to change it all. On the roof of the apartment house they set up a baby-garden with fifteen babies, run by Julia's mother-in-law. Julia returns to her music and thus relieves Frank of his obligation to be sole breadwinner. Everybody does what he/she is best suited for, and the children are happy because they are with other babies while being cared for by a competent person, who is not their mother.

"An Honest Woman" is a "fallen" woman who gets up. Deserted by the man she loved and lived with (though he could not marry her), Mary Cameron puts her life together, defying the conventional notion that, as one person observes, "you can't reform spilled milk." She is Gilman's answer to Nathaniel Hawthorne. Unlike Hester Prynne, who carries her humiliation with dignity, Mary Cameron refuses to carry it at all. She feels grief but no shame, for she is an honest woman, even if the world would not define her so. Trained to be independent by her father, a freethinker, she fell in love with a "glib young phrenologist," a man able to fool her because he had considerable experience with women. When the blackguard returns years later to be forgiven and declares his love, she refuses him, asserting that his love and need for her "does not make me love you again." Over and over, Gilman evokes the image of the attractive seducer, the man who makes women follow him because of his ardent passion, not theirs. (Walter Stetson pursued a reluctant Charlotte Perkins for years, finally persuading her only when he suffered a dreadful personal setback that aroused her compassion.)

Adultery was a subject genteel folk avoided talking about, except to denounce the women who engaged in it. In "Turned," Mrs. Marroner (a Ph.D. formerly on a college faculty) discovers that her husband has seduced and impregnated their docile, trusting servant girl, Gerta. Initially enraged at the girl's disloyalty, Mrs. Marroner soon turns her fury on the husband who took advantage of the girl's innocence without even loving her. Had he loved the girl, his wife would have suffered but understood. It is the seduction she cannot forgive, the use of power against a helpless victim. It is an "offense against all women and against the unborn child." The two women unite and together confront the villainous man.

Gilman was well past forty when she wrote most of her fiction, and her age is reflected in her unusual concern for the lives of middle-aged and older women. The last two stories describe different choices and different life problems. In "The Widow's Might" the mature woman, having spent her adult life devoted to husband and children, decides it is time to go off and play, to run her own business, to do whatever she chooses. Not a helpless, broken, distraught woman after her husband's death, she discovers resources within herself never before explored.

Mr. Peebles in "Mr. Peebles' Heart" is a fiftyish, grayish, stoutish man who has spent his life doing his duty, which meant essentially supporting women—his mother, his wife, his daughters—by running a store that he detested. He is persuaded by his sister-in-law, who is a doctor and a "new woman," to take off and travel. He does, and returns "enlarged, refreshed, and stimulated." His wife, left to take care of herself, also changes and grows in his absence. As a result, a tired and conventional marriage, built on unarticulated assumptions that did not help either party develop, gains a new life when the people involved learn that their possibilities are limitless.

Gilman's message is essentially just that: our possibilities for change are limitless, if we want them. How to achieve those changes is examined on a small scale in the short stories, and in a considerably more complicated way in the novels, seven of which are excerpted in this collection. The first three "realistic" novels are followed by excerpts from her only detective story. The last three are her utopian visions. Together they constitute her strategy for getting from the realistic present to the feasible future.

The Crux, serialized in 1910 and published as a book in 1911, takes another look at innocence betrayed—or almost betrayed. Again innocence has no charm. Innocent women are created in a male image to be fragile and vulnerable. What women need is education, sophistication, world experience, adventure—tools for their own protection. Gilman snorts at the idea that women need to be protected *by* men. Women need to be protected *from* men, and that protection must come from the self.

The novel is about the growing up of Vivian Lane, a sheltered, smothered, New England girl, who defies her parents by leaving home to go West. A group of women, including her zesty grandmother, are inspired to move to Colorado by a woman doctor, who is tough, breezy, powerful, and unmarried. Vivian is torn between her attraction to this model and to that offered by Adela St. Cloud, who flutters, is soft and misty, sinks into cushions, and is entrancing to young men—the embodiment of conventional feminine qualities. Then there are the men. Morton, whom Vivian has promised to marry, is fast, racy, wild, "practiced in the art of pleasing women." Mrs. St. Cloud advises Vivian to devote her life to Morton, to reshape him. It is "the most beautiful work on earth . . . to be the guiding star, the inspiration of a man's life." And Vivian is drawn to that role, so much does she want to be needed and loved. Gilman skillfully draws the appeal of that kind of man, showing how a woman can choose to thwart her own needs and talents by focusing on her role as his helpmate. The other major male character is Dr. Richard Hale, independent, slightly cantankerous, somewhat misogynistic.

The crux of the story is that Morton has venereal disease. The excerpt in this volume shows the confrontation between the two doctors, the conventional male and the socially conscious female, on the question of Morton's disease and the subsequent painful disclosure made to Vivian. The section ends with the doctor's words to Vivian and Gilman's admonition to us all: "Beware of a biological sin, my dear; for it there is no forgiveness."

In Gilman's day, venereal disease was an important social issue and the subject of extensive discussion. Syphilis and gonorrhea were difficult to diagnose and cure. Penicillin was not developed until 1942. Salvarsan, used in the treatment of syphilis before then, was not available until approximately 1910, and in any case had only limited success as well as dangerous side effects. The Wasserman test for syphilis was developed in 1906, but there is still no easy means of detecting gonorrhea.[5]

Others before Gilman had used venereal disease as a subject in their fiction. In 1874, Dr. Dio Lewis published *Chastity: Or Our Secret Sins*, in which a syphilitic man, warned by his doctor of the risk to his beautiful and pure fiancée, marries anyway. Years later the doctor observes their daughter. "That little girl's eyeballs, gums, and breath are a painful fulfillment of my prophecy." The doctor had urged that the mother be told "the source of the poison" so that "she could then cooperate with us in forestalling the development of the horrid taint in future children," but the father "never would give his consent," and so the doctor withheld his knowledge.[6] Gilman created a woman doctor who refuses to be bound by tradition, although as author she shied away from direct challenge to medical protocol; Morton was not the woman doctor's patient.

Vivian sends Morton away only to discover how deeply she misses him. Though she knows he is a scoundrel, she had not realized how "large a part in her life [his] constant attention and admiration had become." Slowly Vivian rebuilds her world. She discovers the pleasures of the outdoor life in the West. She establishes a kindergarten and is gratified by her work. She learns that twenty-seven is not so old after all. Very slowly love grows between Dr. Hale and Vivian Lane. Their love is based on affection, respect, and shared interests. It is rooted in experience and wisdom. No less ardent for being wiser, it is indeed deeper.

What Diantha Did, published in 1912, juxtaposes the ordinary way of doing things, that is, the irrational way, against the sensible, useful way, which is unconventional and therefore shocking. Diantha Bell also escapes her home, leaving behind a "virtuous" mother, a good, self-sacrificing New England woman, and her father, who is a run-of-the-mill tyrant. Diantha is a schoolteacher who hates teaching; her father is a businessman who hates business; her mother is a housekeeper who hates keeping house. Diantha also parts from her lover, Ross, who supports four able-bodied sisters and a healthy mother by running the family store, which he hates.

Diantha breaks out. She begins her career as an apprentice-housekeeper in the home of a young couple with a child. The lady of the house is an architect, who loves her husband and loves her child, but does not love keeping house. When he wanted to marry me he asked if I loved him, she wails, not if I would be his cook and his chambermaid. "Can't a woman enjoy her home, just as a man does, without running the shop?"

Eventually Diantha puts her domestic skills and her business head to professional use in what Gilman calls domestic specialization. Diantha elevates domestic service to "world service" by treating it as any other kind of specialized skill. She organizes the servant girls of her new community—although it is in a form of "company union"—and establishes a community center, a union hall, where the girls live and from which they work out, offering food service and housecleaning service. Diantha takes them out of the private homes in which they live and in which they are economically and sexually exploited, and she gives them a home, a community, privacy, and autonomy. To each of the girls as she starts the day, Diantha says: "You are not servants—you are employees. . . . Each of us must do our best to make this new kind of work valued and respected." Men no longer make their own shoes or build their own houses, she explains; women should no longer do their own housework. Nobody brags about home brewing or home tailoring or home shoemaking, why home cooking? Why connect food to love?

Diantha Bell runs her food-preparation and housecleaning services like high-powered businesses. She even rents out the community house in the daytime for businessmen's lunches and in the evenings for meetings and dances. She uses the latest technological advances to send her delectable and inexpensive foods to her customers: aluminum containers lined with asbestos!

Eventually Diantha manages an entire hotel complex, complete with housekeeping cottages, child-care facilities, and food service.

Benigna Machiavelli, the next selection, creates a special Gilman character, a kind of female Huck Finn, but one with a social conscience and a large view; one who ultimately agrees to grow up, but on her own terms. She is bright, mischievous, manipulative, and not especially honest, but she is essentially good, a good Iago, a good Machiavelli.

There is very little coming-of-age literature written for and about women. In this short novel Gilman offers a model of girl-into-womanhood, a road to autonomy, a system to develop independence and courage, a way to handle difficult parents without irreconcilable tensions. Its autobiographical quality comes not, as in "The Yellow Wallpaper," from its similarity to Gilman's experiences, but as a projection of the kind of person she would have liked to have been, and of the kind of childhood and adolescence she would have liked to have lived through. Benigna's life is hardly easy. She is burdened with a tyrannical, alcoholic father, a self-denying and ineffectual mother, and a vacuous older sister. It is Benigna's survival that is the center of the book.

A homily that Gilman printed in *The Forerunner* gives a clue to her portrayal of Benigna:

All pain is personal. It is between You and the Thing that Hurts. You may not be able to move the Thing—but You are movable.

Benigna is movable, and Gilman demonstrates how she manages her life. As always, everything ends well, not because of magic, but because people have changed themselves and thereby resolved their dilemmas.

Gilman's fiction can end cheerfully because she ordinarily presents problems that can be resolved by individual will. Firmly believing that we can, in some fashion, shape our lives, she had to avoid creating situations that lacked that fundamental possibility. Inevitably her people are middle or lower-middle class, and primarily of Northern European background. Most of the seemingly hopeless situations involve people with some maneuvering space: they are widows, or are secure financially, or are young and without responsibilities, so that with reason and enterprise and lots of hard work, they can triumph. Her characters are feminist Horatio Algers, but their aim is not wealth and worldly success; their aim is autonomy and the facility to use their gifts for the social good. When the situation is genuinely overwhelming—a young, helpless girl, pregnant and abandoned, or an abused wife oppressed by a vicious husband—then some competent, knowledgeable woman intercedes.

We can get out from the worst traps, Gilman suggests, if we start from there and make the best use of our skills and options. For most untrained women that means a boardinghouse, the very symbol of the home and domestic service. But the boardinghouse is not for the private service of a single family; it is socialized, servicing many people and offering independence to those who run it and work in it.

While Gilman showed that economic independence frequently comes to women who select some business enterprise, such as Diantha did, her overriding commitment was to a combination of what she called humanism and we call feminism, and socialism, by which she meant a form of social cooperation, based on the socialization of private property and the establishment of collective organization and social relations. She dissociated herself from Marxist parties and Marxist ideology, primarily because she rejected the idea of class struggle and class violence. She was closer ideologically to the English Fabians than to any other group, but for most of her life she remained unidentified politically and even ideologically.[7] She wrote books and made speeches in an effort to persuade people, mostly but not only women, that they needed to be rid of the social constraints that prevented their full development; that they alone could make the necessary changes that would bring about their freedom; and that the only kind of society that would permit the full flourishing of human potential, for men and women, would be a socialized society. Beyond that, it would be dangerous to try to place Gilman in any ideological camp. The arena in which her struggle essentially took place was the fictional one, and the form it sometimes took was the utopian novel. She wrote three: *Moving the Mountain*, 1911; *Herland*, 1915; and its sequel, *With Her in Ourland*, 1916.[8]

The first is set in the United States in 1940, the American people having chosen socialism twenty years before. This new world is revealed through the perceptions of a man, John Robertson, who has been lost in Tibet for thirty years and for whom, consequently, the old world is gone. He is skeptical about the new humanist-socialist one. Many of the conversations that present the new society occur between Robertson and his brother-in-law; thus the new world, in which women play a major part, is seen through the words and eyes of men, one a convert and one yet to be converted.

In the excerpt presented, one can see much about the way the new society is organized. Families remain intact, the girl-children taking their mothers' names and the boy-children their fathers'. Gilman, despite her radical stance on many issues, never questioned the desirability of the nuclear family or monogamous marriage. What is stripped from the family is household chores. The home, removed entirely from the process of production, can, for the first time, be what it always claimed to be: a refuge of love and affection, a place to leave and return to, not a place where any family member carries out his or her work. Remove the profit motive and the food is better and cheaper. It becomes what it is meant to be, sustenance and nourishment, not a commodity to buy and sell. The technology, none of which is in the realm of fantasy, is put to human needs. From Gilman's descriptions we are meant to get a sense of what might be feasible and possible now were social organization to be altered.

The architecture of the apartment complex is reshaped to aid in the creation and maintenance of a community. The roof, a baby-garden by day, becomes an adult recreation center in the evening. Though people live both in families and alone, the basic social unit is larger than either. Gilman popularized demands for domestic reform that feminists had long urged and even acted upon, for many experiments had established community kitchens and dining halls before Diantha did. Architects had incorporated these ideas into plans for urban and suburban development before Gilman; and the tradition continued well into the 1920s with a variety of architectural plans that highlighted the kitchenless home.[9]

In Gilman's utopian America, the key to creating a changed consciousness is the education of the young, and the mother is the key to the child. Motherhood remains a revered status; it is socialized, however, for not all mothers can or want to spend their workday with children. The institution of motherhood, which in the real world isolates women and children in the private home, becomes a collective enterprise, the heart of the community, the vehicle for the expansion and growth of women and children.

If *Moving the Mountain* reflects a society in transition, "a baby-Utopia" as Gilman called it, then *Herland* is utopia complete. There is total privacy and there is community. No family mediates, no family exists except where the entire community acts as one. There are no last names because the final product, the child-into-adult, is a collective product, not a private one, and there are no men, at least until three Americans stumble into Herland. Reproduction is achieved parthenogenically, inspired by desire and longing for motherhood. Thus, women are freed, not from childbirth, as technological solutions from Aldous Huxley to Shulamith Firestone envision, but from male sexuality.[10]

The story, like *Moving the Mountain*, unwinds as an odyssey, a spiritual odyssey, in the course of which the skeptics, again men, are educated. Although *Moving the Mountain* relies, as do many utopian novels, on long-winded dialogues, *Herland* persuades the male intruders, and the reader, by way of dramatic action. As *Herland* ends, each of the three men has reacted differently to this world of women. Jeff has accommodated without struggle; Terry, having attempted to rape his wife—a crime punishable by Herland's most severe sentence, exile—is straining to leave; and Van, the Intelligence, the man of reason, having been persuaded that Herland is a better and more humane world, is nevertheless about to return to his American home with his Herland wife, Ellador. The future of the young couple is unclear. It never occurs to Van that he will not return permanently to his American home some day, but Ellador expects to go back to Herland with the new discoveries, experiences, and knowledge she is about to encounter.

In *Ourland*, the happy couple wanders the globe, Ellador setting for herself the job of diagnosing the world's social ills to

report back to her people. Gilman relies on wide-eyed innocence and a fresh approach to the familiar to startle the reader
into a different consciousness. Conversations between Ellador
and Van explore a variety of Gilman's concerns: the ethic of
individualism as it operates against the social good; emotion as
companion, not enemy, to reason; the superiority of heterosex-
ual love; historical roles of men and women so vastly different as
to make generalizations suspect. Most surprising, perhaps, are
the sharply critical judgments directed at women, judgments
illustrated through a favorite Gilman device of turnabout. What
would you think about men if they allowed themselves to be
kept by Herland women as fragile and delicate pets, Ellador asks
Van. Even as early as 1915 Gilman saw the enormous impact yet
to be felt as growing numbers of women participated in public
life through paid work. The excerpts as well as the book itself
end on a droll note. Just as Van's universe has expanded
through knowledge of Ellador and her world, so too has Ellador
grown with experience. She learns that "men are people, too,
just as much as women are."

In this book, as well as in other published and private writings, Gilman articulated certain ideas that, however characteris-
tic of her time and however dominant in intellectual circles of
the period, still are strikingly jarring and offensive. Despite her
genuine commitment to humanism and socialism, Gilman
voiced opinions that are racist, chauvinist, and anti-Semitic. The
decision to exclude selections from *Ourland* that would illustrate
these ideas flowed not from the desire to hide that side of her
thought but from the belief that her valuable ideas better deserve remembering and repeating.

Unpunished, Gilman's only detective novel, was completed by
1929 and, despite Gilman's effort and interest, was never published. Her attempt to write a racy, clever piece is not successful.
She is not comfortable with the language or structure of sus-
pense stories. *Unpunished* suffers, more than does most of her
fiction, from hasty writing. It is not a bad first draft, which is
probably what it was, but she had no patience to work at it
persistently. Still, its ideas are intriguing, and the manuscript
presents the culmination of a number of key themes in her
writing.

The excerpt chosen here introduces the family: Wade Vaughn, prosperous criminal lawyer who supports his dead wife's sister, Jacqueline Warner, crippled and scarred from an automobile accident years before; her son, Hal, nineteen when the story opens; and his cousin, Iris, eighteen, Vaughn's stepdaughter. Bess and Jim Hunt, a detective duo like Dashiell Hammett's Nick and Nora Charles, are the narrators through whom the story takes form. Their friend, Dr. Ross Akers, physician to Vaughn and friend to the family, introduces the Hunts to the problem. The problem is that Vaughn has been murdered—many times. He has been shot, garroted, smashed on the head, and poisoned.

Vaughn is Gilman's embodiment of all conceivable villainy, although he appears to the world as a benevolent protector of a crippled woman and two defenseless children and as a reliable criminal attorney, defender of those in legal trouble. In reality he is a hideous and depraved tyrant who has driven his wife to suicide and then continues to torment her surviving crippled sister and the children. He uses his professional position to blackmail his victims, whom he takes pleasure in humiliating and abusing, sexually if they are attractive women. Everyone who knows him well has reason to want him dead. The questions are: Who killed him first? Is it a crime to kill a man already dead? And is it morally acceptable to kill a person so wicked and corrupt? To begin with the last, Charlotte Gilman, in the tradition of Agatha Christie's *Murder on the Orient Express*, asserts that Vaughn's murder was morally justifiable. Initially it is only Bess Hunt who insists that "if any people had a right to kill a man, they had," while her husband accuses her of having lost her moral sense. But when Vaughn's base and diabolical qualities are disclosed, even Jim is convinced. "I regret that Mr. Vaughn is dead," he says, " . . . so I cannot have the pleasure of killing him." Thus, the detached observers, the Hunts, make the moral judgment about Vaughn's "badness" and Jacqueline Warner's "goodness." Of her, Bess says, "I'm sure she's good. Those children wouldn't love her so if she wasn't."

Vaughn and his family stand as a parody, a caricature, of the nurturing and loving home. Jacqueline Warner is forced, by her helpless condition and the needs of two young children, to accept Vaughn's terms: she must be submissive and obedient, which are, after all, the rules for all traditional wifely behavior, in fiction and out. When Iris, the unstable wife Vaughn later drove to suicide, sought her sister's protection, Vaughn threatened to deal with Iris's nervous condition by consulting "any examining physician" who would agree that "restraint was necessary, and seclusion"—a harkening back to "The Yellow Wallpaper" and to Walter Stetson and S. Weir Mitchell. Just as Iris and Jacqueline's despotic father tried to force them to marry against their will and then threatened to punish them financially if they refused (which they did, and he did), so Vaughn, in the next generation of tyrannical and wicked fathers, tries to force fragile young Iris to marry a brute. The intended bridegroom justifies the forced marriage on the grounds that he adores her so much he has the right to follow any course to win her. And indeed Iris agrees to the marriage to protect her cousin and her aunt, whom Vaughn will otherwise evict. Thus we see marriage used as a weapon by fathers against daughters and husbands against wives; we see women forced to enter marriages for reasons that have little to do with their own desire.

If Bess Hunt is Gilman's voice, one that relies on cleverness, dry humor, and detached observation, then Jacqueline Warner is Gilman's model of awesome womanly behavior. "Here is this woman," Bess says to her husband, "widowed, crippled, disfigured, disinherited, and the only person on earth to look out for those two children. Even if she could have escaped with them, any sort of court would have given them back to him. What could she bring against him that would hold?"

And how does she survive? As all Gilman heroines do. She recognizes, first, the need to maintain her health and her strength: she exercises as best she can from a wheelchair; she studies nutrition; she keeps the windows open, to compensate for her limited access to the outside. Even crippled and imprisoned women can create their own space. To make herself indispensable, she masters all the skills of an efficient housekeeper. Most important, she teaches herself and Iris typing and stenography, so that when they can make their escape, both women will be able to support themselves, one inside the home as a typist, the other out of it as a secretary.

The core of this story is the connection between two women, Jacqueline Warner, who frees herself, and Bess Hunt, who presents that struggle to the reader. Bess Hunt sees her role not as reconstructing a crime, because she does not view Vaughn's murder as a crime. She is "reconstructing the virtue" of a tormented woman, living in isolation, hiding her real feelings from her children, appearing to be submissive, making it possible for her children (and both are "her" children, though only one is biologically so) to grow and develop in this hideous environment.

There is both a happy ending and a surprise ending. Iris and Hal marry, thus uniting first cousins in fiction, as Gilman did many times, to reproduce Charlotte and Houghton Gilman's first-cousin marriage. Jacqueline Warner marries Dr. Akers. Before they wed, Jacqueline insists upon a long separation from Akers and her children so she can have the surgery that will restore her beauty. Akers teases her: "And you are going to desert your children, you unnatural mother," indicating how long-lasting and deep must have been the pain Gilman felt from that decades-old criticism. Jacqueline, forty-three at the time of her marriage, demonstrates the pleasures possible for women of middle age.

The surprise ending reclaims some semblance of traditional morality. The coroner's report returns a dull and commonplace verdict: Vaughn died of a heart attack. It is not till the very end that we learn the rest of Jacqueline Warner's story, for truth goes beyond medical testimony. Preparing to escape from Vaughn's home, Jacqueline had wished to leave behind a legacy of fear. Wearing her sister's death mask, and a black and white scarf identical to the one Iris hanged herself with, Jacqueline had appeared as her sister, standing for a moment (after months of practice) before her tormentor. He died of shock.

In detective stories, everybody is always guilty. The question is who is guilty of the specific crime. To discover the truth involves exposing concealed knowledge, in the course of which the familiar becomes strange and the strange becomes familiar.[11] In Gilman's story, the familiar is the home; but one is not really "at home" until one leaves one's home. In *Unpunished*, the scarred and physically grotesque person who conceals the crime is "guilty," but not in moral terms. At the end she not only regains her beauty but achieves a genuine home. She does so by leaving behind the home in which she was grotesque, in which she could never be herself, but always had to behave publicly in a way to conceal her real self, a home in which the tyrannical and cruel father-uncle-husband dominated. All the good people in that perverted home had to conceal their real identities in order to survive. Only by rejecting that home and the family provided by the villain could they achieve real community and real family, and then only by destroying the force that had defiled them.

Never in her fiction, and this was her last fictional work, did Gilman remove her villain with such direct violence. Destruction replaced persuasion. *Unpunished,* written when Gilman was in her last years, perhaps voices the frustration she experienced at having devoted a life to struggling for changes that did not occur.

Gilman's fictional work, when viewed as a whole, erases the distinction between realistic fiction, which mediates struggles, and fantasies, which eliminate them. If you take what Diantha did and socialize it, you walk into *Herland.* If you take Dr. Hale from *The Crux* and put him on location in *Moving the Mountain,* he will change. Gilman's utopia leads us back to reality. Her reality moves us on into a future vision. It is an attainable, feasible vision, she insists. It can happen if we do it. We need not abandon the real world to enter into imaginary ones, Lewis Mumford reminds us, "for it is out of the first that the second are always coming." Like all socialists, from scientific to utopian, from Saint-Simon to Marx, Gilman knew that the success of her socialist-feminist idea depended on convincing a sizable portion of the world of its soundness.

Her fiction was a grand strategy for the women's movement as well. Most of her fictional writing appeared in the first two decades of the twentieth century and can be read as an effort to expand the suffrage struggle: to encourage the women's movement to address larger issues; to persuade women to use the important political organization they had developed for purposes beyond the vote. The women's movement was strong in the early part of the century. A powerful socialist movement was also gaining momentum in the same period. Gilman tried to use her fictional world to offer them a way to unite.

Gilman developed a strong repugnance toward Freud's ideas, or at least the Freudianism that invaded the United States. This repugnance was not rooted in a denial of the power of the emotional life. Quite the contrary, her reliance on reason came out of her fear of submitting to one's emotions, for one cannot assume feelings will lead to action in one's interest. "To love the child does not serve the child," she said many times, and she knew from her own life, as a daughter and as a mother, how inadequate love could be. Of her own mother, Gilman wrote, "My mother, devoted soul that she was, hurt me more than anyone else ever did."

To break out of the prison of outworn beliefs, one must decide on a course of action and discipline the emotions, subordinating them to that decision. In time the emotions will be reconditioned. Such a course is particularly necessary for women, who are forever falling in love with the wrong men, sexual attraction being essentially the working out of cultural values. Diantha must assert herself, against her family and the man she loves, to do what she knows is right for her, though her feelings often pull her back and make her want to quit. Vivian must break with Morton, although she is in pain at having to do so. The girl in the pink hat follows her passion and is almost done in. Julia tries to do her duty, as she was trained to do, and raise her child, and in the process makes everybody miserable, including the child she loves.

The murky world of the unconscious must have frightened Charlotte Gilman. Conceding to these subterranean forces, the very ones that almost destroyed her, she saw as a denial of one's unique quality as a thinking creature. The psychiatric notions of her day, particularly when she was a young woman, certainly had proved themselves dangerous to her.

The entire arena of sexuality in Gilman's private life and in her public work is far too complicated for casual commentary here.[12] "Voluntary motherhood," a phrase used by the women's movement in the last half of the nineteenth century, incorporated a spirit of choice for women,[13] and in general Gilman can be placed in this community. These women opposed contraceptive devices and abortion because they saw both as encouraging female sexuality outside of marriage and as a threat to the primacy of the mother in the family, the source of power for most women. However, they directly defied Victorian insistence on wifely submission, asserting the right of abstinence, the right of a wife to refuse her husband, and the right of a mother to decide when to bear a child. In this way they stood for advanced notions of women's rights. It was not just that many of these women—and I place Gilman gingerly among them—probably disliked sexual intercourse. Many women of the time did, for sex was defined by men and by what men saw as their needs and their rights, and it always meant the possibility of pregnancy, abortion, or venereal disease. Most observers of the time and later commentators would agree with reformer-physician Nicholas Cooke, author of *Satan in Society* (published in 1870) when he asserted that "the simple fact remains that the majority perhaps—or certainly an immense proportion—of those who have borne children are innocent of the faintest ray of sexual pleasure."[14]

In this context, the demand for abstinence, whatever the psychological scars, had feminist implications. Contemporary feminists advance sexual freedom as a demand. In the years of Gilman's early womanhood, sexual freedom was seen by many women, Gilman among them, as another way for men to control women. Autonomy began, not with sexual freedom, but with economic independence. In Gilman's fictional world, sexuality is not a prime concern. The pleasures of love, marriage, work, children, and community dominate. She does not directly confront the matter of sexuality and its place in women's lives. And no wonder. Prevailing cultural attitudes during the years when she came of age did not recognize women as having sexual drives of any kind. Even the "radicals" in the free-love movement had notions of sexual behavior which are perplexingly conventional to contemporary eyes and which, in addition, did not offer much independence to women. Many free-lovers, even those in the "sinful" wing of that amorphous movement—that is, those who believed in the right to a free and varied choice of sexual partners—argued that variety was desirable, so long as sexual indulgence was practiced for purposes of procreation only, which meant not very often. Most of the free-lovers believed in monogamy, fidelity, and continence, except when pregnancy was desired. In what the public saw as the "cesspool of sexual experiment in America,"[15] the Oneida community in upstate New York, women's sexual pleasure seems to have been a goal, but certainly not women's autonomy.

Relations between men and women in a particular historical context of power set limits on the degree of autonomy that women can forge for themselves. The sexual bind that nineteenth-century Americans, men and women, inherited as part of their culture was exacerbated in Gilman's personal history. Her father abandoned her mother, she recounts in her autobiography, because another pregnancy would have been fatal. Thus, daughters menace their mothers' lives by the very act of their birth. Sex brings with it not only a frightening pregnancy but the likelihood of death; yet sex is so necessary in a marriage that without it, men desert their families. She grew up in a household where she may have believed herself in some way responsible for her father's abandonment and her mother's depression and bitterness. Gilman described in painful detail her mother's decision to deny all affection to her children, so that they would early in life be steeled to its absence and thus not suffer, as she did, when love was removed. Whether or not these descriptions were accurate, they surely had a psychological reality in her early years. It is not surprising then that Charlotte Anna Perkins (and many others like her) emerged into womanhood with an ambivalent and uncomfortable sense of her own sexuality; it is, in fact, astonishing that genuine sexual pleasure was ever achieved.

In a sentimental era, family and home were sacred, and yet in Gilman's fictional world the home is a place from which one must flee. Historically, the home has never been the haven its supporters have claimed it to be, not for women, not for children, and often not even for men. Gilman's families are rarely evil: they smother creativity and withhold affection and stifle growth, but they are ordinary and they operate within widely shared conventional values. So Benigna Machiavelli's family includes a drunken father, a self-sacrificing mother who denies her own humanity by behaving like a dutiful wife, and a foolish sister ready to run off with a rogue in order to escape her parental prison. Diantha's well-meaning parents insist her place is at home and in good conscience deny her an education. Diantha's father, with no business aptitude, refuses his wife a role in his business because her work is in the home. Diantha's lover, burdened by the responsibility of supporting five adult women, does not think to challenge the prerogatives of women of his class. Mr. Peebles and Ross Akers spend years taking care of women who should be taking care of themselves.

The message from Gilman persists. One must leave the family in order to grow. One must go into the world and do things. The family, as presently constituted, embodies deadening tradition, foolish obedience, unexamined belief. The family breeds authoritarianism and tyranny by training boys and men to rule and girls and women to submit to that rule. But we are social beings and so we must create new families from remnants of the old, and from friends, colleagues at work, neighbors, and folks from the boardinghouse. The boardinghouse is often instrumental in Gilman's family-building. Once women and children, and occasionally men, flee the parental home, new social forms must be created to construct humane social relationships and institutions, as are suggested in the utopian works.

For Gilman, in fiction as in life, a favorite place of flight is the West. Gilman's West is a metaphor, an idea, a process, and a place. It is not Frederick Jackson Turner's West, the frontier where the trappings of a decaying civilization are discarded and a new, essentially male and capitalist American culture is reshaped. Gilman's is an urban West. Western cities are a place for the new, the untried; rules there are stretchable. Men far outnumber women, so women can select their mates from competing males, which Gilman believed to be the traditional way in nature. The West is the great leveler, and its cities, a powerful source of community and civilization. The West is where Gilman went to regain her emotional strength, where her daughter lived her long life, where Gilman chose to die. The West is also an idea, not just for Horace Greeley's young men, but for Charlotte Gilman's young women, and middle-aged women, and elderly women; in fact, for anyone struggling to escape confining convention.

Gilman used the variously common fictional forms to propagandize for her humanist vision. *Benigna Machiavelli* can be read as a satire of *Little Women*: the sentimental, self-sacrificing Marmee is an accomplice in her own humiliation by refusing to confront the abusive, selfish father, which Bronson Alcott surely was in reality. Gilman demonstrates that the domestic novel need not be trivial. After all, hadn't her aunt Harriet Beecher Stowe set an example by infusing that form with an anti-slavery message?

There is a good deal of tongue-in-cheek Horatio Alger in Gilman's stories, but without the crucial reliance on luck. Her characters make their own luck. To grow and develop, they must poke holes in all the pieties: fidelity to parents; patience as a desirable woman's virtue, or as anybody's virtue; honesty under all circumstances; woman's work as defined by marriage and motherhood. Everything gets turned around: sometimes couples should live apart to be happily married, he in the country and she in the city; sometimes she should run the business and he should set up a laboratory in the basement, or just loaf; Diantha should quit teaching and become a domestic servant. People should do whatever they want, whatever is useful, whatever will gratify. We should not do what conventional wisdom teaches or what the experts advise, because such advice is almost always wrong. The ministers know nothing of morality; the parents know little of child-rearing; the neurologists know nothing of women's ailments. Gilman respected expertise and skill but not the contemporary system of credentials or training.

The women in Gilman's fictional world struggle to reach a new sense of themselves, but not through sexual awakening, not as Kate Chopin's heroine or Anna Karenina or Emma Bovary relates to her world, by defying conventions that define women's sexual place. Gilman's women, through struggle and hardship, ultimately achieve autonomy, usually through their work. With that autonomy, they are then complete enough to love and to be loved. Gilman's heroines often do not marry the most sympathetic men. They come to love the men who have to change; and those men do change ultimately, a hint to women readers that it is possible to persuade men to think and to behave differently.

In general, male authors are naturally concerned primarily with problems faced commonly by men. Female writers tend to create female characters who respond, more often than not tragically or painfully, to the male world. Gilman created models of women who do all sorts of things; they do not exclusively react to the men in their lives. They are depicted in confrontation with uniquely female concerns, as they affect pregnancy, careers, marriage, or family relations. She tried to shape a female culture sharing center stage with a male world. Her women characters are creative, ingenious, adventurous, manipulative, self-indulgent, nasty, smug, curious, dependent: they are all manner of things unto themselves, not primarily the mirror for men. One can read Gilman's fiction as an effort to create a literary genre where woman's business is the business of the story, and that business ironically is often narrated through male characters. In her fictional writing Gilman tried to create a consciousness that defines and defends values and a projected society that is yet to be realized. It is the imaginative demands, not the literary skill, that make reading her fiction informing.

Gilman used the common vocabulary of her time to convey her ideas in a popular mode. She tried to rescue what she called the female qualities of love and cooperation from the camp of the reactionaries, who used them to hold women in their place. Her goal was not to replace the Victorian notion of selfless, patient, self-sacrificing womanhood with pleasure-seeking, self-involved individualism. It was not the idea of service to which she objected, but the objects of that service—husband and children. Service is for the community, the world, not simply for the family, and it should dominate equally the lives of men and women.

Although the ideology of individualism is at the foundation of American capitalist society, oddly it is the family, not the individual, that is seen as the basic social unit. Gilman, with her commitment to a socialist society, saw the flowering of the individual as the best way to achieve genuine community. So long as the family remains the social unit, the woman is tied to it and in it. She is kept from pursuing her individual gifts and her individual choices.

Gilman's social product, her work, is always traceable to her own experiences. If she had been able to pluck her father from the Boston Public Library and put him down in their home in Providence, as she desperately wished she could as a girl, he would have been indistinguishable as a day-to-day father from those tyrants in her books. (Perhaps for her the only thing worse than a father who deserted his family was one who did not.) Her mother, self-sacrificing and submissive, took the anger that needed to be usefully directed to free her from her husband, and turned it instead into bitterness, which spilled over to damage her children, while she continued to "love" her absent and rejecting husband. Charlotte Gilman initially took her own anger, which might earlier have helped her to strike out on her own, and turned it upon herself, in deep, prolonged, and debilitating depressions. In her private correspondence it is sadly clear that she saw her emotional illness as a sign of personal weakness and responded with shame and guilt; but in her external product, "The Yellow Wallpaper," she examined and understood the social roots of mental illness and was able to show how the emotions ultimately are not a private affair at all.

In her fiction Gilman constructed a world in which her own sorrows would have been largely eliminated and her unique gifts cherished and encouraged. She drew upon the unbearable and destructive elements in her own inner and outer life, and managed them through her fiction. By frequently confronting her life through resolutions achieved in her work, Gilman was able to achieve stability and gratification in her mature years.

Notes

1. Renewed interest in Gilman can be marked from the 1966 reissue of *Women and Economics*, with an introductory essay by Carl Degler.

2. See Dolores Hayden, "Charlotte Perkins Gilman: Domestic Revolution or Domestic Evolution," paper read at the 1978 Berkshire Conference on the History of Women, to be published in the *Radical History Review*, 21, issue devoted to "The Politics of Space." Hayden's description of Gilman's novel *What Diantha Did*, excerpted in this volume, as a "belated and conservative expression" or "maternal capitalism" caused me to reexamine my interpretation, and I am indebted to Dolores Hayden for persuading me to look afresh at Gilman's ideas.

3. My thanks to Paul Buhle for providing this piece of information.

4. The word "psychiatry" was not used in the nineteenth century, but phy-

sicians like Mitchell, who sought to understand the links between physical and emotional disorders, are precursors of the contemporary psychiatric profession. Sigmund Freud, for example, trained as a neurologist.

5. See James Reed, *From Private Vice to Public Virtue: The Birth Control Movement and American Society Since 1830* (New York: Basic Books, Inc., 1978), pp. 39 and 392. Gilman's assertion in *The Crux* that most of the male population suffered from some form of venereal disease may not be much exaggerated.

6. Quoted in Taylor Stoehr, *Free Love in America: A Documentary History* (New York: AMS Press Inc., 1979), p. 209.

7. She was, for a time, a member of the Socialist party.

8. For a fuller discussion of the utopia in Gilman's fiction, see my introduction to *Herland*, published by Pantheon Books in 1979.

9. Dolores Hayden has written extensively on the subject. See "Redesigning the Domestic Workplace," *Chrysalis*, no. 1 (1977): 19–30; "Melusina Fay Peirce and Cooperative Housekeeping," *International Journal of Urban and Regional Research*, 2, no. 3 (1978): 404–20; "Two Utopian Feminists and Their Programs for Kitchenless Houses," *Signs*, 4 (Winter 1978): 274–90; *Seven American Utopias: The Architecture of Communitarian Socialism, 1790–1935* (Cambridge, Mass.: MIT Press, 1976).

10. Gilman would be amused to learn that in the last twenty years biologists have discovered that in some species of lizards when the female is in total isolation over a period of time she reproduces parthenogenically and when the male is reintroduced, the female reverts to bisexual reproduction. See Charles C. Cole, "The Value of Virgin Birth," *Natural History*, (January 1978): 56–62.

11. Some of these ideas were inspired by Maria Tatar in a talk she gave to The Bunting Institute of Radcliffe College on May 2, 1979, entitled "The Houses of Fiction: Toward a Definition of the Uncanny."

12. I will explore the subject more fully in my forthcoming biography of Gilman.

13. My interpretation rests on the persuasive discussions by Daniel Scott Smith in "Family Limitation, Sexual Control and Domestic Feminism in Victorian America," *Feminist Studies*, Vol. 1, Nos. 3-4, Winter-Spring 1973, and by Linda Gordon in *Woman's Body, Woman's Right: A Social History of Birth Control in America* (New York: Grossman Publishers, 1976).

14. Quoted in Stoehr, *Free Love in America*, p. 196.

15. Stoehr, *Free Love in America*, p. 344. An extended discussion of the freelove movement can be found in Stoehr's book and in Hal D. Sears, *The Sex Radicals: Free Love in High Victorian America* (Lawrence, Kansas: The Regents Press of Kansas, 1977). Neither author reads the material in quite the way I do, however.

THE CHARLOTTE PERKINS GILMAN READER

THE
YELLOW
WALLPAPER *

It is very seldom that mere ordinary people like John and myself secure ancestral halls for the summer.

A colonial mansion, a hereditary estate, I would say a haunted house and reach the height of romantic felicity—but that would be asking too much of fate!

Still I will proudly declare that there is something queer about it.

Else, why should it be let so cheaply? And why have stood so long untenanted?

John laughs at me, of course, but one expects that.

John is practical in the extreme. He has no patience with faith, an intense horror of superstition, and he scoffs openly at any talk of things not to be felt and seen and put down in figures.

John is a physician, and *perhaps*—(I would not say it to a living soul, of course, but this is dead paper and a great relief to my mind)—*perhaps* that is one reason I do not get well faster.

You see, he does not believe I am sick! And what can one do?

If a physician of high standing, and one's own husband, assures friends and relatives that there is really nothing the matter

---

*"The Yellow Wallpaper" appeared originally in the January 1892 issue of The New England Magazine.

with one but temporary nervous depression—a slight hysterical tendency—what is one to do?

My brother is also a physician, and also of high standing, and he says the same thing.

So I take phosphates or phosphites—whichever it is—and tonics, and air and exercise, and journeys, and am absolutely forbidden to "work" until I am well again.

Personally, I disagree with their ideas.

Personally, I believe that congenial work, with excitement and change, would do me good.

But what is one to do?

I did write for a while in spite of them; but it *does* exhaust me a good deal—having to be so sly about it, or else meet with heavy opposition.

I sometimes fancy that in my condition, if I had less opposition and more society and stimulus—but John says the very worst thing I can do is to think about my condition, and I confess it always makes me feel bad.

So I will let it alone and talk about the house.

The most beautiful place! It is quite alone, standing well back from the road, quite three miles from the village. It makes me think of English places that you read about, for there are hedges and walls and gates that lock, and lots of separate little houses for the gardeners and people.

There is a *delicious* garden! I never saw such a garden—large and shady, full of box-bordered paths, and lined with long grape-covered arbors with seats under them.

There were greenhouses, but they are all broken now.

There was some legal trouble, I believe, something about the heirs and co-heirs; anyhow, the place has been empty for years.

That spoils my ghostliness, I am afraid, but I don't care—there is something strange about the house—I can feel it.

I even said so to John one moonlight evening, but he said what I felt was a draught, and shut the window.

I get unreasonably angry with John sometimes. I'm sure I never used to be so sensitive. I think it is due to this nervous condition.

But John says if I feel so I shall neglect proper self-control; so I take pains to control myself—before him, at least, and that makes me very tired.

I don't like our room a bit. I wanted one downstairs that opened onto the piazza and had roses all over the window, and such pretty old-fashioned chintz hangings! But John would not hear of it.

He said there was only one window and not room for two beds, and no near room for him if he took another.

He is very careful and loving, and hardly lets me stir without special direction.

I have a schedule prescription for each hour in the day; he takes all care from me, and so I feel basely ungrateful not to value it more.

He said he came here solely on my account, that I was to have perfect rest and all the air I could get. "Your exercise depends on your strength, my dear," said he, "and your food somewhat on your appetite; but air you can absorb all the time." So we took the nursery at the top of the house.

It is a big, airy room, the whole floor nearly, with windows that look all ways, and air and sunshine galore. It was nursery first, and then playroom and gymnasium, I should judge, for the windows are barred for little children, and there are rings and things in the walls.

The paint and paper look as if a boys' school had used it. It is stripped off—the paper—in great patches all around the head of my bed, about as far as I can reach, and in a great place on the other side of the room low down. I never saw a worse paper in my life. One of those sprawling, flamboyant patterns committing every artistic sin.

It is dull enough to confuse the eye in following, pronounced enough constantly to irritate and provoke study, and when you follow the lame uncertain curves for a little distance they suddenly commit suicide—plunge off at outrageous angles, destroy themselves in unheard-of contradictions.

The color is repellent, almost revolting: a smouldering unclean yellow, strangely faded by the slow-turning sunlight. It is a dull yet lurid orange in some places, a sickly sulphur tint in others.

No wonder the children hated it! I should hate it myself if I had to live in this room long.

There comes John, and I must put this away—he hates to have me write a word.

We have been here two weeks, and I haven't felt like writing before, since that first day.

I am sitting by the window now, up in this atrocious nursery, and there is nothing to hinder my writing as much as I please, save lack of strength.

John is away all day, and even some nights when his cases are serious.

I am glad my case is not serious!

But these nervous troubles are dreadfully depressing.

John does not know how much I really suffer. He knows there is no reason to suffer, and that satisfies him.

Of course it is only nervousness. It does weigh on me so not to do my duty in any way!

I meant to be such a help to John, such a real rest and comfort, and here I am a comparative burden already!

Nobody would believe what an effort it is to do what little I am able—to dress and entertain, and order things.

It is fortunate Mary is so good with the baby. Such a dear baby!

And yet I *cannot* be with him, it makes me so nervous.

I suppose John never was nervous in his life. He laughs at me so about this wallpaper!

At first he meant to repaper the room, but afterward he said that I was letting it get the better of me, and that nothing was worse for a nervous patient than to give way to such fancies.

He said that after the wallpaper was changed it would be the heavy bedstead, and then the barred windows, and then that gate at the head of the stairs, and so on.

"You know the place is doing you good," he said, "and really, dear, I don't care to renovate the house just for a three months' rental."

"Then do let us go downstairs," I said. "There are such pretty rooms there."

Then he took me in his arms and called me a blessed little goose, and said he would go down cellar, if I wished, and have it whitewashed into the bargain.

But he is right enough about the beds and windows and things.

It is as airy and comfortable a room as anyone need wish, and, of course, I would not be so silly as to make him uncomfortable just for a whim.

I'm really getting quite fond of the big room, all but that horrid paper.

Out of one window I can see the garden—those mysterious deep-shaded arbors, the riotous old-fashioned flowers, and bushes and gnarly trees.

Out of another I get a lovely view of the bay and a little private wharf belonging to the estate. There is a beautiful shaded lane that runs down there from the house. I always fancy I see people walking in these numerous paths and arbors, but John has cautioned me not to give way to fancy in the least. He says that with my imaginative power and habit of story-making, a nervous weakness like mine is sure to lead to all manner of excited fancies, and that I ought to use my will and good sense to check the tendency. So I try.

I think sometimes that if I were only well enough to write a little it would relieve the press of ideas and rest me.

But I find I get pretty tired when I try.

It is so discouraging not to have any advice and companionship about my work. When I get really well, John says we will ask Cousin Henry and Julia down for a long visit; but he says he would as soon put fireworks in my pillow-case as to let me have those stimulating people about now.

I wish I could get well faster.

But I must not think about that. This paper looks to me as if it *knew* what a vicious influence it had!

There is a recurrent spot where the pattern lolls like a broken neck and two bulbous eyes stare at you upside down.

I get positively angry with the impertinence of it and the everlastingness. Up and down and sideways they crawl, and those absurd unblinking eyes are everywhere. There is one place where two breadths didn't match, and the eyes go all up and down the line, one a little higher than the other.

I never saw so much expression in an inanimate thing before, and we all know how much expression they have! I used to lie awake as a child and get more entertainment and terror out of blank walls and plain furniture than most children could find in a toy-store.

I remember what a kindly wink the knobs of our big old

bureau used to have, and there was one chair that always seemed like a strong friend.

I used to feel that if any of the other things looked too fierce I could always hop into that chair and be safe.

The furniture in this room is no worse than inharmonious, however, for we had to bring it all from downstairs. I suppose when this was used as a playroom they had to take the nursery things out, and no wonder! I never saw such ravages as the children have made here.

The wallpaper, as I said before, is torn off in spots, and it sticketh closer than a brother—they must have had perseverance as well as hatred.

Then the floor is scratched and gouged and splintered, the plaster itself is dug out here and there, and this great heavy bed, which is all we found in the room, looks as if it had been through the wars.

But I don't mind it a bit—only the paper.

There comes John's sister. Such a dear girl as she is, and so careful of me! I must not let her find me writing.

She is a perfect and enthusiastic housekeeper, and hopes for no better profession. I verily believe she thinks it is the writing which made me sick!

But I can write when she is out, and see her a long way off from these windows.

There is one that commands the road, a lovely shaded winding road, and one that just looks off over the country. A lovely country, too, full of great elms and velvet meadows.

This wallpaper has a kind of sub-pattern in a different shade, a particularly irritating one, for you can only see it in certain lights, and not clearly then.

But in the places where it isn't faded and where the sun is just so—I can see a strange, provoking, formless sort of figure that seems to skulk about behind that silly and conspicuous front design.

There's sister on the stairs!

Well, the Fourth of July is over! The people are all gone, and I am tired out. John thought it might do me good to see a little company, so we just had Mother and Nellie and the children down for a week.

Of course I didn't do a thing. Jennie sees to everything now. But it tired me all the same.

John says if I don't pick up faster he shall send me to Weir Mitchell in the fall.

But I don't want to go there at all. I had a friend who was in his hands once, and she says he is just like John and my brother, only more so!

Besides, it is such an undertaking to go so far.

I don't feel as if it was worthwhile to turn my hand over for anything, and I'm getting dreadfully fretful and querulous.

I cry at nothing, and cry most of the time.

Of course I don't when John is here, or anybody else, but when I am alone.

And I am alone a good deal just now. John is kept in town very often by serious cases, and Jennie is good and lets me alone when I want her to.

So I walk a little in the garden or down that lovely lane, sit on the porch under the roses, and lie down up here a good deal.

I'm getting really fond of the room in spite of the wallpaper. Perhaps *because* of the wallpaper.

It dwells in my mind so!

I lie here on this great immovable bed—it is nailed down, I believe—and follow that pattern about by the hour. It is as good as gymnastics, I assure you. I start, we'll say, at the bottom, down in the corner over there where it has not been touched, and I determine for the thousandth time that I *will* follow that pointless pattern to some sort of a conclusion.

I know a little of the principle of design, and I know this thing was not arranged on any laws of radiation, or alternation, or repetition, or symmetry, or anything else that I ever heard of.

It is repeated, of course, by the breadths, but not otherwise.

Looked at in one way, each breadth stands alone; the bloated curves and flourishes—a kind of "debased Romanesque" with delirium tremens—go waddling up and down in isolated columns of fatuity.

But, on the other hand, they connect diagonally, and the sprawling outlines run off in great slanting waves of optic horror, like a lot of wallowing sea-weeds in full chase.

The whole thing goes horizontally, too, at least it seems so, and I exhaust myself trying to distinguish the order of its going in that direction.

They have used a horizontal breadth for a frieze, and that adds wonderfully to the confusion.

There is one end of the room where it is almost intact, and there, when the crosslights fade and the low sun shines directly upon it, I can almost fancy radiation after all—the interminable grotesque seems to form around a common center and rush off in headlong plunges of equal distraction.

It makes me tired to follow it. I will take a nap, I guess.

I don't know why I should write this.

I don't want to.

I don't feel able.

And I know John would think it absurd. But I *must* say what I feel and think in some way—it is such a relief!

But the effort is getting to be greater than the relief.

Half the time now I am awfully lazy, and lie down ever so much. John says I mustn't lose my strength, and has me take cod liver oil and lots of tonics and things, to say nothing of ale and wine and rare meat.

Dear John! He loves me very dearly, and hates to have me sick. I tried to have a real earnest reasonable talk with him the other day, and tell him how I wish he would let me go and make a visit to Cousin Henry and Julia.

But he said I wasn't able to go, nor able to stand it after I got there; and I did not make out a very good case for myself, for I was crying before I had finished.

It is getting to be a great effort for me to think straight. Just this nervous weakness, I suppose.

And dear John gathered me up in his arms, and just carried me upstairs and laid me on the bed, and sat by me and read to me till it tired my head.

He said I was his darling and his comfort and all he had, and that I must take care of myself for his sake, and keep well.

He says no one but myself can help me out of it, that I must use my will and self-control and not let any silly fancies run away with me.

There's one comfort—the baby is well and happy, and does not have to occupy this nursery with the horrid wallpaper.

If we had not used it, that blessed child would have! What a fortunate escape! Why, I wouldn't have a child of mine, an impressionable little thing, live in such a room for worlds.

I never thought of it before, but it is lucky that John kept me here after all; I can stand it so much easier than a baby, you see.

Of course I never mention it to them any more—I am too wise—but I keep watch for it all the same.

There are things in that wallpaper that nobody knows about but me, or ever will.

Behind that outside pattern the dim shapes get clearer every day.

It is always the same shape, only very numerous.

And it is like a woman stooping down and creeping about behind that pattern. I don't like it a bit. I wonder—I begin to think—I wish John would take me away from here!

It is so hard to talk with John about my case, because he is so wise, and because he loves me so.

But I tried it last night.

It was moonlight. The moon shines in all around just as the sun does.

I hate to see it sometimes, it creeps so slowly, and always comes in by one window or another.

John was asleep and I hated to waken him, so I kept still and watched the moonlight on that undulating wallpaper till I felt creepy.

The faint figure behind seemed to shake the pattern, just as if she wanted to get out.

I got up softly and went to feel and see if the paper *did* move, and when I came back John was awake.

"What is it, little girl?" he said. "Don't go walking about like that—you'll get cold."

I thought it was a good time to talk, so I told him that I really was not gaining here, and that I wished he would take me away.

"Why, darling!" said he. "Our lease will be up in three weeks, and I can't see how to leave before.

"The repairs are not done at home, and I cannot possibly leave town just now. Of course, if you were in any danger, I could and would, but you really are better, dear, whether you can see it or not. I am a doctor, dear, and I know. You are gaining flesh and color, your appetite is better, I feel really much easier about you."

"I don't weigh a bit more," said I, "nor as much; and my appetite may be better in the evening when you are here but it is worse in the morning when you are away!"

"Bless her little heart!" said he with a big hug. "She shall be as sick as she pleases! But now let's improve the shining hours by going to sleep, and talk about it in the morning!"

"And you won't go away?" I asked gloomily.

"Why, how can I, dear? It is only three weeks more and then we will take a nice little trip of a few days while Jennie is getting the house ready. Really, dear, you are better!"

"Better in body perhaps—" I began, and stopped short, for he sat up straight and looked at me with such a stern, reproachful look that I could not say another word.

"My darling," said he, "I beg of you, for my sake and for our child's sake, as well as for your own, that you will never for one instant let that idea enter your mind! There is nothing so dangerous, so fascinating, to a temperament like yours. It is a false and foolish fancy. Can you not trust me as a physician when I tell you so?"

So of course I said no more on that score, and we went to sleep before long. He thought I was asleep first, but I wasn't, and lay there for hours trying to decide whether that front pattern and the back pattern really did move together or separately.

On a pattern like this, by daylight, there is a lack of sequence, a defiance of law, that is a constant irritant to a normal mind.

The color is hideous enough, and unreliable enough, and infuriating enough, but the pattern is torturing.

You think you have mastered it, but just as you get well under way in following, it turns a back-somersault and there you are. It slaps you in the face, knocks you down, and tramples upon you. It is like a bad dream.

The outside pattern is a florid arabesque, reminding one of a fungus. If you can imagine a toadstool in joints, an interminable string of toadstools, budding and sprouting in endless convolutions—why, that is something like it.

That is, sometimes!

There is one marked peculiarity about this paper, a thing nobody seems to notice but myself, and that is that it changes as the light changes.

When the sun shoots in through the east window—I always watch for that first long, straight ray—it changes so quickly that I never can quite believe it.

That is why I watch it always.

By moonlight—the moon shines in all night when there is a moon—I wouldn't know it was the same paper.

At night in any kind of light, in twilight, candlelight, lamplight, and worst of all by moonlight, it becomes bars! The outside pattern, I mean, and the woman behind it is as plain as can be.

I didn't realize for a long time what the thing was that showed behind, that dim sub-pattern, but now I am quite sure it is a woman.

By daylight she is subdued, quiet. I fancy it is the pattern that keeps her so still. It is so puzzling. It keeps me quiet by the hour.

I lie down ever so much now. John says it is good for me, and to sleep all I can.

Indeed he started the habit by making me lie down for an hour after each meal.

It is a very bad habit, I am convinced, for you see, I don't sleep.

And that cultivates deceit, for I don't tell them I'm awake—oh, no!

The fact is I am getting a little afraid of John.

He seems very queer sometimes, and even Jennie has an inexplicable look.

It strikes me occasionally, just as a scientific hypothesis, that perhaps it is the paper!

I have watched John when he did not know I was looking, and come into the room suddenly on the most innocent excuses, and I've caught him several times *looking at the paper!* And Jennie too. I caught Jennie with her hand on it once.

She didn't know I was in the room, and when I asked her in a quiet, a very quiet voice, with the most restrained manner possible, what she was doing with the paper, she turned around as if she had been caught stealing, and looked quite angry—asked me why I should frighten her so!

Then she said that the paper stained everything it touched, that she had found yellow smooches on all my clothes and John's and she wished we would be more careful!

Did not that sound innocent? But I know she was studying that pattern, and I am determined that nobody shall find it out but myself!

Life is very much more exciting now than it used to be. You see, I have something more to expect, to look forward to, to watch. I really do eat better, and am more quiet than I was.

John is so pleased to see me improve! He laughed a little the other day, and said I seemed to be flourishing in spite of my wallpaper.

I turned it off with a laugh. I had no intention of telling him it was *because* of the wallpaper—he would make fun of me. He might even want to take me away.

I don't want to leave now until I have found it out. There is a week more, and I think that will be enough.

I'm feeling so much better!

I don't sleep much at night, for it is so interesting to watch developments; but I sleep a good deal during the daytime.

In the daytime it is tiresome and perplexing.

There are always new shoots on the fungus, and new shades of yellow all over it. I cannot keep count of them, though I have tried conscientiously.

It is the strangest yellow, that wallpaper! It makes me think of all the yellow things I ever saw—not beautiful ones like butter-cups, but old, foul, bad yellow things.

But there is something else about that paper—the smell! I noticed it the moment we came into the room, but with so much air and sun it was not bad. Now we have had a week of fog and rain, and whether the windows are open or not, the smell is here.

It creeps all over the house.

I find it hovering in the dining-room, skulking in the parlor, hiding in the hall, lying in wait for me on the stairs.

It gets into my hair.

Even when I go to ride, if I turn my head suddenly and sur-prise it—there is that smell!

Such a peculiar odor, too! I have spent hours in trying to analyze it, to find what it smelled like.

It is not bad—at first—and very gentle, but quite the subtlest, most enduring odor I ever met.

In this damp weather it is awful. I wake up in the night and find it hanging over me.

It used to disturb me at first. I thought seriously of burning the house—to reach the smell.

But now I am used to it. The only thing I can think of that it is like is the *color* of the paper! A yellow smell.

There is a very funny mark on this wall, low down, near the mopboard. A streak that runs round the room. It goes behind every piece of furniture, except the bed, a long, straight, even *smooch*, as if it had been rubbed over and over.

I wonder how it was done and who did it, and what they did it for. Round and round and round—round and round and round—it makes me dizzy!

I really have discovered something at last.

Through watching so much at night, when it changes so, I have finally found out.

The front pattern *does* move—and no wonder! The woman behind shakes it!

Sometimes I think there are a great many women behind, and sometimes only one, and she crawls around fast, and her crawling shakes it all over.

Then in the very bright spots she keeps still, and in the very shady spots she just takes hold of the bars and shakes them hard.

And she is all the time trying to climb through. But nobody could climb through that pattern—it strangles so; I think that is why it has so many heads.

They get through, and then the pattern strangles them off and turns them upside down, and makes their eyes white!

If those heads were covered or taken off it would not be half so bad.

I think that woman gets out in the daytime!

And I'll tell you why—privately—I've seen her!

I can see her out of every one of my windows!

It is the same woman, I know, for she is always creeping, and most women do not creep by daylight.

I see her in that long shaded lane, creeping up and down. I see her in those dark grape arbors, creeping all around the garden.

I see her on that long road under the trees, creeping along, and when a carriage comes she hides under the blackberry vines.

I don't blame her a bit. It must be very humiliating to be caught creeping by daylight!

I always lock the door when I creep by daylight. I can't do it at night, for I know John would suspect something at once.

And John is so queer now that I don't want to irritate him. I wish he would take another room! Besides, I don't want anybody to get that woman out at night but myself.

I often wonder if I could see her out of all the windows at once.

But, turn as fast as I can, I can only see out of one at one time.

And though I always see her, she *may* be able to creep faster than I can turn! I have watched her sometimes away off in the open country, creeping as fast as a cloud shadow in a wind.

If only that top pattern could be gotten off from the under one! I mean to try it, little by little.

I have found out another funny thing, but I shan't tell it this time! It does not do to trust people too much.

There are only two more days to get this paper off, and I believe John is beginning to notice. I don't like the look in his eyes.

And I heard him ask Jennie a lot of professional questions about me. She had a very good report to give.

She said I slept a good deal in the daytime.

John knows I don't sleep very well at night, for all I'm so quiet!

He asked me all sorts of questions, too, and pretended to be very loving and kind.

As if I couldn't see through him!

Still, I don't wonder he acts so, sleeping under this paper for three months.

It only interests me, but I feel sure John and Jennie are affected by it.

▼ ▼ ▼ ▼ ▼

Hurrah! This is the last day, but it is enough. John is to stay in town over night, and won't be out until this evening.

Jennie wanted to sleep with me—the sly thing; but I told her I should undoubtedly rest better for a night all alone.

That was clever, for really I wasn't alone a bit! As soon as it was moonlight and that poor thing began to crawl and shake the pattern, I got up and ran to help her.

I pulled and she shook. I shook and she pulled, and before morning we had peeled off yards of that paper.

A strip about as high as my head and half around the room.

And then when the sun came and that awful pattern began to laugh at me, I declared I would finish it today!

We go away tomorrow, and they are moving all my furniture down again to leave things as they were before.

Jennie looked at the wall in amazement, but I told her merrily that I did it out of pure spite at the vicious thing.

She laughed and said she wouldn't mind doing it herself, but I must not get tired.

How she betrayed herself that time!

But I am here, and no person touches this paper but Me—not *alive!*

She tried to get me out of the room—it was too patent! But I said it was so quiet and empty and clean now that I believed I would lie down again and sleep all I could, and not to wake me even for dinner—I would call when I woke.

So now she is gone, and the servants are gone, and the things are gone, and there is nothing left but that great bedstead nailed down, with the canvas mattress we found on it.

We shall sleep downstairs tonight, and take the boat home tomorrow.

I quite enjoy the room, now it is bare again.

How those children did tear about here!

This bedstead is fairly gnawed!

But I must get to work.

I have locked the door and thrown the key down into the front path.

I don't want to go out, and I don't want to have anybody come in, till John comes.

I want to astonish him.

I've got a rope up here that even Jennie did not find. If that woman does get out, and tries to get away, I can tie her!

But I forgot I could not reach far without anything to stand on!

This bed will *not* move!

I tried to lift and push it until I was lame, and then I got so angry I bit off a little piece at one corner—but it hurt my teeth.

Then I peeled off all the paper I could reach standing on the floor. It sticks horribly and the pattern just enjoys it! All those strangled heads and bulbous eyes and waddling fungus growths just shriek with derision!

I am getting angry enough to do something desperate. To jump out of the window would be admirable exercise, but the bars are too strong even to try.

Besides I wouldn't do it. Of course not. I know well enough that a step like that is improper and might be misconstrued.

I don't like to *look* out of the windows even—there are so many of those creeping women, and they creep so fast.

I wonder if they all come out of that wallpaper as I did?

But I am securely fastened now by my well-hidden rope—you don't get *me* out in the road there!

I suppose I shall have to get back behind the pattern when it comes night, and that is hard!

It is so pleasant to be out in this great room and creep around as I please!

I don't want to go outside. I won't, even if Jennie asks me to.

For outside you have to creep on the ground, and everything is green instead of yellow.

But here I can creep smoothly on the floor, and my shoulder just fits in that long smooch around the wall, so I cannot lose my way.

Why, there's John at the door!

It is no use, young man, you can't open it!

How he does call and pound!

Now he's crying to Jennie for an axe.

It would be a shame to break down that beautiful door!

"John, dear!" said I in the gentlest voice. "The key is down by the front steps, under a plantain leaf!"

That silenced him for a few moments.

Then he said, very quietly indeed, "Open the door, my darling!"

"I can't," said I. "The key is down by the front door under a plantain leaf!" And then I said it again, several times, very gently and slowly, and said it so often that he had to go and see, and he got it of course, and came in. He stopped short by the door.

"What is the matter?" he cried. "For God's sake, what are you doing!"

I kept on creeping just the same, but I looked at him over my shoulder.

"I've got out at last," said I, "in spite of you and Jane. And I've pulled off most of the paper, so you can't put me back!"

Now why should that man have fainted? But he did, and right across my path by the wall, so that I had to creep over him every time!

Why I Wrote "The Yellow Wallpaper"?*

Many and many a reader has asked that. When the story first came out, in the New England Magazine about 1891, a Boston physician made protest in The Transcript. Such a story ought not to be written, he said; it was enough to drive anyone mad to read it.

Another physician, in Kansas I think, wrote to say that it was the best description of incipient insanity he had ever seen, and—begging my pardon—had I been there?

Now the story of the story is this:

For many years I suffered from a severe and continuous nervous breakdown tending to melancholia—and beyond. During about the third year of this trouble I went, in devout faith and some faint stir of hope, to a noted specialist in nervous diseases, the best known in the country. This wise man put me to bed and applied the rest cure, to which a still-good physique responded so promptly that he concluded there was nothing much the matter with me, and sent me home with solemn advice to

---

*"Why I Wrote 'The Yellow Wallpaper'?" appeared in the October 1913 issue of The Forerunner.

"live as domestic a life as far as possible," to "have but two hours' intellectual life a day," and "never to touch pen, brush, or pencil again" as long as I lived. This was in 1887.

I went home and obeyed those directions for some three months, and came so near the borderline of utter mental ruin that I could see over.

Then, using the remnants of intelligence that remained, and helped by a wise friend, I cast the noted specialist's advice to the winds and went to work again—work, the normal life of every human being; work, in which is joy and growth and service, without which one is a pauper and a parasite—ultimately recovering some measure of power.

Being naturally moved to rejoicing by this narrow escape, I wrote "The Yellow Wallpaper," with its embellishments and additions, to carry out the ideal (I never had hallucinations or objections to my mural decorations) and sent a copy to the physician who so nearly drove me mad. He never acknowledged it.

The little book is valued by alienists and as a good specimen of one kind of literature. It has, to my knowledge, saved one woman from a similar fate—so terrifying her family that they let her out into normal activity and she recovered.

But the best result is this. Many years later I was told that the great specialist had admitted to friends of his that he had altered his treatment of neurasthenia since reading "The Yellow Wallpaper."

It was not intended to drive people crazy, but to save people from being driven crazy, and it worked.

WHEN I WAS A WITCH *

If I had understood the terms of that one-sided contract with Satan, the Time of Witching would have lasted longer—you may be sure of that. But how was I to tell? It just happened, and has never happened again, though I've tried the same preliminaries as far as I could control them.

The thing began all of a sudden, one October midnight—the 30th, to be exact. It had been hot, really hot, all day, and was sultry and thunderous in the evening—no air stirring, and the whole house stewing with that ill-advised activity which always seems to move the steam radiator when it isn't wanted.

I was in a state of simmering rage—hot enough, even without the weather and the furnace—and I went up on the roof to cool off. A top-floor apartment has that advantage, among others—you can take a walk without the mediation of an elevator boy!

There are things enough in New York to lose one's temper over at the best of times, and on this particular day they seemed to all happen at once, and some fresh ones. The night before, cats and dogs had broken my rest, of course. My morning paper was more than usually mendacious; and my neighbor's morning paper—more visible than my own as I went downtown—was

---

*"When I Was a Witch" appeared in the May 1910 issue of The Forerunner, 1-6.

more than usually salacious. My cream wasn't cream—my egg was a relic of the past. My "new" napkins were giving out.

Being a woman, I'm supposed not to swear; but when the motorman disregarded my plain signal, and grinned as he rushed by; when the subway guard waited till I was just about to step on board, and then slammed the door in my face— standing behind it calmly for some minutes before the bell rang to warrant his closing—I desired to swear like a mule-driver.

At night it was worse. The way people paw one's back in the crowd! The cow-puncher who packs the people in or jerks them out—the men who smoke and spit, law or no law—the women whose saw-edged cartwheel hats, swashing feathers, and deadly pins add so to one's comfort inside.

Well, as I said, I was in a particularly bad temper, and went up on the roof to cool off. Heavy black clouds hung low overhead, and lightning flickered threateningly here and there.

A starved black cat stole from behind a chimney and mewed dolefully. Poor thing! She had been scalded.

The street was quiet for New York. I leaned over a little and looked up and down the long parallels of twinkling lights. A belated cab drew near, the horse so tired he could hardly hold his head up.

Then the driver, with a skill born of plenteous practice, flung out his long-lashed whip and curled it under the poor beast's belly with a stinging cut that made me shudder. The horse shuddered too, poor wretch, and jingled his harness with an effort at a trot.

I leaned over the parapet and watched that man with a spirit of unmitigated ill-will.

"I wish," said I, slowly—and I did wish it with all my heart— "that every person who strikes or otherwise hurts a horse unnecessarily shall feel the pain intended—and the horse not feel it!"

It did me good to say it, anyhow, but I never expected any result. I saw the man swing his great whip again, and lay on heartily. I saw him throw up his hands—heard him scream—but I never thought what the matter was, even then.

The lean black cat, timid but trustful, rubbed against my skirt and mewed.

"Poor Kitty!" I said. "Poor Kitty! It is a shame!" And I thought tenderly of all the thousands of hungry, hunted cats who slink and suffer in a great city.

Later, when I tried to sleep, and up across the stillness rose the raucous shrieks of some of these same sufferers, my pity turned cold. "Any fool that will try to keep a cat in a city!" I muttered, angrily.

Another yell—a pause—an ear-torturing, continuous cry. "I wish," I burst forth, "that every cat in the city was comfortably dead!"

A sudden silence fell, and in the course of time I got to sleep.

Things went fairly well next morning, till I tried another egg. They were expensive eggs, too.

"I can't help it!" said my sister, who keeps house.

"I know you can't," I admitted. "But somebody could help it. I wish the people who are responsible had to eat their old eggs, and never got a good one till they sold good ones!"

"They'd stop eating eggs, that's all," said my sister, "and eat meat."

"Let 'em eat meat!" I said, recklessly. "The meat is as bad as the eggs! It's so long since we've had a clean, fresh chicken that I've forgotten how they taste!"

"It's cold storage," said my sister. She is a peaceable sort; I'm not.

"Yes, cold storage!" I snapped. "It ought to be a blessing—to tide over shortages, equalize supplies, and lower prices. What does it do? Corner the market, raise prices the year round, and make all the food bad!"

My anger rose. "If there was any way of getting at them!" I cried. "The law doesn't touch 'em. They need to be cursed somehow! I'd like to do it! I wish the whole crowd that profit by this vicious business might taste their bad meat, their old fish, their stale milk—whatever they ate. Yes, and feel the prices as we do!"

"They couldn't, you know; they're rich," said my sister.

"I know that, " I admitted sulkily. "There's no way of getting at 'em. But I wish they could. And I wish they knew how people hated 'em, and felt that too—till they mended their ways!"

When I left for my office I saw a funny thing. A man who

drove a garbage cart took his horse by the bits and jerked and wrenched brutally. I was amazed to see him clap his hands to his own jaws with a moan, while the horse philosophically licked his chops and looked at him.

The man seemed to resent his expression, and struck him on the head, only to rub his own poll and swear amazedly, looking around to see who had hit him. The horse advanced a step, stretching a hungry nose toward a garbage pail crowned with cabbage leaves, and the man, recovering his sense of proprietorship, swore at him and kicked him in the ribs. That time he had to sit down, turning pale and weak. I watched with growing wonder and delight.

A market wagon came clattering down the street, the hard-faced young ruffian fresh for his morning task. He gathered the ends of the reins and brought them down on the horse's back with a resounding thwack. The horse did not notice this at all, but the boy did. He yelled!

I came to a place where many teamsters were at work hauling dirt and crushed stone. A strange silence and peace hung over the scene where usually the sound of the lash and sight of brutal blows made me hurry by. The men were talking together a little, and seemed to be exchanging notes. It was too good to be true. I gazed and marvelled, waiting for my car.

It came, merrily running along. It was not full. There was one not far ahead, which I had missed in watching the horses; there was no other near it in the rear.

Yet the coarse-faced person in authority who ran it went gaily by without stopping, though I stood on the track almost, and waved my umbrella.

A hot flush of rage surged to my face. "I wish you felt the blow you deserve," said I, viciously, looking after the car. "I wish you'd have to stop, and back to here, and open the door and apologize. I wish that would happen to all of you, every time you play that trick."

To my infinite amazement, that car stopped and backed up till the front door was before me. The motorman opened it, holding his hand to his cheek. "Beg your pardon, madam!" he said.

I passed in, dazed, overwhelmed. Could it be? Could it possibly be that—that what I wished came true? The idea sobered me, but I dismissed it with a scornful smile. "No such luck!" said I.

Opposite me sat a person in petticoats. She was of a sort I particularly detest. No real body of bones and muscles, but the contours of grouped sausages. Complacent, gaudily dressed, heavily wigged and ratted, with powder and perfume and flowers and jewels—and a dog.

A poor, wretched, little, artificial dog—alive, but only so by virtue of man's insolence—not a real creature that God made. And the dog had clothes on—and a bracelet! His fitted jacket had a pocket—and a pocket-handkerchief! He looked sick and unhappy.

I meditated on his pitiful position, and that of all the other poor chained prisoners, leading unnatural lives of enforced celibacy, cut off from sunlight, fresh air, the use of their limbs; led forth at stated intervals by unwilling servants, to defile our streets; over-fed, under-exercised, nervous, and unhealthy.

"And we say we love them!" said I, bitterly to myself. "No wonder they bark and howl and go mad. No wonder they have almost as many diseases as we do! I wish—" Here the thought I had dismissed struck me again. "I wish that all the unhappy dogs in cities would die at once!"

I watched the sad-eyed little invalid across the car. He dropped his head and died. She never noticed it till she got off; then she made fuss enough.

The evening papers were full of it. Some sudden pestilence had struck both dogs and cats, it would appear. Red headlines struck the eye, big letters, and columns were filled out of the complaints of those who had lost their "pets," of the sudden labors of the board of health, and of interviews with doctors.

All day, as I went through the office routine, the strange sense of this new power struggled with reason and common knowledge. I even tried a few furtive test "wishes"—wished that the wastebasket would fall over, that the inkstand would fill itself; but they didn't.

I dismissed the idea as pure foolishness, till I saw those newspapers and heard people telling worse stories.

One thing I decided at once—not to tell a soul. "Nobody'd believe me if I did," said I to myself. "And I won't give 'em the chance. I've scored on cats and dogs, anyhow—and horses."

As I watched the horses at work that afternoon, and thought of all their unknown sufferings from crowded city stables, bad air, and insufficient food, and from the wearing strain of asphalt pavements in wet and icy weather, I decided to have another try on horses.

"I wish," said I, slowly and carefully, but with a fixed intensity of purpose, "that every horse owner, keeper, hirer, and driver or rider, might feel what the horse feels, when he suffers at our hands. Feel it keenly and constantly till the case is mended."

I wasn't able to verify this attempt for some time; but the effect was so general that it got widely talked about soon; and this "new wave of humane feeling" soon raised the status of horses in our city. Also it diminished their numbers. People began to prefer motor drays—which was a mighty good thing.

Now I felt pretty well assured in my own mind, and kept my assurance to myself. Also I began to make a list of my cherished grudges, with a fine sense of power and pleasure.

"I must be careful," I said to myself, "very careful; and, above all things, 'make the punishment fit the crime.' "

The subway crowding came to my mind next—both the people who crowd because they have to, and the people who make them. "I musn't punish anybody for what they can't help," I mused. "But when it's pure meanness!" Then I bethought me of the remote stockholders, of the more immediate directors, of the painfully prominent officials and insolent employees—and got to work.

"I might as well make a good job of it while this lasts," said I to myself. "It's quite a responsibility, but lots of fun." And I wished that every person responsible for the condition of our subways might be mysteriously compelled to ride up and down in them continuously during rush hours.

This experiment I watched with keen interest, but for the life of me I could see little difference. There were a few more well-dressed persons in the crowds, that was all. So I came to the conclusion that the general public was mostly to blame, and carried their daily punishment without knowing it.

For the insolent guards and cheating ticket-sellers who give you short change, very slowly, when you are dancing on one foot and your train is there, I merely wished that they might feel the pain their victims would like to give them, short of real injury. They did, I guess.

Then I wished similar things for all manner of corporations and officials. It worked. It worked amazingly. There was a sudden conscientious revival all over the country. The dry bones rattled and sat up. Boards of directors, having troubles enough of their own, were aggravated by innumerable communications from suddenly sensitive stockholders.

In mills and mines and railroads, things began to mend. The country buzzed. The papers fattened. The churches sat up and took the credit for themselves. I was incensed at this, and, after brief consideration, wished that every minister would preach to his congregation exactly what he believed and what he thought of them.

I went to six services the next Sunday—about ten minutes each, for two sessions. It was most amusing. A thousand pulpits were emptied forthwith, refilled, reemptied, and so on, from week to week. People began to go to church—men largely; women didn't like it as well. They had always supposed the ministers thought more highly of them than now appeared to be the case.

One of my oldest grudges was against the sleeping-car people; and I now began to consider them. How often I had grinned and borne it—with other thousands—submitting helplessly.

Here is a railroad—a common carrier—and you have to use it. You pay for your transportation, a good round sum.

Then if you wish to stay in the sleeping car during the day, they charge you another $2.50 for the privilege of sitting there, whereas you have paid for a seat when you bought your ticket. That seat is now sold to another person—twice sold. Five dollars for twenty-four hours in a space six feet by three by three at night, and one seat by day; twenty-four of these privileges to a car—$120 a day for the rent of the car—and the passengers to pay the porter besides. That makes $44,800 a year.

Sleeping cars are expensive to build, they say. So are hotels; but they do not charge at such a rate. Now, what could I do to get even? Nothing could ever put back the dollars into the millions of pockets; but it might be stopped now, this beautiful process.

So I wished that all persons who profited by this performance might feel a shame so keen that they would make public avowal and apology, and, as partial restitution, offer their wealth to promote the cause of free railroads!

Then I remembered parrots. This was lucky, for my wrath flamed again. It was really cooking, as I tried to work out responsibility and adjust penalties. But parrots! Any person who wants to keep a parrot should go and live on an island alone with their preferred conversationalist!

There was a huge, squawky parrot right across the street from me, adding its senseless, rasping cries to the more necessary evils of other noises.

I had also an aunt with a parrot. She was a wealthy, ostentatious person, who had been an only child and inherited her money.

Uncle Joseph hated the yelling bird, but that didn't make any difference to Aunt Mathilda.

I didn't like this aunt, and wouldn't visit her, lest she think I was truckling for the sake of her money; but after I had wished this time, I called at the time set for my curse to work; and it did work with a vengeance. There sat poor Uncle Joe, looking thinner and meeker than ever; and my aunt, like an over-ripe plum, complacent enough.

"Let me out!" said Polly, suddenly. "Let me out to take a walk!"

"The clever thing!" said Aunt Mathilda. "He never said that before."

She let him out. Then he flapped up on the chandelier and sat among the prisms, quite safe.

"What an old pig you are, Mathilda!" said the parrot.

She started to her feet—naturally.

"Born a pig—trained a pig—a pig by nature and education!" said the parrot. "Nobody'd put up with you, except for your money, unless it's this long-suffering husband of yours. He wouldn't, if he hadn't the patience of Job!"

"Hold your tongue!" screamed Aunt Mathilda. "Come down from there! Come here!"

Polly cocked his head and jingled the prisms. "Sit down, Mathilda!" he said, cheerfully. "You've got to listen. You are fat and homely and selfish. You are a nuisance to everybody about you. You have got to feed me and take care of me better than ever—and you've got to listen to me when I talk. Pig!"

I visited another person with a parrot the next day. She put a cloth over his cage when I came in.

"Take it off!" said Polly. She took it off.

"Won't you come into the other room?" she asked me, nervously.

"Better stay here!" said her pet. "Sit still—sit still!"

She sat still.

"Your hair is mostly false," said pretty Poll. "And your teeth—and your outlines. You eat too much. You are lazy. You ought to exercise, and don't know enough. Better apologize to this lady for backbiting! You've got to listen."

The trade in parrots fell off from that day; they say there is no call for them. But the people who kept parrots keep them yet—parrots live a long time.

Bores were a class of offenders against whom I had long borne undying enmity. Now I rubbed my hands and began on them, with this simple wish: that every person whom they bored should tell them the plain truth.

There is one man whom I have specially in mind. He was blackballed at a pleasant club, but continues to go there. He isn't a member—he just goes; and no one does anything to him.

It was very funny after this. He appeared that very night at a meeting, and almost every person present asked him how he came there. "You're not a member, you know," they said. "Why do you butt in? Nobody likes you."

Some were more lenient with him. "Why don't you learn to be more considerate of others, and make some real friends?" they said. "To have a few friends who do enjoy your visits ought to be pleasanter than being a public nuisance."

He disappeared from that club, anyway.

I began to feel very cocky indeed.

In the food business there was already a marked improvement, and in transportation. The hubbub of reformation waxed louder daily, urged on by the unknown sufferings of all the profiters by iniquity.

The papers thrived on all this; and as I watched the loud-voiced protestations of my pet abomination in journalism, I had a brilliant idea, literally.

Next morning I was downtown early, watching the men open their papers. My abomination was shamefully popular, and never more so than this morning. Across the top was printed in gold letters:

All intentional lies, in adv., editorial, news, or any other
    column . . . . Scarlet
All malicious matter . . . . Crimson
All careless or ignorant mistakes . . . . Pink
All for direct self-interest of owner . . . . Dark green
All mere bait to sell the paper . . . . Bright green
All advertising, primary or secondary . . . . Brown
All sensational and salacious matter . . . . Yellow
All hired hypocrisy . . . . Purple
Good fun, instruction, and entertainment . . . . Blue
True and necessary news and honest editorials . . . . Ordinary print

You never saw such a crazy quilt of a paper. They were bought like hot cakes for some days; but the real business fell off very soon. They'd have stopped it all if they could; but the papers looked all right when they came off the press. The color scheme flamed out only to the bona-fide reader.

I let this work for about a week, to the immense joy of all the other papers, and then turned it on to them, all at once. Newspaper reading became very exciting for a little, but the trade fell off. Even newspaper editors could not keep on feeding a market like that. The blue printed and ordinary printed matter grew from column to column and page to page. Some papers—small, to be sure, but refreshing—began to appear in blue and black alone.

This kept me interested and happy for quite a while, so much so that I quite forgot to be angry at other things. There was *such* a change in all kinds of business, following the mere printing of truth in the newspapers. It began to appear as if we had lived in a sort of delirium—not really knowing the facts about anything.

As soon as we really knew the facts, we began to behave very differently, of course.

What really brought all my enjoyment to an end was women. Being a woman, I was naturally interested in them, and could see some things more clearly than men could. I saw their real power, their real dignity, their real responsibility in the world; and then the way they dress and behave used to make me fairly frantic. 'Twas like seeing archangels playing jackstraws—or real horses used only as rocking-horses. So I determined to get after them.

How to manage it! What to hit first! Their hats—their ugly, inane, outrageous hats—that is what one thinks of first. Their silly, expensive clothes—their diddling beads and jewelry—their greedy childishness—mostly of the women provided for by rich men.

Then I thought of all the other women, the real ones, the vast majority, patiently doing the work of servants without even a servant's pay—and neglecting the noblest duties of motherhood in favor of house-service; the greatest power on earth, blind, chained, untaught, in a treadmill. I thought of what they might do, compared to what they did do, and my heart swelled with something that was far from anger.

Then I wished—with all my strength—that women, all women, might realize Womanhood at last; its power and pride and place in life; that they might see their duty as mothers of the world—to love and care for everyone alive; that they might see their duty to men—to choose only the best, and then to bear and rear better ones; that they might see their duty as human beings, and come right out into full life and work and happiness!

I stopped, breathless, with shining eyes. I waited, trembling, for things to happen.

Nothing happened.

You see, this magic which had fallen on me was black magic—and I had wished white.

It didn't work at all, and, what was worse, it stopped all the other things that were working so nicely.

Oh, if I had only thought to wish permanence for those lovely punishments! If only I had done more while I could do it, had half appreciated my privileges when I was a witch!

IF I WERE A MAN *

"If I were a man, . . ." that was what pretty little Mollie Mathewson always said when Gerald would not do what she wanted him to—which was seldom.

That was what she said this bright morning, with a stamp of her little high-heeled slipper, just because he had made a fuss about that bill, the long one with the "account rendered," which she had forgotten to give him the first time and been afraid to the second—and now he had taken it from the postman himself.

Mollie was "true to type." She was a beautiful instance of what is reverentially called "a true woman." Little, of course— no true woman may be big. Pretty, of course—no true woman could possibly be plain. Whimsical, capricious, charming, changeable, devoted to pretty clothes and always "wearing them well," as the esoteric phrase has it. (This does not refer to the clothes—they do not wear well in the least—but to some special grace of putting them on and carrying them about, granted to but few, it appears.)

She was also a loving wife and a devoted mother possessed of "the social gift" and the love of "society" that goes with it, and, with all these was fond and proud of her home and managed it as capably as—well, as most women do.

* "If I Were a Man" was published in the July 1914 issue of Physical Culture, 31–34.

If ever there was a true woman it was Mollie Mathewson, yet she was wishing heart and soul she was a man.

And all of a sudden she was!

She was Gerald, walking down the path so erect and square-shouldered, in a hurry for his morning train, as usual, and, it must be confessed, in something of a temper.

Her own words were ringing in her ears—not only the "last word," but several that had gone before, and she was holding her lips tight shut, not to say something she would be sorry for. But instead of acquiescence in the position taken by that angry little figure on the veranda, what she felt was a sort of superior pride, a sympathy as with weakness, a feeling that "I must be gentle with her," in spite of the temper.

A man! Really a man—with only enough subconscious memory of herself remaining to make her recognize the differences.

At first there was a funny sense of size and weight and extra thickness, the feet and hands seemed strangely large, and her long, straight, free legs swung forward at a gait that made her feel as if on stilts.

This presently passed, and in its place, growing all day, wherever she went, came a new and delightful feeling of being *the right size*.

Everything fitted now. Her back snugly against the seat-back, her feet comfortably on the floor. Her feet? . . . His feet! She studied them carefully. Never before, since her early school days, had she felt such freedom and comfort as to feet—they were firm and solid on the ground when she walked; quick, springy, safe—as when, moved by an unrecognizable impulse, she had run after, caught, and swung aboard the car.

Another impulse fished in a convenient pocket for change—instantly, automatically, bringing forth a nickel for the conductor and a penny for the newsboy.

These pockets came as a revelation. Of course she had known they were there, had counted them, made fun of them, mended them, even envied them; but she never had dreamed of how it *felt* to have pockets.

Behind her newspaper she let her consciousness, that odd mingled consciousness, rove from pocket to pocket, realizing the armored assurance of having all those things at hand, instantly get-at-able, ready to meet emergencies. The cigar case gave her a warm feeling of comfort—it was full; the firmly held fountain pen, safe unless she stood on her head; the keys, pencils, letters, documents, notebook, checkbook, bill folder—all at once, with a deep rushing sense of power and pride, she felt what she had never felt before in all her life—the possession of money, of her own earned money—hers to give or to withhold, not to beg for, tease for, wheedle for—hers.

That bill—why, if it had come to her—to him, that is—he would have paid it as a matter of course, and never mentioned it—to her.

Then, being he, sitting there so easily and firmly with his money in his pockets, she wakened to his life-long consciousness about money. Boyhood—its desires and dreams, ambitions. Young manhood—working tremendously for the wherewithal to make a home—for her. The present years with all their net of cares and hopes and dangers; the present moment, when he needed every cent for special plans of great importance, and this bill, long overdue and demanding payment, meant an amount of inconvenience wholly unnecessary if it had been given him when it first came; also, the man's keen dislike of that "account rendered."

"Women have no business sense!" she found herself saying. "And all that money just for hats—idiotic, useless, ugly things!"

With that she began to see the hats of the women in the car as she had never seen hats before. The men's seemed normal, dignified, becoming, with enough variety for personal taste, and with distinction in style and in age, such as she had never noticed before. But the women's—

With the eyes of a man and the brain of a man; with the memory of a whole lifetime of free action wherein the hat, close-fitting on cropped hair, had been no handicap; she now perceived the hats of women.

The massed fluffed hair was at once attractive and foolish, and on that hair, at every angle, in all colors, tipped, twisted, tortured into every crooked shape, made of any substance chance might offer, perched these formless objects. Then, on their formlessness the trimmings—these squirts of stiff feathers, these violent outstanding bows of glistening ribbon, these swaying, projecting masses of plumage which tormented the faces of bystanders.

Never in all her life had she imagined that this idolized millinery could look, to those who paid for it, like the decorations of an insane monkey.

And yet, when there came into the car a little woman, as foolish as any, but pretty and sweet-looking, up rose Gerald Mathewson and gave her his seat. And, later, when there came in a handsome red-cheeked girl, whose hat was wilder, more violent in color and eccentric in shape than any other—when she stood nearby and her soft curling plumes swept his cheek once and again—he felt a sense of sudden pleasure at the intimate tickling touch—and she, deep down within, felt such a wave of shame as might well drown a thousand hats forever.

When he took his train, his seat in the smoking car, she had a new surprise. All about him were the other men, commuters too, and many of them friends of his.

To her, they would have been distinguished as "Mary Wade's husband," "the man Belle Grant is engaged to," "that rich Mr. Shopworth," or "that pleasant Mr. Beale." And they would all have lifted their hats to her, bowed, made polite conversation if near enough—especially Mr. Beale.

Now came the feeling of open-eyed acquaintance, of knowing men—as they were. The mere amount of this knowledge was a surprise to her—the whole background of talk from boyhood up, the gossip of barber-shop and club, the conversation of morning and evening hours on trains, the knowledge of political affiliation, of business standing and prospects, of character—in a light she had never known before.

They came and talked to Gerald, one and another. He seemed quite popular. And as they talked, with this new memory and new understanding, an understanding which seemed to include all these men's minds, there poured in on the submerged consciousness beneath a new, a startling knowledge—what men really think of women.

Good, average, American men were there; married men for the most part, and happy—as happiness goes in general. In the minds of each and all there seemed to be a two-story department, quite apart from the rest of their ideas, a separate place where they kept their thoughts and feelings about women.

In the upper half were the tenderest emotions, the most exquisite ideals, the sweetest memories, all lovely sentiments as to "home" and "mother," all delicate admiring adjectives, a sort of sanctuary, where a veiled statue, blindly adored, shared place with beloved yet commonplace experiences.

In the lower half—here that buried consciousness woke to keen distress—they kept quite another assortment of ideas. Here, even in this clean-minded husband of hers, was the memory of stories told at men's dinners, of worse ones overheard in street or car, of base traditions, coarse epithets, gross experiences—known, though not shared.

And all these in the department "woman," while in the rest of the mind—here was new knowledge indeed.

The world opened before her. Not the world she had been reared in—where Home had covered all the map, almost, and the rest had been "foreign," or "unexplored country," but the world as it was—man's world, as made, lived in, and seen, by men.

It was dizzying. To see the houses that fled so fast across the car window, in terms of builders' bills, or of some technical insight into materials and methods; to see a passing village with lamentable knowledge of who "owned it" and of how its Boss was rapidly aspiring in state power, or of how that kind of paving was a failure; to see shops, not as mere exhibitions of desirable objects, but as business ventures, many mere sinking ships, some promising a profitable voyage—this new world bewildered her.

She—as Gerald—had already forgotten about that bill, over which she—as Mollie—was still crying at home. Gerald was "talking business" with this man, "talking politics" with that, and now sympathizing with the carefully withheld troubles of a neighbor.

Mollie had always sympathized with the neighbor's wife before.

She began to struggle violently with this large dominant masculine consciousness. She remembered with sudden clearness things she had read, lectures she had heard, and resented with increasing intensity this serene masculine preoccupation with the male point of view.

Mr. Miles, the little fussy man who lived on the other side of the street, was talking now. He had a large complacent wife;

Mollie had never liked her much, but had always thought him rather nice—he was so punctilious in small courtesies.

And here he was talking to Gerald—such talk!

"Had to come in here," he said. "Gave my seat to a dame who was bound to have it. There's nothing they won't get when they make up their minds to it—eh?"

"No fear!" said the big man in the next seat. "They haven't much mind to make up, you know—and if they do, they'll change it."

"The real danger," began the Rev. Alfred Smythe, the new Episcopal clergyman, a thin, nervous, tall man with a face several centuries behind the times, "is that they will overstep the limits of their God-appointed sphere."

"Their natural limits ought to hold 'em, I think," said cheerful Dr. Jones. "You can't get around physiology, I tell you."

"I've never seen any limits, myself, not to what they want, anyhow," said Mr. Miles. "Merely a rich husband and a fine house and no end of bonnets and dresses, and the latest thing in motors, and a few diamonds—and so on. Keeps us pretty busy."

There was a tired gray man across the aisle. He had a very nice wife, always beautifully dressed, and three unmarried daughters, also beautifully dressed—Mollie knew them. She knew he worked hard, too, and she looked at him now a little anxiously.

But he smiled cheerfully.

"Do you good, Miles," he said. "What else would a man work for? A good woman is about the best thing on earth."

"And a bad one's the worst, that's sure," responded Miles.

"She's a pretty weak sister, viewed professionally," Dr. Jones averred with solemnity, and the Rev. Alfred Smythe added, "She brought evil into the world."

Gerald Mathewson sat up straight. Something was stirring in him which he did not recognize—yet could not resist.

"Seems to me we all talk like Noah," he suggested drily. "Or the ancient Hindu scriptures. Women have their limitations, but so do we, God knows. Haven't we known girls in school and college just as smart as we were?"

"They cannot play our games," coldly replied the clergyman.

Gerald measured his meager proportions with a practiced eye.

"I never was particularly good at football myself," he modestly admitted, "but I've known women who could outlast a man in all-round endurance. Besides—life isn't spent in athletics!"

This was sadly true. They all looked down the aisle where a heavy ill-dressed man with a bad complexion sat alone. He had held the top of the columns once, with headlines and photographs. Now he earned less than any of them.

"It's time we woke up," pursued Gerald, still inwardly urged to unfamiliar speech. "Women are pretty much *people*, seems to me. I know they dress like fools—but who's to blame for that? We invent all those idiotic hats of theirs, and design their crazy fashions, and, what's more, if a woman is courageous enough to wear common-sense clothes—and shoes—which of us wants to dance with her?

"Yes, we blame them for grafting on us, but are we willing to let our wives work? We are not. It hurts our pride, that's all. We are always criticizing them for making mercenary marriages, but what do we call a girl who marries a chump with no money? Just a poor fool, that's all. And they know it.

"As for Mother Eve—I wasn't there and can't deny the story, but I will say this. If she brought evil into the world, we men have had the lion's share of keeping it going ever since—how about that?"

They drew into the city, and all day long in his business, Gerald was vaguely conscious of new views, strange feelings, and the submerged Mollie learned and learned.

THE GIRL IN THE PINK HAT *

My sister Polly and I had a "stateroom," but we did not sit in it all the time. The car was not at all full, and I like to move about and look at the scenery from all sides.

Polly is a dear girl, but her best friends admit she is a trifle odd in appearance. She will wear her red hair pulled down over her ears and forehead and neck—that's a switch, too; with a squushy hat drooping over the whole; and big yellow-glassed shell goggles and a veil besides. Also one of those long traveling cloaks, sort of black silk duster. I never could see how people can stand veils over their eyes, and mouths, and noses—especially noses; they tickle so.

But I'm very fond of Polly, and she is really a good-looking girl, when properly dressed. She's a romantic soul, and good as gold. I am romantic, too—but not good.

We were coming home from a long trip, away out to the Coast and back, and the home stretch was tiresome. Somewhere about Schenectady it was. Polly was reading another of her interminable magazines, and I was prowling about after variety and amusement.

*"The Girl in the Pink Hat" appeared in the February 1916 issue of The Forerunner, 29–33.

There was a day-coach just ahead, and I slipped in there for a change, and found an empty seat.

Just in front sat a young couple, with their heads pretty close together, and I watched them idly, for she was a pretty, eager-looking girl in a soft pink hat, and he quite an impressive fellow—rather too much so, I thought.

Presently I caught a note of trouble in her voice, and a low insistence in his—low, but quite audible to me. The seat in front of them was empty, and I dare say he thought the one behind was too; at any rate they talked, and I couldn't help hearing them.

The amazing way in which people bare their hearts to one another, in streetcars or steam cars, or in steamer chairs, has always been a wonder to me. You cannot accuse the traveling public of eavesdropping when it hears the immediate fellow sufferers in the New York subway explaining their economic disabilities or their neighbors in the day-coach exhibiting a painful degree of marital infelicity.

In my own travels I become an unwilling mother confessor to all about me, for my ears are unusually keen, and seem especially so on the cars. Perhaps it is because the speakers, to overcome the noise of the wheels, raise their voices or sharpen them to a peculiarly penetrating pitch. At any rate I can hear them, right and left, front and rear, which is sometimes interesting, sometimes tedious, sometimes acutely disagreeable.

This time it was interesting, very.

"I tell you it is not my fault," he was saying, in a low restrained voice, but as one whose patience was wearing thin. "I couldn't help it if the car was stalled, could I? And then we *had* to catch this train. I have an engagement in the city I can't afford to miss."

"You can't attend to it tonight, can you?" she asked, evidently trying to keep control of herself, not to be frightened, and not to lose faith in him. Yet a note of suspicion would struggle through in spite of her.

"Why can't we stop off at Albany and—" she spoke low, but I heard it, the little hesitant girlish voice, with a touch of awe at the words "—be married, and then take a later train to New York?"

"What *is* the difference, my dear," he protested, "whether we're married in Albany or in New York?"

"What time do we get to New York?" she asked.

"About nine," he said, and then I became really alert, for I knew it would be about eleven.

"And you can arrange for it then—tonight?" she persisted. "Isn't your license for Ohio?"

"What a careful soul you are, my dear," he replied airily. "Yes, that license was for Ohio, of course, and I could hardly get one in New York tonight. But there are more ways than one of being married in New York, you will find. People can be married, legally and properly married, before a notary public, and I have a friend who is one. Nothing could be simpler. We call him up, take a taxi to his apartment, make our deposition and have it all properly set down with a big red seal—tonight. Then if you want to go to The Little Church Around the Corner tomorrow and have it 'solemnized,' you may."

He talked too much. Also, though I sat behind, I could "smell his breath." And I saw that the girl was not satisfied. Evidently she was not as green as he had thought her. Either from romances or at "the movies" she had known things of this sort to be done—with sad results.

It must be a terrible thing in the mind of an affectionate young girl to have to distrust her lover. I judged, from what I had gathered, that she had planned a perfectly good marriage, in her home state, before starting on this journey; that some trifle about that incident of the stalled car had upset her, started her to thinking, and that his drinking, on their wedding trip, seemed a suspicious circumstance to her.

She was visibly alarmed, yet striving still to keep her trust, not to accept the horrible alternative which forced itself upon her mind. She sat still for a minute or two, looking out of the window, while he fondled her in a vain attempt to substitute caresses she did not want for the reassurance he could not give.

She made up her mind presently.

It was a very firm little chin I now observed, as she turned squarely toward him, a face pale but quite determined. She smiled too, trying hard to hold her illusions.

"A bride has *some* privileges, surely," she suggested with an effect of buoyancy, "even an eloping bride. I prefer to be married in Albany, if you please, my dear."

It was a pity for this gentleman's purposes that he had taken that drink, or those drinks. It was a little too much, or not quite enough. It made him irritable.

"But I don't please," he said testily. "I did all I could to please you—fixed up to have it all done in Elyria this morning. But we slipped up on that—and now I don't propose to stop over in Albany. It's all nonsense, Jess—only means delay and trouble— I don't know anybody in Albany, and I know plenty in New York. And I tell you I've got to be there in the morning, and I will. And you'll be Mrs. Marsh before midnight, all right, all right—"

"I know somebody in Albany," she answered. "I have an old friend there; she was my Sunday school teacher. I can stay there over night, or for some days, and you can come up with another license and marry me."

Even then, if he had been quite sober he could have satisfied her. She was fairly trembling at her own daring, and quite ready to break down and cry on his shoulder and own she was a goose—if he said the right thing.

But he did not. He tried to assert a premature authority.

"You'll do nothing of the sort," he told her sharply. "You're my wife, or will be in a few hours, and you're going with me to New York."

She lifted her head at that.

"I am going to get off at Albany," she answered.

"You haven't so much as a nickel, my dear," he said disagreeably, "to 'phone with even, or take a car."

"I'll walk!" she said.

"You haven't your bag either," he told her. "It's in the baggage car and I've got the checks."

"I don't care—Miss Pierce will take care of me."

"And suppose Miss Pierce happens not to be there," he suggested. "A nice pickle you'd be in—in Albany—at night— alone—no money and no bag—eh, my dear!"

He put his arm about her and hugged her close. She permitted it, but returned to her plea.

"Julius! You'll stop if I want to, surely! Or if you can't, you'll let me. Just get my bag for me, and give me a dollar or two—you're not going to try to *make* me go to New York—against my will?"

"I'm tired of this," he replied, with sudden irritability. "Of course you are coming to New York. Now just make up your mind to it."

"Julius—I'm sorry to—to—set myself against you so, but I have made up my mind. I mean to get off at Albany. If you won't get my bag, I shall appeal to the conductor—"

He sat up at that, squared his shoulders, and laid an arm across the back of the seat, bending towards her, and speaking low. But I could still hear.

"We've had all we're going to of this—do you hear? You don't know it, but I'm what they call a 'plainclothesman.' Do you see that star?" From his gesture, and the direction of her frightened eyes, her little gasp, I felt as if I saw it too. "Now, you sit tight and make no more fuss till we get to the city," he muttered. "If you appeal to the conductor—or anybody else, I'll simply tell 'em that you're a well-known criminal I'm taking back. And if you raise any rough stuff I've got the bracelets—see?"

She saw. I heard them chink in his pocket.

"Shall I put them on, or will you be quiet?" he asked, and she sank down defeated.

"Now a fellow can get a little peace, I guess?" said Mr. Marsh, and leaned his head back on the red plush.

He kept stern watch of her as we drew toward Albany. I knew he would, and I slipped silently out to consult with Polly. She was immensely excited, and full of plans for a dramatic rescue, but I persuaded her it was not safe.

"He's got the star and the handcuffs," I told her. "The girl has nothing but her word—we couldn't do it—not and be sure of it. And besides, it would make a terrible scene—she'd never get over the publicity. Wait now—I see how we can work it. Would you be willing to get off at Poughkeepsie—take a later train or stop over night, as you like?"

"What for?" demanded Polly. "Of course I'm willing—but how does it help her?"

"Why, he'll be watching so that she can't get off—but he wouldn't stop you. Here—give me that writing tablet, please. I'll tell you directly—but I want to get this done before we're in—or I'll lose that seat. I'll come back as quick as I can and tell you—I'm sure we can do it."

So I took paper and pencils, and slipped softly back into the seat behind them.

After we left Albany his vigilance relaxed, and presently he was dozing beside her, a sufficient obstacle to her exit.

I swiftly wrote a careful explanation of my overhearing them, of my appreciation of her difficult position, and of her inevitable wish to avoid a noisy scene. Then I proposed my plan—simple enough and calling only for a little courage and firmness on her part—and slipped it in near the window; he couldn't see it—even if awake.

"Have you a watch?" I wrote. "If you have, look at it now, please." And I had the pleasure of seeing her do so.

"We get to Poughkeepsie at nine," I wrote. "At about fifteen minutes before then, say that you must go to the dressing-room—he can't refuse that privilege. Go in there first, and shut the door. Take your hat off, and hide it under your dress. I shall be down near there, and when I open the door, you crouch down and slip through into the next car, into the stateroom—this end, close to the door, you know. You'll see my sister there—red hair, veil, yellow glasses. She'll tell you what to do. You can look around and see if you think I'm trustworthy. If you think so, you can nod."

She looked presently, and I'm sure my good-natured, strong-lined, spinsterish face seemed reliable. So she nodded, with determination.

Then I went back to Polly and explained all that I had in mind, the two of us engaging in eager preparations. As the time approached, I entered the day-coach once more, taking the little shut-in seat just opposite the woman's retiring-room, and was all eyes and ears for my plan's fulfillment.

Sure enough, I saw her coming down the aisle, holding the seat backs as the car swung forward. He was watching her too, saw her safely inside with the door shut, and seemed satisfied. He knew she could not get off the train going at that rate.

Then I rose, as if to enter the little place myself, and un-latched the door. Finding it occupied, I came forward a little and stood by the water-cooler, my coat on my arm, filling as much of the aisle as possible. She slipped out like a sly child, and I presently followed, stopping to try to enter the dressing-room in vain; opening and closing the rear door with easy indifference.

Before we ran into Poughkeepsie, he must have become anxious, for he started to search the train.

Ours was the next car, our stateroom the first place to look, and he looked accordingly. He saw only a lady with low-curved red hair, a squushy hat, yellow glasses, a veil, a long duster coat, reading her magazine, and my spinsterish self, knitting for the soldiers.

I watched him go down the aisle, questioning a lady near the door—had she seen a girl in a pink hat go through the car? She had not, and resented being asked.

He rushed into the next one, soon came back, again questioning and searching—and as the train stopped, leaped to the platform. Small chance would any pink-hatted, light-coated girl have had of escape on that platform. Only a few got off and he watched every one of them. But naturally he would not know my sister in a neat traveling hat and waterproof coat. How should he?

And as naturally, he would not know my sister, or what certainly appeared to be my sister, wearing that long red switch of which my sister was so proud, her squushy hat, her long duster, her yellow glasses, and her veil. She sat reading as before, and when our friend came through the train again, this time accompanied by the conductor, she barely looked up from her page.

"You need not intrude upon these ladies," said the conductor, glancing at us. "I recognize them both."

"She may have hidden herself in their dressing-room," the man insisted. But that was easily shown to be empty, and he backed out, muttering apologies.

"Steady, my dear, steady," I urged, as I saw her trembling with the excitement of that search. "That's the last of it, I'm sure. He'll go all over the train—and then he'll think he must have missed you at Poughkeepsie."

We had closed our door by this time, and she could breathe in peace, and speak even, though she would not raise her voice above a whisper.

"He'll be waiting when we get off—he'll be sure to know me then. I'm so afraid!" she said.

"You haven't a thing to be afraid of, my dear child," I told her. "My car will be there. You shall come home with me for tonight, and tomorrow we'll talk of the future plans. Or—if you prefer—we'll buy a return ticket to Elyria, and you shall be home again tomorrow."

"I can't think," she said. "I'm so frightened. It has been—just awful! You see, I—I *loved* him! I was going to *marry* him—and to have all that turned into—into this!"

"See here, child, you mustn't talk about it now. You've got to keep a straight face and be Sister Polly till we're out of the woods. Just read one of those foolish stories—it'll take up your mind."

And happening on one of Leroy Scott's doubly involved detective stories, she actually did forget her own distresses for a while following those of other people.

As we proceeded in a dignified manner up the long platform, attended by two red-capped porters, her hand upon my arm, I felt her start slightly.

"There he is," she said. "He's just inside the gate. But how funny! He's got another hat—and another coat—how funny! But I'd know his moustache anywhere."

It was funny, even funnier than she thought. Sister Polly in Poughkeepsie had not been idle, and my young brother, Hugh, had received a telegram as long as a letter and marked "Rush!" He was on hand, standing near the gate, and looking sharply about him and behind him were two other men who also seemed interested in the crowd.

As we came through, the sharp eyes of Mr. Marsh caught the look of terror in the face beside me, and recognized it in spite of all Polly's wrappings. He started towards her, and she shrank against me with a pitiful little cry, but Mr. Marsh was checked in his career by a strong hand on either arm.

"That's him, and he's wanted all right," said one of his captors, while the other, not too gently, removed his moustache.

Then my young brother, Hugh, with a quizzical smile, took the handcuffs out of that threatening pocket, and they were slipped in place by experienced hands.

"You've certainly had one narrow escape, child," said Hugh to our young guest.

THE COTTAGETTE *

"hy not?" said Mr. Mathews "It is far too small for a house, too pretty for a hut, too—unusual—for a cottage."

"Cottagette, by all means," said Lois, seating herself on a porch chair. "But it is larger than it looks, Mr. Mathews. How do you like it, Malda?"

I was delighted with it. More than delighted. Here this tiny shell of fresh unpainted wood peeped out from under the trees, the only house in sight except the distant white specks on far-off farms, and the little wandering village in the river-threaded valley. It sat right on the turf—no road, no path even, and the dark woods shadowed the back windows.

"How about meals?" asked Lois.

"Not two minutes' walk," he assured her, and showed us a little furtive path between the trees to the place where meals were furnished.

We discussed and examined and exclaimed, Lois holding her pongee skirts close about her—she needn't have been so careful, there wasn't a speck of dust—and presently decided to take it.

---

*"The Cottagette" appeared in the August 1910 issue of The Forerunner, 1-5.

Never did I know the real joy and peace of living, before that blessed summer at High Court. It was a mountain place, easy enough to get to, but strangely big and still and far away when you were there.

The working basis of the establishment was an eccentric woman named Caswell, a sort of musical enthusiast, who had a summer school of music and the "higher thought." Malicious persons, not able to obtain accommodations there, called the place High C.

I liked the music very well, and kept my thoughts to myself, both high and low, but the Cottagette I loved unreservedly. It was so little and new and clean, smelling only of its fresh-planed boards—they hadn't even stained it.

There was one big room and two little ones in the tiny thing, though from the outside you wouldn't have believed it, it looked so small; but small as it was, it harbored a miracle—a real bathroom with water piped from mountain springs. Our windows opened into the green shadiness, the soft brownness, the bird-inhabited, quiet, flower-starred woods. But in front we looked across whole counties—over a far-off river—into another state. Off and down and away—it was like sitting on the roof of something—something very big.

The grass swept up to the doorstep, to the walls—only it wasn't just grass, of course, but such a procession of flowers as I had never imagined could grow in one place.

You had to go quite a way through the meadow, wearing your own narrow faintly marked streak in the grass, to reach the town-connecting road below. But in the woods was a little path, clear and wide, by which we went to meals.

For we ate with the highly thoughtful musicians, and highly musical thinkers, in their central boardinghouse nearby. They didn't call it a boardinghouse, which is neither high nor musical; they called it the Calceolaria. There was plenty of that growing about, and I didn't mind what they called it so long as the food was good—which it was, and the prices reasonable—which they were.

The people were extremely interesting—some of them at least; and all of them were better than the average of summer boarders.

But if there hadn't been any interesting ones, it didn't matter while Ford Mathews was there. He was a newspaper man, or rather an ex-newspaper man, then becoming a writer for magazines, with books ahead.

He had friends at High Court—he liked music, he liked the place, and he liked us. Lois liked him too, as was quite natural. I'm sure I did.

He used to come up evenings and sit on the porch and talk.

He came daytimes and went on long walks with us. He established his workshop in a most attractive little cave not far beyond us—the country there is full of rocky ledges and hollows—and sometimes asked us over to an afternoon tea, made on a gipsy fire.

Lois was a good deal older than I, but not really old at all, and she didn't look her thirty-five by ten years. I never blamed her for not mentioning it, and I wouldn't have done so myself on any account. But I felt that together we made a safe and reasonable household. She played beautifully, and there was a piano in our big room. There were pianos in several other little cottages about—but too far off for any jar of sound. When the wind was right, we caught little wafts of music now and then; but mostly it was still, blessedly still, about us. And yet that Calceolaria was only two minutes off—and with raincoats and rubbers we never minded going to it.

We saw a good deal of Ford, and I got interested in him; I couldn't help it. He was big. Not extra big in pounds and inches, but a man with a big view and grip—with purpose and real power. He was going to do things. I thought he was doing them now, but he didn't—this was all like cutting steps in the ice-wall, he said. It had to be done, but the road was long ahead. And he took an interest in my work too, which is unusual for a literary man.

Mine wasn't much. I did embroidery and made designs.

It is such pretty work! I like to draw from flowers and leaves and things about me—conventionalize them sometimes, and sometimes paint them just as they are, in soft silk stitches.

All about up here were the lovely small things I needed; and not only these, but the lovely big things that make one feel so strong and able to do beautiful work.

Here was the friend I lived so happily with, and all this fairy-land of sun and shadow, the free immensity of our view, and the dainty comfort of the Cottagette. We never had to think of ordinary things till the soft musical thrill of the Japanese gong stole through the trees, and we trotted off to the Calceolaria.

I think Lois knew before I did.

We were old friends and trusted each other, and she had had experience too.

"Malda," she said, "let us face this thing and be rational." It was a strange thing that Lois should be so rational and yet so musical—but she was, and that was one reason I liked her so much.

"You are beginning to love Ford Mathews—do you know it?"

I said yes, I thought I was.

"Does he love you?"

That I couldn't say. "It is early yet," I told her. "He is a man, he is about thirty I believe, he has seen more of life and probably loved before—it may be nothing more than friendliness with him."

"Do you think it would be a good marriage?" she asked. We had often talked of love and marriage, and Lois had helped me to form my views—hers were very clear and strong.

"Why yes—if he loves me," I said. "He has told me quite a bit about his family, good Western farming people, real Americans. He is strong and well—you can read clean living in his eyes and mouth." Ford's eyes were as clear as a girl's, the whites of them were clear. Most men's eyes, when you look at them critically, are not like that. They may look at you very expressively, but when you look at them, just as features, they are not very nice.

I liked his looks, but I liked him better.

So I told her that as far as I knew, it would be a good marriage—if it was one.

"How much do you love him?" she asked.

That I couldn't quite tell—it was a good deal—but I didn't think it would kill me to lose him.

"Do you love him enough to do something to win him—to really put yourself out somewhat for that purpose?"

"Why—yes—I think I do. If it was something I approved of. What do you mean?"

Then Lois unfolded her plan. She had been married—unhappily married, in her youth; that was all over and done with years ago. She had told me about it long since, and she said she did not regret the pain and loss because it had given her experience. She had her maiden name again—and freedom. She was so fond of me she wanted to give me the benefit of her experience—without the pain.

"Men like music," said Lois. "They like sensible talk; they like beauty, of course, and all that—"

"Then they ought to like you!" I interrupted, and, as a matter of fact, they did. I knew several who wanted to marry her, but she said "once was enough." I don't think they were "good marriages," though.

"Don't be foolish, child," said Lois. "This is serious. What they care for most, after all, is domesticity. Of course they'll fall in love with anything; but what they want to marry is a home-maker. Now we are living here in an idyllic sort of way, quite conducive to falling in love, but no temptation to marriage. If I were you—if I really loved this man and wished to marry him—I would make a home of this place."

"Make a home? Why, it *is* a home. I never was so happy anywhere in my life. What on earth do you mean, Lois?"

"A person might be happy in a balloon, I suppose," she replied, "but it wouldn't be a home. He comes here and sits talking with us, and it's quiet and feminine and attractive—and then we hear that big gong at the Calceolaria, and off we go slopping through the wet woods—and the spell is broken. Now you can cook." I could cook. I could cook excellently. My esteemed Mama had rigorously taught me every branch of what is now called domestic science; and I had no objection to the work, except that it prevented my doing anything else. And one's hands are not so nice when one cooks and washes dishes—I need nice hands for my needlework. But if it was a question of pleasing Ford Mathews—

Lois went on calmly. "Miss Caswell would put on a kitchen for us in a minute; she said she would, you know, when we took the cottage. Plenty of people keep house up here—we can if we want to."

"But we don't want to," I said. "We never have wanted to.

The very beauty of the place is that it never had any housekeeping about it. Still, as you say, it would be cosy on a wet night, we could have delicious little suppers, and have him stay—"

"He told me he had never known a home since he was eighteen," said Lois.

That was how we came to install a kitchen in the Cottagette. The men put it up in a few days, just a lean-to with a window, sink, and two doors. I did the cooking. We had nice things, there is no denying that: good fresh milk and vegetables particularly. Fruit is hard to get in the country, and meat too—still we managed nicely; the less you have, the more you have to manage— it takes time and brains, that's all.

Lois likes to do housework, but it spoils her hands for practicing, so she can't and I was perfectly willing to do it—it was all in the interest of my own heart. Ford certainly enjoyed it. He dropped in often, and ate things with undeniable relish. So I was pleased, though it did interfere with my work a good deal. I always work best in the morning; but of course housework has to be done in the morning too; and it is astonishing how much work there is in the littlest kitchen. You go in for a minute, and you see this thing and that thing and the other thing to be done, and your minute is an hour before you know it.

When I was ready to sit down, the freshness of the morning was gone somehow. Before, when I woke up, there was only the clean wood smell of the house, and then the blessed out-of-doors; now I always felt the call of the kitchen as soon as I woke. An oil stove will smell a little, either in or out of the house; and soap, and—well, you know if you cook in a bedroom how it makes the room feel differently? Our house had been only bedroom and parlor before.

We baked too—the baker's bread was really pretty poor, and Ford did enjoy my whole wheat, and brown, and especially hot rolls and gems. It was a pleasure to feed him, but it did heat up the house, and me. I never could work much—at my work— baking days. Then, when I did get to work, the people would come with things—milk or meat or vegetables, or children with berries; and what distressed me most was the wheelmarks on our meadow. They soon made quite a road—they had to, of course, but I hated it. I lost that lovely sense of being on the last edge and looking over—we were just a bead on a string like other houses. But it was quite true that I loved this man, and would do more than this to please him. We couldn't go off so freely on excursions as we used, either; when meals are to be prepared, someone has to be there, and to take in things when they come. Sometimes Lois stayed in, she always asked to, but mostly I did. I couldn't let her spoil her summer on my account. And Ford certainly liked it.

He came so often that Lois said she thought it would look better if we had an older person with us, and that her mother could come if I wanted her, and she could help with the work of course. That seemed reasonable, and she came. I wasn't very fond of Lois's mother, Mrs. Fowler, but it did seem a little conspicuous, Mr. Mathews eating with us more than he did at the Calceolaria. There were others of course, plenty of them dropping in, but I didn't encourage it much, it made so much more work. They would come in to supper, and then we would have musical evenings. They offered to help me wash dishes, some of them, but a new hand in the kitchen is not much help. I preferred to do it myself; then I knew where the dishes were.

Ford never seemed to want to wipe dishes, though I often wished he would.

So Mrs. Fowler came. She and Lois had one room, they had to—and she really did a lot of the work; she was a very practical old lady.

Then the house began to be noisy. You hear another person in a kitchen more than you hear yourself, I think—and the walls were only boards. She swept more than we did too. I don't think much sweeping is needed in a clean place like that; and she dusted all the time, which I know is unnecessary. I still did most of the cooking, but I could get off more to draw, out-of-doors, and to walk. Ford was in and out continually, and, it seemed to me, was really coming nearer. What was one summer of interrupted work, of noise and dirt and smell and constant meditation on what to eat next, compared to a lifetime of love? Besides—if he married me—I should have to do it always, and might as well get used to it.

Lois kept me contented, too, telling me nice things that Ford said about my cooking. "He does appreciate it so," she said.

One day he came around early and asked me to go up Hugh's Peak with him. It was a lovely climb and took all day. I demurred a little; it was Monday. Mrs. Fowler thought it was cheaper to have a woman come and wash, and we did, but it certainly made more work.

"Never mind," he said. "What's washing day or ironing day or any of that old foolishness to us? This is walking day—that's what it is." It was really, cool and sweet and fresh—it had rained in the night—and brilliantly clear.

"Come along!" he said. "We can see as far as Patch Mountain I'm sure. There'll never be a better day."

"Is anyone else going?" I asked.

"Not a soul. It's just us. Come."

I came gladly, only suggesting—"Wait, let me put up a lunch."

"I'll wait just long enough for you to put on knickers and a short skirt," said he. "The lunch is all in the basket on my back. I know how long it takes for you women to 'put up' sandwiches and things."

We were off in ten minutes, light-footed and happy; and the day was all that could be asked. He brought a perfect lunch, too, and had made it all himself. I confess it tasted better to me than my own cooking; but perhaps that was the climb.

When we were nearly down, we stopped by a spring on a broad ledge, and supped, making tea as he liked to do out-of-doors. We saw the round sun setting at one end of a world view, and the round moon rising at the other, calmly shining each on each.

And then he asked me to be his wife.

We were very happy.

"But there's a condition!" said he, all at once, sitting up straight and looking very fierce. "You mustn't cook!"

"What!" said I. "Mustn't cook?"

"No," said he, "you must give it up—for my sake."

I stared at him dumbly.

"Yes, I know all about it," he went on. "Lois told me. I've seen a good deal of Lois—since you've taken to cooking. And since I would talk about you, naturally I learned a lot. She told me how you were brought up, and how strong your domestic instincts were—but bless your artist soul, dear girl, you have some others!" Then he smiled rather queerly and murmured, "Surely in vain the net is spread in the sight of any bird.

"I've watched you, dear, all summer," he went on. "It doesn't agree with you.

"Of course the things taste good—but so do my things! I'm a good cook myself. My father was a cook, for years—at good wages. I'm used to it, you see.

"One summer when I was hard up I cooked for a living—and saved money instead of starving."

"Oh ho!" said I. "That accounts for the tea—and the lunch!"

"And lots of other things," said he.

"But you haven't done half as much of your lovely work since you started this kitchen business, and—you'll forgive me, dear—it hasn't been as good. Your work is quite too good to lose; it is a beautiful and distinctive art, and I don't want you to let it go. What would you think of me if I gave up my hard long years of writing for the easy competence of a well-paid cook!"

I was still too happy to think very clearly. I just sat and looked at him. "But you want to marry me?" I said.

"I want to marry you, Malda—because I love you—because you are young and strong and beautiful—because you are wild and sweet and—fragrant, and—elusive, like the wildflowers you love. Because you are so truly an artist in your special way, seeing beauty and giving it to others. I love you because of all this, because you are rational and high-minded and capable of friendship—and in spite of your cooking!"

"But—how do you want to live?"

"As we did here—at first," he said. "There was peace, exquisite silence. There was beauty—nothing but beauty. There were the clean wood odors and flowers and fragrances and sweet wild wind. And there was you—your fair self, always delicately dressed, with white firm fingers sure of touch in delicate true work. I loved you then. When you took to cooking, it jarred on me. I have been a cook, I tell you, and I know what it is. I hated it—to see my woodflower in a kitchen. But Lois told me about how you were brought up to it and loved it, and I said to myself, 'I love this woman; I will wait and see if I love her even as a cook.' And I do, darling: I withdraw the condition. I will love you always, even if you insist on being my cook for life!"

"Oh, I don't insist!" I cried. "I don't want to cook—I want to draw! But I thought—Lois said—How she has misunderstood you!"

"It is not true, always, my dear," said he, "that the way to a man's heart is through his stomach; at least it's not the only way. Lois doesn't know everything; she is young yet! And perhaps for my sake you can give it up. Can you, sweet?"

Could I? Could I? Was there ever a man like this?

THE UNNATURAL MOTHER *

"Don't tell me!" said old Mis' Briggs, with a forbidding shake of the head. "No mother that was a mother would desert her own child for anything on earth!"

"And leaving it a care on the town, too!" put in Susannah Jacobs. "As if we hadn't enough to do to take care of our own!"

Miss Jacobs was a well-to-do old maid, owning a comfortable farm and homestead, and living alone with an impoverished cousin acting as general servant, companion, and protégée. Mis' Briggs, on the contrary, had had thirteen children, five of whom remained to bless her, so that what maternal feeling Miss Jacobs might lack, Mis' Briggs could certainly supply.

"I should think," piped little Martha Ann Simmons, the village dressmaker, "that she might 'a saved her young one first and then tried what she could do for the town."

Martha had been married, had lost her husband, and had one sickly boy to care for.

The youngest Briggs girl, still unmarried at thirty-six, and in her mother's eyes a most tender infant, now ventured to make a remark.

---

* *"The Unnatural Mother" appeared in the November 1916 issue of* The Forerunner, *281–285.*

"You don't any of you seem to think what she did for all of us—if she hadn't left hers we should all have lost ours, sure."

"You ain't no call to judge, Maria 'Melia," her mother hastened to reply. "You've no children of your own, and you can't judge of a mother's duty. No mother ought to leave her child, whatever happens. The Lord gave it to her to take care of—he never gave her other people's. You needn't tell me!"

"She was an unnatural mother," repeated Miss Jacobs harshly, "as I said to begin with!"

"What is the story?" asked the City Boarder. The City Boarder was interested in stories from a business point of view, but they did not know that. "What did this woman do?" she asked.

There was no difficulty in eliciting particulars. The difficulty was rather in discriminating amidst their profusion and contradictoriness. But when the City Boarder got it clear in her mind, it was somewhat as follows:

The name of the much-condemned heroine was Esther Greenwood, and she lived and died here in Toddsville.

Toddsville was a mill village. The Todds lived on a beautiful eminence overlooking the little town, as the castles of robber barons on the Rhine used to overlook their little towns. The mills and the mill hands' houses were built close along the bed of the river. They had to be pretty close, because the valley was a narrow one, and the bordering hills were too steep for travel, but the water power was fine. Above the village was the reservoir, filling the entire valley save for a narrow road beside it, a fair blue smiling lake, edged with lilies and blue flag, rich in pickerel and perch. This lake gave them fish, it gave them ice, it gave the power that ran the mills that gave the town its bread. Blue Lake was both useful and ornamental.

In this pretty and industrious village Esther had grown up, the somewhat neglected child of a heart-broken widower. He had lost a young wife, and three fair babies before her—this one was left him, and he said he meant that she should have all the chance there was.

"That was what ailed her in the first place!" they all eagerly explained to the City Boarder. "She never knew what 'twas to have a mother, and she grew up a regular tomboy! Why, she used to roam the country for miles around, in all weather like an Injun! And her father wouldn't take no advice!"

This topic lent itself to eager discussion. The recreant father, it appeared, was a doctor, not their accepted standby, the resident physician of the neighborhood, but an alien doctor, possessed of "views."

"You never heard such things as he advocated," Miss Jacobs explained. "He wouldn't give no medicines, hardly; said 'nature' did the curing—he couldn't."

"And he couldn't either—that was clear," Mrs. Briggs agreed. "Look at his wife and children dying on his hands, as it were! 'Physician, heal thyself,' I say."

"But, Mother," Maria Amelia put in, "she was an invalid when he married her, they say; and those children died of polly—polly—what's that thing that nobody can help?"

"That may all be so," Miss Jacobs admitted, "but all the same, it's a doctor's business to give medicine. If 'nature' was all that was wanted, we needn't have any doctor at all!"

"I believe in medicine and plenty of it. I always gave my children a good clearance, spring and fall, whether anything ailed 'em or not, just to be on the safe side. And if there was anything the matter with 'em, they had plenty more. I never had anything to reproach myself with on that score," stated Mrs. Briggs, firmly. Then as a sort of concession to the family graveyard, she added piously, "The Lord giveth and the Lord taketh away."

"You should have seen the way he dressed that child!" pursued Miss Jacobs. "It was a reproach to the town. Why, you couldn't tell at a distance whether it was a boy or a girl. And barefoot! He let that child go barefoot till she was so big we was actually mortified to see her."

It appeared that a wild, healthy childhood had made Esther very different in her early womanhood from the meek, well-behaved damsels of the little place. She was well enough liked by those who knew her at all, and the children of the place adored her, but the worthy matrons shook their heads and prophesied no good of a girl who was "queer."

She was described with rich detail in reminiscence, how she wore her hair short till she was fifteen—"just shingled like a boy's—it did seem a shame that girl had no mother to look after her—and her clo'se was almost a scandal, even when she did put on shoes and stockings. Just gingham—brown gingham—and *short!"*

"I think she was a real nice girl," said Maria Amelia. "I can remember her just as well! She was *so* nice to us children. She was five or six years older than I was, and most girls that age won't have anything to do with little ones. But she was kind and pleasant. She'd take us berrying and on all sorts of walks, and teach us new games and tell us things. I don't remember anyone that ever did us the good she did!"

Maria Amelia's thin chest heaved with emotion, and there were tears in her eyes; but her mother took her up somewhat sharply.

"That sounds well I must say—right before your own mother that's toiled and slaved for you! It's all very well for a young thing that's got nothing on earth to do to make herself agreeable to young ones. That poor blinded father of hers never taught her to do the work a girl should—naturally he couldn't."

"At least he might have married again and given her another mother," said Susannah Jacobs, with decision, with so much decision, in fact, that the City Boarder studied her expression for a moment and concluded that if this recreant father had not married again it was not for lack of opportunity.

Mrs. Simmons cast an understanding glance upon Miss Jacobs, and nodded wisely.

"Yes, he ought to have done that, of course. A man's not fit to bring up children, anyhow. How can they? Mothers have the instinct—that is, all natural mothers have. But, dear me! There's some as don't seem to *be* mothers—even when they have a child!"

"You're quite right, Mis' Simmons," agreed the mother of thirteen. "It's a divine instinct, I say. I'm sorry for the child that lacks it. Now this Esther. We always knew she wan't like other girls—she never seemed to care for dress and company and things girls naturally do, but was always philandering over the hills with a parcel of young ones. There wan't a child in town but would run after her. She made more trouble 'n a little in families, the young ones quotin' what Aunt Esther said, and tellin' what Aunt Esther did to their own mothers, and she only a young girl. Why, she actually seemed to care more for them children than she did for beaux or anything—it wasn't natural!"

"But she did marry?" pursued the City Boarder.

"Marry! Yes, she married finally. We all thought she never would, but she did. After the things her father taught her, it did seem as if he'd ruined *all* her chances. It's simply terrible the way that girl was trained."

"Him being a doctor," put in Mrs. Simmons, "made it different, I suppose."

"Doctor or no doctor," Miss Jacobs rigidly interposed, "it was a crying shame to have a young girl so instructed."

"Maria 'Melia," said her mother, "I want you should get me my smelling salts. They're up in the spare chamber, I believe. When your Aunt Marcia was here she had one of her spells— don't you remember?—and she asked for salts. Look in the top bureau drawer—they must be there."

Maria Amelia, thirty-six but unmarried, withdrew dutifully, and the other ladies drew closer to the City Boarder.

"It's the most shocking thing I ever heard of," murmured Mrs. Briggs. "Do you know he—a father—actually taught his daughter how babies come!"

There was a breathless hush.

"He did," eagerly chimed in the little dressmaker. "All the particulars. It was perfectly awful!"

"He said," continued Mrs. Briggs, "that he expected her to be a mother and that she ought to understand what was before her!"

"He was waited on by a committee of ladies from the church, married ladies, all older than he was," explained Miss Jacobs severely. "They told him it was creating a scandal in the town— and what do you think he said?"

There was another breathless silence.

Above, the steps of Maria Amelia were heard, approaching the stairs.

"It ain't there, Ma!"

"Well, you look in the highboy and in the top drawer; they're somewhere up there," her mother replied.

Then, in a sepulchral whisper:

"He told us—yes, ma'am, I was on that committee—he told us that until young women knew what was before them as mothers, they would not do their duty in choosing a father for their children! That was his expression—'choosing a father'! A nice thing for a young girl to be thinking of—a father for her children!"

"Yes, and more than that," inserted Miss Jacobs, who, though not on the committee, seemed familiar with its workings. "He told them—" But Mrs. Briggs waved her aside and continued swiftly—

"He taught that innocent girl about—the Bad Disease! Actually!"

"He did!" said the dressmaker. "It got out, too, all over town. There wasn't a man here would have married her after that."

Miss Jacobs insisted on taking up the tale. "I understand that he said it was 'to protect her'! Protect her, indeed! Against matrimony! As if any man alive would want to marry a young girl who knew all the evil of life! I was brought up differently, I assure you!"

"Young girls should be kept innocent!" Mrs. Briggs solemnly proclaimed. "Why, when I was married I knew no more what was before me than a babe unborn, and my girls were all brought up so, too!"

Then, as Maria Amelia returned with the salts, she continued more loudly. "But she did marry after all. And a mighty queer husband she got, too. He was an artist or something, made pictures for the magazines and such as that, and they do say she met him first out in the hills. That's the first 'twas known of it here, anyhow—them two traipsing about all over; him with his painting things! They married and just settled down to live with her father, for she vowed she wouldn't leave him; and he said it didn't make no difference where he lived, he took his business with him."

"They seemed very happy together," said Maria Amelia.

"Happy! Well, they might have been, I suppose. It was a pretty queer family, I think." And her mother shook her head in retrospection. "They got on all right for a while; but the old man died, and those two—well, I don't call it housekeeping—the way they lived!"

"No," said Miss Jacobs. "They spent more time out-of-doors than they did in the house. She followed him around everywhere. And for open lovemaking—"

They all showed deep disapproval at this memory. All but the City Boarder and Maria Amelia.

"She had one child, a girl," continued Mrs. Briggs, "and it was just shocking to see how she neglected that child from the beginnin'. She never seemed to have no maternal feelin' at all!"

"But I thought you said she was very fond of children," remonstrated the City Boarder.

"Oh, *children*, yes. She'd take up with any dirty-faced brat in town, even them Canucks. I've seen her again and again with a whole swarm of the mill hands' young ones round her, goin' on some picnic or other—'open air school,' she used to call it— *such* notions as she had. But when it come to her own child! Why—" Here the speaker's voice sank to a horrified hush. "She never had no baby clo'se for it! Not a single sock!"

The City Boarder was interested. "Why, what did she do with the little thing?"

"The Lord knows!" answered old Mis' Briggs. "She never would let us hardly see it when 'twas little. 'Shamed too, I don't doubt. But that's strange feelin's for a mother. Why, I was so proud of my babies! And I kept 'em lookin' so pretty! I'd 'a sat up all night and sewed and washed, but I'd 'a had my children look well!" And the poor old eyes filled with tears as she thought of the eight little graves in the churchyard, which she never failed to keep looking pretty, even now. "She just let that young one roll round in the grass like a puppy with hardly nothin' on! Why, a squaw does better! She does keep 'em done up for a spell! That child was treated worse 'n an Injun! We all done what we could, of course. We felt it no more 'n right. But she was real hateful about it, and we had to let her be."

"The child died?" asked the City Boarder.

"Died! Dear no! That's it you saw going by; a great strappin' girl she is, too, and promisin' to grow up well, thanks to Mrs. Stone's taking her. Mrs. Stone always thought a heap of Esther. It's a mercy to the child that she lost her mother, I do believe! How she ever survived that kind of treatment beats all! Why, that woman never seemed to have the first spark of maternal feeling to the end! She seemed just as fond of the other young ones after she had her own as she was before, and that's against nature. The way it happened was this. You see, they lived up the valley nearer to the lake than the village. He was away, and was coming home that night, it seems, driving from Drayton along the lake road. And she set out to meet him. She must 'a walked up to the dam to look for him; and we think maybe she saw the team clear across the lake. Maybe she thought he could get to the house and save little Esther in time—that's the only explanation we ever could put on it. But this is what she did; and you can judge for yourselves if any mother in her senses *could* 'a done such a thing! You see 'twas the time of that awful disaster, you've read of it, likely, that destroyed three villages. Well, she got to the dam and seen that 'twas givin' way—she was always great for knowin' all such things. And she just turned and ran. Jake Elder was up on the hill after a stray cow, and he seen her go. He was too far off to imagine what ailed her, but he said he never saw a woman run so in his life.

"And, if you'll believe it, she run right by her own house— never stopped—never looked at it. Just run for the village. Of course, she may have lost her head with the fright, but that wasn't like her. No, I think she had made up her mind to leave that innocent baby to die! She just ran down here and give warnin', and, of course, we sent word down valley on horse-back, and there was no lives lost in all three villages. She started to run back as soon as we was 'roused, but 'twas too late then.

"Jake saw it all, though he was too far off to do a thing. He said he couldn't stir a foot, it was so awful. He seen the wagon drivin' along as nice as you please till it got close to the dam, and then Greenwood seemed to see the danger and shipped up like mad. He was the father, you know. But he wasn't quite in time—the dam give way and the water went over him like a tidal wave. She was almost to the gate when it struck the house and her—and we never found her body nor his for days and days. They was washed clear down river.

"Their house was strong, and it stood a little high and had some big trees between it and the lake, too. It was moved off the place and brought up against the side of the stone church down yonder, but 'twant wholly in pieces. And that child was found swimmin' round in its bed, most drowned, but not quite. The wonder is, it didn't die of a cold, but it's here yet—must have a strong constitution. Their folks never did nothing for it—so we had to keep it here."

"Well, now, Mother," said Maria Amelia Briggs. "It does seem to me that she did her duty. You know yourself that if she hadn't give warnin' all three of the villages would 'a been cleaned out—a matter of fifteen hundred people. And if she'd stopped to lug that child, she couldn't have got here in time. Don't you believe she was thinkin' of those mill hands' children?"

"Maria 'Melia, I'm ashamed of you!" said old Mis' Briggs. "But you ain't married and ain't a mother. A mother's duty is to her own child! She neglected her own to look after other folks'—the Lord never gave her them other children to care for!"

"Yes," said Miss Jacobs, "and here's her child, a burden on the town! She was an unnatural mother!"

MAKING
A CHANGE *

W a-a-a-a-a! Waa-a-a-aaa!"
Frank Gordins set down his coffee cup so hard
that it spilled over into the saucer.

"Is there no way to stop that child crying?" he demanded.

"I do not know of any," said his wife, so definitely and politely that the words seemed cut off by machinery.

"I *do*," said his mother with even more definiteness, but less
politeness.

Young Mrs. Gordins looked at her mother-in-law from under
her delicate level brows, and said nothing. But the weary lines
about her eyes deepened; she had been kept awake nearly all
night, and for many nights.

So had he. So, as a matter of fact, had his mother. She had not
the care of the baby—but lay awake wishing she had.

"There's no use talking about it," said Julia. "If Frank is not
satisfied with the child's mother, he must say so—perhaps we
can make a change."

This was ominously gentle. Julia's nerves were at the breaking
point. Upon her tired ears, her sensitive mother's heart, the grat-

*"Making a Change" appeared in the December 1911 issue of The Forerunner,
311–315.

ing wail from the next room fell like a lash—burnt in like fire. Her ears were hypersensitive, always. She had been an ardent musician before her marriage, and had taught quite successfully on both piano and violin. To any mother a child's cry is painful; to a musical mother it is torment.

But if her ears were sensitive, so was her conscience. If her nerves were weak, her pride was strong. The child was her child, it was her duty to take care of it, and take care of it she would. She spent her days in unremitting devotion to its needs and to the care of her neat flat; and her nights had long since ceased to refresh her.

Again the weary cry rose to a wail.

"It does seem to be time for a change of treatment," suggested the older woman acidly.

"Or a change of residence," offered the younger, in a deadly quiet voice.

"Well, by Jupiter! There'll be a change of some kind, and p. d. q.!" said the son and husband, rising to his feet.

His mother rose also, and left the room, holding her head high and refusing to show any effects of that last thrust.

Frank Gordins glared at his wife. His nerves were raw, too. It does not benefit anyone in health or character to be continuously deprived of sleep. Some enlightened persons use that deprivation as a form of torture.

She stirred her coffee with mechanical calm, her eyes sullenly bent on her plate.

"I will not stand having Mother spoken to like that," he stated with decision.

"I will not stand having her interfere with my methods of bringing up children."

"Your methods! Why, Julia, my mother knows more about taking care of babies than you'll ever learn! She has the real love of it—and the practical experience. Why can't you *let* her take care of the kid—and we'll all have some peace!"

She lifted her eyes and looked at him; deep inscrutable wells of angry light. He had not the faintest appreciation of her state of mind. When people say they are "nearly crazy" from weariness, they state a practical fact. The old phrase which describes reason as "tottering on her throne" is also a clear one.

Julia was more near the verge of complete disaster than the family dreamed. The conditions were so simple, so usual, so inevitable.

Here was Frank Gordins, well brought up, the only son of a very capable and idolatrously affectionate mother. He had fallen deeply and desperately in love with the exalted beauty and fine mind of the young music teacher, and his mother had approved. She too loved music and admired beauty.

Her tiny store in the savings bank did not allow of a separate home, and Julia had cordially welcomed her to share in their household.

Here was affection, propriety, and peace. Here was a noble devotion on the part of the young wife, who so worshipped her husband that she used to wish she had been the greatest musician on earth—that she might give it up for him! She had given up her music, perforce, for many months, and missed it more than she knew.

She bent her mind to the decoration and artistic management of their little apartment, finding her standards difficult to maintain by the ever-changing inefficiency of her help. The musical temperament does not always include patience, nor, necessarily, the power of management.

When the baby came, her heart overflowed with utter devotion and thankfulness; she was his wife—the mother of his child. Her happiness lifted and pushed within till she longed more than ever for her music, for the free-pouring current of expression, to give forth her love and pride and happiness. She had not the gift of words.

So now she looked at her husband, dumbly, while wild visions of separation, of secret flight—even of self-destruction— swung dizzily across her mental vision. All she said was, "All right, Frank. We'll make a change. And you shall have—some peace."

"Thank goodness for that, Jule! You do look tired, girlie—let Mother see to His Nibs, and try to get a nap, can't you?"

"Yes," she said. "Yes . . . I think I will." Her voice had a peculiar note in it. If Frank had been an alienist, or even a general physician, he would have noticed it. But his work lay in electric coils, in dynamos and copper wiring—not in women's nerves—and he did not notice it.

He kissed her and went out, throwing back his shoulders and drawing a long breath of relief as he left the house behind him and entered his own world.

"This being married—and bringing up children—is not what it's cracked up to be." That was the feeling in the back of his mind. But it did not find full admission, much less expression.

When a friend asked him, "All well at home?" he said, "Yes, thank you—pretty fair. Kid cries a good deal—but that's natural, I suppose."

He dismissed the whole matter from his mind and bent his faculties to a man's task—how he can earn enough to support a wife, a mother, and a son.

At home his mother sat in her small room, looking out of the window at the ground-glass one just across the "well," and thinking hard.

By the disorderly little breakfast table his wife remained motionless, her chin in her hands, her big eyes staring at nothing, trying to formulate in her weary mind some reliable reason why she should not do what she was thinking of doing. But her mind was too exhausted to serve her properly.

Sleep—sleep—sleep—that was the one thing she wanted. Then his mother could take care of the baby all she wanted to, and Frank could have some peace. . . . Oh, dear! It was time for the child's bath.

She gave it to him mechanically. On the stroke of the hour, she prepared the sterilized milk and arranged the little one comfortably with his bottle. He snuggled down, enjoying it, while she stood watching him.

She emptied the tub, put the bath apron to dry, picked up all the towels and sponges and varied appurtenances of the elaborate performance of bathing the first-born, and then sat staring straight before her, more weary than ever, but growing inwardly determined.

Greta had cleared the table, with heavy heels and hands, and was now rattling dishes in the kitchen. At every slam, the young mother winced, and when the girl's high voice began a sort of doleful chant over her work, young Mrs. Gordins rose to her feet with a shiver and made her decision.

She carefully picked up the child and his bottle, and carried him to his grandmother's room.

"Would you mind looking after Albert?" she asked in a flat, quiet voice. "I think I'll try to get some sleep."

"Oh, I shall be delighted," replied her mother-in-law. She said it in a tone of cold politeness, but Julia did not notice. She laid the child on the bed and stood looking at him in the same dull way for a little while, then went out without another word.

Mrs. Gordins, senior, sat watching the baby for some long moments. "He's a perfectly lovely child!" she said softly, gloating over his rosy beauty. "There's not a *thing* the matter with him! It's just her absurd ideas. She's so irregular with him! To think of letting that child cry for an hour! He is nervous because she is. And of course she couldn't feed him till after his bath— of course not!"

She continued in these sarcastic meditations for some time, taking the empty bottle away from the small wet mouth, that sucked on for a few moments aimlessly and then was quiet in sleep.

"I could take care of him so that he'd *never* cry!" she continued to herself, rocking slowly back and forth. "And I could take care of twenty like him—and enjoy it! I believe I'll go off somewhere and do it. Give Julia a rest. Change of residence, indeed!"

She rocked and planned, pleased to have her grandson with her, even while asleep.

Greta had gone out on some errand of her own. The rooms were very quiet. Suddenly the old lady held up her head and sniffed. She rose swiftly to her feet and sprang to the gas jet— no, it was shut off tightly. She went back to the dining-room— all right there.

"That foolish girl has left the range going and it's blown out!" she thought, and went to the kitchen. No, the little room was fresh and clean, every burner turned off.

"Funny! It must come in from the hall." She opened the door. No, the hall gave only its usual odor of diffused basement. Then the parlor—nothing there. The little alcove called by the renting agent "the music room," where Julia's closed piano and violin case stood dumb and dusty—nothing there.

"It's in her room—and she's asleep!" said Mrs. Gordins, senior; and she tried to open the door. It was locked. She

knocked—there was no answer; knocked louder—shook it—
rattled the knob. No answer.

Then Mrs. Gordins thought quickly. "It may be an accident,
and nobody must know. Frank mustn't know. I'm glad Greta's
out. I *must* get in somehow!" She looked at the transom, and the
stout rod Frank had himself put up for the portieres Julia loved.

"I believe I can do it, at a pinch."

She was a remarkably active woman of her years, but no
memory of earlier gymnastic feats could quite cover the exercise. She hastily brought the step-ladder. From its top she could
see in, and what she saw made her determine recklessly.

Grabbing the pole with small strong hands, she thrust her
light frame bravely through the opening, turning clumsily but
successfully, and dropping breathlessly and somewhat bruised
to the floor, she flew to open the windows and doors.

When Julia opened her eyes she found loving arms around
her, and wise, tender words to soothe and reassure.

"Don't say a thing, dearie—I understand. I *understand*, I tell
you! Oh, my dear girl—my precious daughter! We haven't been
half good enough to you, Frank and I! But cheer up now—I've
got the *loveliest* plan to tell you about! We *are* going to make a
change! Listen now!"

And while the pale young mother lay quiet, petted and waited
on to her heart's content, great plans were discussed and decided on.

Frank Gordins was pleased when the baby "outgrew his crying spells." He spoke of it to his wife.

"Yes," she said sweetly. "He has better care."

"I knew you'd learn," said he, proudly.

"I have!" she agreed. "I've learned—ever so much!"

He was pleased, too, vastly pleased, to have her health improve rapidly and steadily, the delicate pink come back to her
cheeks, the soft light to her eyes; and when she made music for
him in the evening, soft music, with shut doors—not to waken
Albert—he felt as if his days of courtship had come again.

Greta the hammer-footed had gone, and an amazing French
matron who came in by the day had taken her place. He asked
no questions as to this person's peculiarities, and did not know
that she did the purchasing and planned the meals, meals of

such new delicacy and careful variance as gave him much delight. Neither did he know that her wages were greater than her predecessor's. He turned over the same sum weekly, and did not pursue details.

He was pleased also that his mother seemed to have taken a new lease of life. She was so cheerful and brisk, so full of little jokes and stories—as he had known her in his boyhood; and above all she was so free and affectionate with Julia, that he was more than pleased.

"I tell you what it is!" he said to a bachelor friend. "You fellows don't know what you're missing!" And he brought one of them home to dinner—just to show him.

"Do you do all that on thirty-five a week?" his friend demanded.

"That's about it," he answered proudly.

"Well, your wife's a wonderful manager—that's all I can say. And you've got the best cook I ever saw, or heard of, or ate of— I suppose I might say—for five dollars."

Mrs. Gordins was pleased and proud. But he was neither pleased nor proud when someone said to him, with displeasing frankness, "I shouldn't think you'd want your wife to be giving music lessons, Frank!"

He did not show surprise nor anger to his friend, but saved it for his wife. So surprised and so angry was he that he did a most unusual thing—he left his business and went home early in the afternoon. He opened the door of his flat. There was no one in it. He went through every room. No wife; no child; no mother; no servant.

The elevator boy heard him banging about, opening and shutting doors, and grinned happily. When Mr. Gordins came out, Charles volunteered some information.

"Young Mrs. Gordins is out, sir; but old Mrs. Gordins and the baby—they're upstairs. On the roof, I think."

Mr. Gordins went to the roof. There he found his mother, a smiling, cheerful nursemaid, and fifteen happy babies.

Mrs. Gordins, senior, rose to the occasion promptly.

"Welcome to my baby-garden, Frank," she said cheerfully. "I'm so glad you could get off in time to see it."

She took his arm and led him about, proudly exhibiting her sunny roof-garden, her sand-pile and big, shallow, zinc-lined

pool, her flowers and vines, her seesaws, swings, and floor mat-
tresses.

"You see how happy they are," she said. "Celia can manage
very well for a few moments." And then she exhibited to him
the whole upper flat, turned into a convenient place for many
little ones to take their naps or to play in if the weather was bad.

"Where's Julia?" he demanded first.

"Julia will be in presently," she told him, "by five o'clock
anyway. And the mothers come for the babies by then, too. I
have them from nine or ten to five."

He was silent, both angry and hurt.

"We didn't tell you at first, my dear boy, because we knew
you wouldn't like it, and we wanted to make sure it would go
well. I rent the upper flat, you see—it is forty dollars a month,
same as ours—and pay Celia five dollars a week, and pay Dr.
Holbrook downstairs the same for looking over my little ones
every day. She helped me to get them, too. The mothers pay me
three dollars a week each, and don't have to keep a nursemaid.
And I pay ten dollars a week board to Julia, and still have about
ten of my own."

"And she gives music lessons?"

"Yes, she gives music lessons, just as she used to. She loves it,
you know. You must have noticed how happy and well she is
now—haven't you? And so am I. And so is Albert. You can't feel
very badly about a thing that makes us all happy, can you?"

Just then Julia came in, radiant from a brisk walk, fresh and
cheery, a big bunch of violets at her breast.

"Oh, Mother," she cried, "I've got tickets and we'll all go to
hear Melba—if we can get Celia to come in for the evening."

She saw her husband, and a guilty flush rose to her brow as
she met his reproachful eyes.

"Oh, Frank!" she begged, her arms around his neck. "Please
don't mind! Please get used to it! Please be proud of us! Just
think, we're all so happy, and we earn about a hundred dollars
a week—all of us together. You see, I have Mother's ten to add
to the house money, and twenty or more of my own!"

They had a long talk together that evening, just the two of
them. She told him, at last, what a danger had hung over
them—how near it came.

"And Mother showed me the way out, Frank. The way to

have my mind again—and not lose you! She is a different woman herself now that she has her heart and hands full of babies. Albert does enjoy it so! And *you've* enjoyed it—till you found it out!

"And dear—my own love—I don't mind it now at all! I love my home, I love my work, I love my mother, I love you. And as to children—I wish I had six!"

He looked at her flushed, eager, lovely face, and drew her close to him.

"If it makes all of you as happy as that," he said, "I guess I can stand it."

And in after years he was heard to remark, "This being married and bringing up children is as easy as can be—when you learn how!"

AN
HONEST
WOMAN*

"There's an honest woman if ever there was one!" said the young salesman to the old one, watching their landlady whisk inside the screen door and close it softly without letting in a single fly—those evergreen California flies not mentioned by real estate men.

"What makes you think so?" asked Mr. Burdock, commonly known as Old Burdock, wriggling forward, with alternate jerks, the two hind legs which supported his chair, until its backward tilt was positively dangerous.

"Think!" said young Abramson with extreme decision. "I happen to know. I've put up here for three years past, twice a year; and I know a lot of people in this town—sell to 'em right along."

"Stands well in the town, does she?" inquired the other with no keen interest. He had put up at the Main House for eight years, and furthermore he knew Mrs. Main when she was a child; but he did not mention it. Mr. Burdock made no pretense of virtue, yet if he had one in especial it lay in the art of not saying things.

"I should say she does!" the plump young man replied, straightening his well-curved waistcoat. "None better. She

*"An Honest Woman" appeared in the March 1911 issue of The Forerunner, 59-65.

hasn't a bill standing—settles the day they come in. Pays cash for everything she can. She must make a handsome thing of this house; but it don't go in finery—she's as plain as a hen."

"Why, I should call Mrs. Main rather a good-looking woman," Burdock gently protested.

"Oh yes, good-looking enough; but I mean her style—no show—no expense—no dress. But she keeps up the house all right—everything first class, and reasonable prices. She's got good money in the bank, they tell me. And there's a daughter—away at school somewhere—won't have her brought up in a hotel. She's dead right, too."

"I dunno why a girl couldn't grow up in a hotel—with a nice mother like that," urged Mr. Burdock.

"Oh come! You know better 'n that. Get talked about in any case—probably worse. No sir! You can't be too careful about a girl, and her mother knows it."

"Glad you've got a high opinion of women. I like to see it," and Mr. Burdock tilted softly backward and forward in his chair, a balancing foot thrust forth. He wore large, square-toed, rather thin shoes with the visible outlines of feet in them.

The shoes of Mr. Abramson, on the other hand, had pronounced outlines of their own, and might have been stuffed with anything—that would go in.

"I've got a high opinion of good women," he announced with finality. "As to bad ones, the less said the better!" and he puffed his strong cigar, looking darkly experienced.

"They're doin' a good deal towards reformin' 'em, nowadays, ain't they?" ventured Mr. Burdock.

The young man laughed disagreeably. "You can't reform spilled milk," said he. "But I do like to see an honest, hard-working woman succeed."

"So do I, boy," said his companion, "so do I," and they smoked in silence.

The hotel bus drew up before the house, backed up creakingly, and one passenger descended, bearing a large, lean suitcase showing much wear. He was an elderly man, tall, well-built, but not well-carried, and wore a long, thin beard. Mr. Abramson looked him over, decided that he was neither a buyer nor a seller, and dismissed him from his mind.

Mr. Burdock looked him over and brought the front legs of his chair down with a thump.

"By heck!" said he softly.

The newcomer went in to register.

Mr. Burdock went in to buy another cigar.

Mrs. Main was at the desk alone, working at her books. Her smooth, dark hair curved away from a fine forehead, both broad and high; wide-set, steady gray eyes looked out from under level brows with a clear directness. Her mouth, at thirty-eight, was a little hard.

The tall man scarcely looked at her, as he reached for the register book; but she looked at him, and her color slowly heightened. He signed his name as one of considerable importance, "Mr. Alexander E. Main, Guthrie, Oklahoma."

"I want a sunny room," he said. "A south room, with a fire when I want it. I feel the cold in this climate very much."

"You always did," remarked Mrs. Main quietly.

Then he looked, the pen dropping from his fingers and rolling across the untouched page, making a dotted path of lessening blotches.

Mr. Burdock made himself as small as he could against the cigar stand, but she ruthlessly approached, sold him the cigar he selected, and waited calmly till he started out, the tall man still staring.

Then she turned to him.

"Here is your key," she said. "Joe, take the gentleman's grip."

The boy moved off with the worn suitcase, but the tall man leaned over the counter towards her.

Mr. Burdock was carefully closing the screen door—so carefully that he could still hear.

"Why Mary! Mary! I must see you," the man whispered.

"You may see me at any time," she answered quietly. "Here is my office."

"This evening!" he said excitedly. "I'll come down this evening when it's quiet. I have so much to tell you, Mary."

"Very well," she said. "Room twenty-seven, Joe," and turned away.

Mr. Burdock took a walk, his cigar still unlighted.

"By heck!" said he. "By—heck! And she as cool as a cucumber—That confounded old skeezicks! Hanged if I don't happen to be passin'."

A sturdy, long-legged little girl was Mary Cameron when he first did business with her father in a Kansas country store. Ranch born and bred, a vigorous, independent child, gravely selling knives and sewing silk, writing paper, and potatoes "to help Father."

Father was a freethinker—a man of keen, strong mind, scant education, and opinions which ran away with him. He trained her to think for herself, and she did; to act up to her beliefs, and she did; to worship liberty and the sacred rights of the individual, and she did.

But the store failed, as the ranch had failed before it. Perhaps Old Man Cameron's arguments were too hot for the store loafers; perhaps his freethinking scandalized them. When Burdock saw Mary again, she was working in a San Francisco restaurant. She did not remember him in the least; but he knew one of her friends there and learned of the move to California—the orange failure, the grape failure, the unexpected death of Mr. Cameron, and Mary's self-respecting efficiency since.

"She's doin' well already—got some money ahead—and she's just as straight!" said Miss Josie. "Want to meet her?"

"Oh no," said Mr. Burdock, who was of a retiring disposition. "No, she wouldn't remember me at all."

When he happened into that restaurant again a year later, Mary had gone, and her friend hinted dark things.

"She got to goin' with a married man!" she confided. "Man from Oklahoma—name o' Main. One o' these Healers—great man for talkin'. She's left here, and I don't know where she is."

Mr. Burdock was sorry, very sorry—not only because he knew Mary, but because he knew Mr. Main. First—where had he met that man first? When he was a glib young phrenologist in Cincinnati. Then he'd run against him in St. Louis—a palmist this time; and then in Topeka—"Dr. Alexander," some sort of an "opaththist." Dr. Main's system of therapy varied, it appeared, with circumstances; he treated brains or bones as it happened, and here in San Francisco had made quite a hit, had lectured, had written a book on sex.

That Mary Cameron, with her hard sense and high courage, should take up with a man like that!

But Mr. Burdock continued to travel, and some four years later, coming to a new hotel in San Diego, he had found Mary again, now Mrs. Mary Main, presiding over the affairs of the house, with a small daughter going to school sedately.

Nothing did he say, to or about her. She was closely attending to her business, and he attended to his; but the next time he was in Cincinnati he had no difficulty in hearing of Mrs. Alexander Main—and her three children—in very poor circumstances indeed.

Of Main he had heard nothing for many years—till now.

He returned to the hotel, and walked near the side window of the office. No one there yet. Selecting chewing gum for solace, as tobacco might betray him, he deliberately tucked a camp stool under the shadow of the overhanging rose bush and sat there, somewhat thornily, but well hidden.

"It's none o' my business, but I mean to get the rights o' this," said Mr. Burdock.

She came in about a quarter of ten, as neat, as plain, as quiet as ever, and sat down under the light with her sewing. Many pretty things Mrs. Main made lovingly, but never wore.

She stopped after a little, folded her strong hands in her lap, and sat looking straight before her.

"If I could only see what she's looking at, I'd get the hang of it," thought Mr. Burdock, occasionally peering.

What she was looking at was a woman's life—and she studied it calmly and with impartial justice.

A fearless, independent girl, fond of her father but recognizing his weaknesses, she had taken her life in her own hands at about the age of twenty, finding in her orphanhood mainly freedom. Her mother she hardly remembered. She was not attractive to such youths as she met in the course of business, coldly repellent to all casual advances, and determined inwardly not to marry, at least not till she had made something of herself. She had worked hard, kept her health, saved money, and read much of the "progressive literature" her father loved.

Then came this man who also read—studied—thought, who felt as she felt, who shared her aspirations, who "understood her." (Quite possibly he did—he was a person of considerable experience.)

Slowly she grew to enjoy his society, to depend upon it. When he revealed himself as lonely, not over-strong, struggling with the world, she longed to help him; and when, at last, in a burst of bitter confidence, he had said he must leave her, that she had made life over for him but that he must tear himself away, that she was life and hope to him, but he was not free— she demanded the facts.

He told her a sad tale, seeming not to cast blame on any but himself; but the girl burned deep and hot with indignation at the sordid woman, older than he, who had married him in his inexperienced youth, drained him of all he could earn, blasted his ideals, made his life an unbearable desert waste. She had— but no, he would not blacken her who had been his wife.

"She gives me no provable cause for divorce," he told her. "She will not loosen her grip. I have left her, but she will not let me go."

"Were there any—children?" she asked after a while.

"There was one little girl—" he said with a pathetic pause. "She died—"

He did not feel it necessary to mention that there were three little boys—who had lived, after a fashion.

Then Mary Cameron made a decision which was more credit to her heart than to her head, though she would have warmly denied such a criticism.

"I see no reason why your life—your happiness—your service to the community—should all be ruined and lost because you were foolish as a boy."

"I was," he groaned. "I fell under temptation. Like any other sinner, I must bear my punishment. There is no escape."

"Nonsense," said Mary. "She will not let you go. You will not live with her. You cannot marry me. But I can be your wife—if you want me to."

It was nobly meant. She cheerfully risked all, gave up all, to make up to him for his "ruined life," to give some happiness to one so long unhappy; and when he vowed that he would not take advantage of such sublime unselfishness, she said that it was not in the least unselfish—for she loved him. This was true—she was quite honest about it.

And he? It is perfectly possible that he entered into their "sacred compact" with every intention of respecting it. She made him happier than anyone else ever had, so far.

There were two happy years when Mr. and Mrs. Main—they took themselves quite seriously—lived in their little flat together and worked and studied and thought great thoughts for the advancement of humanity. Also there was a girl child born, and their contentment was complete.

But in time the income earned by Mr. Main fell away more and more; till Mrs. Main went forth again and worked in a hotel, as efficient as ever, and even more attractive.

Then he had become restless and had gone to Seattle to look for employment—a long search, with only letters to fill the void.

And then—the quiet woman's hands were clenched together till the nails were purple and white—then The Letter came.

She was sitting alone that evening, the child playing on the floor. The woman who looked after her in the daytime had gone home. The two "roomers" who nearly paid the rent were out. It was a still, soft evening.

She had not had a letter for a week—and was hungry for it. She kissed the envelope—where his hand had rested. She squeezed it tight in her hands—laid her cheek on it—pressed it to her heart.

The baby reached up and wanted to share in the game. She gave her the envelope.

He was not coming back—ever. . . . It was better that she should know at once. . . . She was a strong woman—she would not be overcome. . . . She was a capable woman—independent—he need not worry about her in that way. . . . They had been mistaken. . . . He had found one that was more truly his. . . . She had been a Great Boon to him. . . . Here was some money for the child. . . . Good-bye.

She sat there, still, very still, staring straight before her, till the child reached up with a little cry.

Then she caught that baby in her arms, and fairly crushed her with passionate caresses till the child cried in good earnest and had to be comforted. Stony-eyed, the mother soothed and rocked her till she slept, and laid her carefully in her little crib. Then she stood up and faced it.

"I suppose I am a ruined woman," she said.

She went to the glass and lit the gas on either side, facing herself with fixed gaze and adding calmly, "I don't look it!"

She did not look it. Tall, strong, nobly built, softer and richer for her years of love, her happy motherhood, the woman she saw in the glass seemed as one at the beginning of a splendid life, not at the end of a bad one.

No one could ever know all that she thought and felt that night, bracing her broad shoulders to meet this unbelievable blow.

If he had died she could have borne it better; if he had disappeared she would at least have had her memories left. But now she had not only grief but *shame*. She had been a fool—a plain, ordinary, old-fashioned, girl fool, just like so many others she had despised. And now?

Under the shock and torture of her shattered life, the brave, practical soul of her struggled to keep its feet, to stand erect. She was not a demonstrative woman. Possibly he had never known how much she loved him, how utterly her life had grown to lean on his.

This thought struck her suddenly and she held her head higher. "Why should he ever know?" she said to herself, and then, "At least I have the child!" Before that night was over, her plans were made.

The money he had sent, which her first feeling was to tear and burn, she now put carefully aside. "He sent it for the child," she said. "She will need it." She sublet the little flat and sold the furniture to a young couple, friends of hers, who were looking for just such a quiet home. She bought a suit of mourning, not too cumbrous, and set forth with little Mollie for the South.

In that fair land to which so many invalids come too late, it is not hard to find incompetent women, widowed and penniless, struggling to make a business of the only art they know— emerging from the sheltered harbor of "keeping house" upon the troubled sea of "keeping boarders."

Accepting moderate terms because of the child, doing good work because of long experience, offering a friendly sympathy out of her own deep sorrow, Mrs. Main made herself indispensable to such a one.

When her new employer asked her about her husband, she

would press her handkerchief to her eyes and say, "He has left me. I cannot bear to speak of him."

This was quite true.

In a year she had saved a little money, and had spent it for a ticket home for the bankrupt lady of the house, who gladly gave her "the goodwill of the business" for it.

Said goodwill was lodged in an angry landlord, a few discontented and largely delinquent boarders, and many unpaid tradesmen. Mrs. Main called a meeting of her creditors in the stiff boardinghouse parlor.

She said, "I have bought this business, such as it is, with practically my last cent. I have worked seven years in restaurants and hotels and know how to run this place better than it has been done so far. If you people will give me credit for six months, and then, if I make good, for six months more, I will assume these back debts—and pay them. Otherwise I shall have to leave here, and you will get nothing but what will come from a forced sale of this third-hand furniture. I shall work hard, for I have this fatherless child to work for." She had the fatherless child at her side—a pretty thing about three years old.

They looked the house over, looked her over, talked a little with the boarder of longest standing, and took up her offer.

She make good in six months, at the end of the year had begun to pay debts, and now—

Mrs. Main drew a long breath and came back to the present.

Mollie, dear Mollie, was a big girl now, doing excellently well at a good school. The Main House was an established success—had been for years. She had some money laid up—for Mollie's college expenses. Her health was good, she liked her work, she was respected and esteemed in the town, a useful member of a liberal church, of the Progressive Woman's Club, of the City Improvement Association. She had won Comfort, Security, and Peace.

His step on the stairs—restrained—uncertain—eager.

Her door was open. He came in, and closed it softly behind him. She rose and opened it.

"That door stands open," she said. "You need not worry. There's no one about."

"Not many, at any rate," thought the unprincipled Burdock.

She sat down again quietly. He wanted to kiss her, to take her in his arms; but she moved back to her seat with a decided step, and motioned him to his.

"You wanted to speak to me, Mr. Main. What about?"

Then he poured forth his heart as he used to, in a flow of strong, convincing words.

He told of his wanderings, his struggles, his repeated failures; of the misery that had overwhelmed him in his last fatal mistake.

"I deserve it all," he said with the quick smile and lift of the head that once was so compelling. "I deserve everything that has come to me. . . . Once to have had you . . . and to be so blind a fool as to let go your hand! I needed it, Mary, I needed it."

He said little of his intermediate years as to facts, much as to the waste of woe they represented.

"Now I am doing better in my business," he said. "I have an established practice in Guthrie, but my health is not good and I have been advised to come to a warmer climate at least for a while."

She said nothing but regarded him with a clear and steady eye. He seemed an utter stranger, and an unattractive one. That fierce leap of the heart, which, in his presence, at his touch, she recalled so well—where was it now?

"Will you not speak to me, Mary?"

"I have nothing to say."

"Can you not—forgive me?"

She leaned forward, dropping her forehead in her hands. He waited breathless; he thought she was struggling with her heart.

In reality she was recalling their life together, measuring its further prospects in the light of what he had told her, and comparing it with her own life since. She raised her head and looked him squarely in the eye.

"I have nothing to forgive," she said.

"Ah, you are too generous, too noble!" he cried. "And I? The burden of my youth is lifted now. My first wife is dead—some years since—and I am free. You are my real wife, Mary, my true and loving wife. Now I can offer you the legal ceremony as well."

"I do not wish it," she answered.

"It shall be as you say," he went on. "But for the child's sake—I wish to be a father to her."

"You are her father," said she. "That cannot be helped."

"But I wish to give her my name."

"She has it. I gave it to her."

"Brave, dear woman! But now I can give it to you."

"I have it also. It has been my name ever since I—according to my conscience—married you."

"But—but—you have no *legal* right to it, Mary."

She smiled, even laughed.

"Better read a little law, Mr. Main. I have used that name for twelve years, am publicly and honorably known by it; it is mine, legally."

"But Mary, I want to help you."

"Thank you. I do not need it."

"But I want to do for the child—my child—our little one!"

"You may," said she. "I want to send her to college. You may help if you like. I should be very glad if Mollie could have some pleasant and honorable memories of her father." She rose suddenly. "You wish to marry me now, Mr. Main?"

"With all my heart I wish it, Mary. You will?—"

He stood up—he held out his arms to her.

"No," said she, "I will not. When I was twenty-four I loved you. I sympathized with you. I was willing to be your wife— truly and faithfully your wife, even though you could not legally marry me—because I loved you. Now I will not marry you because I do not love you. That is all."

He glanced about the quiet, comfortable room; he had already estimated the quiet, comfortable business; and now, from some forgotten chamber of his honeycombed heart, welled up a fierce longing for this calm, strong, tender woman whose power of love he knew so well.

"Mary! You will not turn me away! I love you—I love you as I never loved you before!"

"I'm sorry to hear it," she said. "It does not make me love you again."

His face darkened.

"Do not drive me to desperation," he cried. "Your whole life here rests on a lie, remember. I could shatter it with a word."

She smiled patiently.

"You can't shatter facts, Mr. Main. People here know that you left me years ago. They know how I have lived since. If you try to blacken my reputation here, I think you will find the climate of Mexico more congenial."

On second thought, this seemed to be the opinion of Mr. Main, who presently left for that country.

It was also agreed with by Mr. Burdock, who emerged later, a little chilly and somewhat scratched, and sought his chamber.

"If that galoot says anything against her in this town, he'll find a hotter climate than Mexico—by heck!" said Mr. Burdock to his boots as he set them down softly. And that was all he ever said about it.

TURNED

In her soft-carpeted, thick-curtained, richly furnished chamber, Mrs. Marroner lay sobbing on the wide, soft bed.

She sobbed bitterly, chokingly, despairingly; her shoulders heaved and shook convulsively; her hands were tight-clenched. She had forgotten her elaborate dress, the more elaborate bed-cover; forgotten her dignity, her self-control, her pride. In her mind was an overwhelming, unbelievable horror, an immeasurable loss, a turbulent, struggling mass of emotion.

In her reserved, superior, Boston-bred life, she had never dreamed that it would be possible for her to feel so many things at once, and with such trampling intensity.

She tried to cool her feelings into thoughts; to stiffen them into words; to control herself—and could not. It brought vaguely to her mind an awful moment in the breakers at York Beach, one summer in girlhood when she had been swimming under water and could not find the top.

In her uncarpeted, thin-curtained, poorly furnished chamber on the top floor, Gerta Petersen lay sobbing on the narrow, hard bed.

She was of larger frame than her mistress, grandly built and

*"Turned" appeared in the September 1911 issue of The Forerunner, 227–232.

strong; but all her proud young womanhood was prostrate now, convulsed with agony, dissolved in tears. She did not try to control herself. She wept for two.

If Mrs. Marroner suffered more from the wreck and ruin of a longer love—perhaps a deeper one; if her tastes were finer, her ideals loftier; if she bore the pangs of bitter jealousy and outraged pride, Gerta had personal shame to meet, a hopeless future, and a looming present which filled her with unreasoning terror.

She had come like a meek young goddess into that perfectly ordered house, strong, beautiful, full of goodwill and eager obedience, but ignorant and childish—a girl of eighteen.

Mr. Marroner had frankly admired her, and so had his wife. They discussed her visible perfections and as visible limitations with that perfect confidence which they had so long enjoyed. Mrs. Marroner was not a jealous woman. She had never been jealous in her life—till now.

Gerta had stayed and learned their ways. They had both been fond of her. Even the cook was fond of her. She was what is called "willing," was unusually teachable and plastic; and Mrs. Marroner, with her early habits of giving instruction, tried to educate her somewhat.

"I never saw anyone so docile," Mrs. Marroner had often commented. "It is perfection in a servant, but almost a defect in character. She is so helpless and confiding."

She was precisely that: a tall, rosy-cheeked baby; rich womanhood without, helpless infancy within. Her braided wealth of dead-gold hair, her grave blue eyes, her mighty shoulders and long, firmly moulded limbs seemed those of a primal earth spirit; but she was only an ignorant child, with a child's weakness.

When Mr. Marroner had to go abroad for his firm, unwillingly, hating to leave his wife, he had told her he felt quite safe to leave her in Gerta's hands—she would take care of her.

"Be good to your mistress, Gerta," he told the girl that last morning at breakfast. "I leave her to you to take care of. I shall be back in a month at latest."

Then he turned, smiling, to his wife. "And you must take care of Gerta, too," he said. "I expect you'll have her ready for college when I get back."

This was seven months ago. Business had delayed him from week to week, from month to month. He wrote to his wife, long, loving, frequent letters, deeply regretting the delay, explaining how necessary, how profitable it was, congratulating her on the wide resources she had, her well-filled, well-balanced mind, her many interests.

"If I should be eliminated from your scheme of things, by any of those 'acts of God' mentioned on the tickets, I do not feel that you would be an utter wreck," he said. "That is very comforting to me. Your life is so rich and wide that no one loss, even a great one, would wholly cripple you. But nothing of the sort is likely to happen, and I shall be home again in three weeks—if this thing gets settled. And you will be looking so lovely, with that eager light in your eyes and the changing flush I know so well— and love so well! My dear wife! We shall have to have a new honeymoon—other moons come every month, why shouldn't the mellifluous kind?"

He often asked after "little Gerta," sometimes enclosed a picture postcard to her, joked his wife about her laborious efforts to educate "the child," was so loving and merry and wise—

All this was racing through Mrs. Marroner's mind as she lay there with the broad, hemstitched border of fine linen sheeting crushed and twisted in one hand, and the other holding a sodden handkerchief.

She had tried to teach Gerta, and had grown to love the patient, sweet-natured child, in spite of her dullness. At work with her hands, she was clever, if not quick, and could keep small accounts from week to week. But to the woman who held a Ph.D., who had been on the faculty of a college, it was like baby-tending.

Perhaps having no babies of her own made her love the big child the more, though the years between them were but fifteen.

To the girl she seemed quite old, of course; and her young heart was full of grateful affection for the patient care which made her feel so much at home in this new land.

And then she had noticed a shadow on the girl's bright face.

She looked nervous, anxious, worried. When the bell rang, she seemed startled, and would rush hurriedly to the door. Her peals of frank laughter no longer rose from the area gate as she stood talking with the always admiring tradesmen.

Mrs. Marroner had labored long to teach her more reserve with men, and flattered herself that her words were at last effective. She suspected the girl of homesickness, which was denied. She suspected her of illness, which was denied also. At last she suspected her of something which could not be denied.

For a long time she refused to believe it, waiting. Then she had to believe it, but schooled herself to patience and understanding. "The poor child," she said. "She is here without a mother—she is so foolish and yielding—I must not be too stern with her." And she tried to win the girl's confidence with wise, kind words.

But Gerta had literally thrown herself at her feet and begged her with streaming tears not to turn her away. She would admit nothing, explain nothing, but frantically promised to work for Mrs. Marroner as long as she lived—if only she would keep her.

Revolving the problem carefully in her mind, Mrs. Marroner thought she would keep her, at least for the present. She tried to repress her sense of ingratitude in one she had so sincerely tried to help, and the cold, contemptuous anger she had always felt for such weakness.

"The thing to do now," she said to herself, "is to see her through this safely. The child's life should not be hurt any more than is unavoidable. I will ask Dr. Bleet about it—what a comfort a woman doctor is! I'll stand by the poor, foolish thing till it's over, and then get her back to Sweden somehow with her baby. How they do come where they are not wanted—and don't come where they are wanted!" And Mrs. Marroner, sitting alone in the quiet, spacious beauty of the house, almost envied Gerta.

Then came the deluge.

She had sent the girl out for needed air toward dark. The late mail came; she took it in herself. One letter for her—her husband's letter. She knew the postmark, the stamp, the kind of typewriting. She impulsively kissed it in the dim hall. No one would suspect Mrs. Marroner of kissing her husband's letters—but she did, often.

She looked over the others. One was for Gerta, and not from Sweden. It looked precisely like her own. This struck her as a little odd, but Mr. Marroner had several times sent messages and cards to the girl. She laid the letter on the hall table and took hers to her room.

"My poor child," it began. What letter of hers had been sad enough to warrant that?

"I am deeply concerned at the news you send." What news to so concern him had she written? "You must bear it bravely, little girl. I shall be home soon, and will take care of you, of course. I hope there is not immediate anxiety—you do not say. Here is money, in case you need it. I expect to get home in a month at latest. If you have to go, be sure to leave your address at my office. Cheer up—be brave—I will take care of you."

The letter was typewritten, which was not unusual. It was unsigned, which was unusual. It enclosed an American bill— fifty dollars. It did not seem in the least like any letter she had ever had from her husband, or any letter she could imagine him writing. But a strange, cold feeling was creeping over her, like a flood rising around a house.

She utterly refused to admit the ideas which began to bob and push about outside her mind, and to force themselves in. Yet under the pressure of these repudiated thoughts she went downstairs and brought up the other letter—the letter to Gerta. She laid them side by side on a smooth dark space on the table; marched to the piano and played, with stern precision, refusing to think, till the girl came back. When she came in, Mrs. Marroner rose quietly and came to the table. "Here is a letter for you," she said.

The girl stepped forward eagerly, saw the two lying together there, hesitated, and looked at her mistress.

"Take yours, Gerta. Open it, please."

The girl turned frightened eyes upon her.

"I want you to read it, here," said Mrs. Marroner.

"Oh, ma'am—No! Please don't make me!"

"Why not?"

There seemed to be no reason at hand, and Gerta flushed more deeply and opened her letter. It was long; it was evidently puzzling to her; it began "My dear wife." She read it slowly.

"Are you sure it is your letter?" asked Mrs. Marroner. "Is not this one yours? Is not that one—mine?"

She held out the other letter to her.

"It is a mistake," Mrs. Marroner went on, with a hard quietness. She had lost her social bearings somehow, lost her usual keen sense of the proper thing to do. This was not life; this was a nightmare.

"Do you not see? Your letter was put in my envelope and my letter was put in your envelope. Now we understand it."

But poor Gerta had no antechamber to her mind, no trained forces to preserve order while agony entered. The thing swept over her, resistless, overwhelming. She cowered before the outraged wrath she expected; and from some hidden cavern that wrath arose and swept over her in pale flame.

"Go and pack your trunk," said Mrs. Marroner. "You will leave my house tonight. Here is your money."

She laid down the fifty-dollar bill. She put with it a month's wages. She had no shadow of pity for those anguished eyes, those tears which she heard drop on the floor.

"Go to your room and pack," said Mrs. Marroner. And Gerta, always obedient, went.

Then Mrs. Marroner went to hers, and spent a time she never counted, lying on her face on the bed.

But the training of the twenty-eight years which had elapsed before her marriage; the life at college, both as student and teacher; the independent growth which she had made, formed a very different background for grief from that in Gerta's mind.

After a while Mrs. Marroner arose. She administered to herself a hot bath, a cold shower, a vigorous rubbing. "Now I can think," she said.

First she regretted the sentence of instant banishment. She went upstairs to see if it had been carried out. Poor Gerta! The tempest of her agony had worked itself out at last as in a child, and left her sleeping, the pillow wet, the lips still grieving, a big sob shuddering itself off now and then.

Mrs. Marroner stood and watched her, and as she watched she considered the helpless sweetness of the face; the defenseless, unformed character; the docility and habit of obedience which made her so attractive—and so easily a victim. Also she thought of the mighty force which had swept over her; of the great process now working itself out through her; of how pitiful and futile seemed any resistance she might have made.

She softly returned to her own room, made up a little fire, and sat by it, ignoring her feelings now, as she had before ignored her thoughts.

Here were two women and a man. One woman was a wife: loving, trusting, affectionate. One was a servant: loving, trusting, affectionate—a young girl, an exile, a dependent; grateful for any kindness; untrained, uneducated, childish. She ought, of course, to have resisted temptation; but Mrs. Marroner was wise enough to know how difficult temptation is to recognize when it comes in the guise of friendship and from a source one does not suspect.

Gerta might have done better in resisting the grocer's clerk; had, indeed, with Mrs. Marroner's advice, resisted several. But where respect was due, how could she criticize? Where obedience was due, how could she refuse—with ignorance to hold her blinded—until too late?

As the older, wiser woman forced herself to understand and extenuate the girl's misdeed and foresee her ruined future, a new feeling rose in her heart, strong, clear, and overmastering: a sense of measureless condemnation for the man who had done this thing. He knew. He understood. He could fully foresee and measure the consequences of his act. He appreciated to the full the innocence, the ignorance, the grateful affection, the habitual docility, of which he deliberately took advantage.

Mrs. Marroner rose to icy peaks of intellectual apprehension, from which her hours of frantic pain seemed far indeed removed. He had done this thing under the same roof with her—his wife. He had not frankly loved the younger woman, broken with his wife, made a new marriage. That would have been heart-break pure and simple. This was something else.

That letter, that wretched, cold, carefully guarded, unsigned letter, that bill—far safer than a check—these did not speak of affection. Some men can love two women at one time. This was not love.

Mrs. Marroner's sense of pity and outrage for herself, the wife, now spread suddenly into a perception of pity and outrage for the girl. All that splendid, clean young beauty, the hope of a happy life, with marriage and motherhood, honorable independence, even—these were nothing to that man. For his own pleasure he had chosen to rob her of her life's best joys.

He would "take care of her," said the letter. How? In what capacity?

And then, sweeping over both her feelings for herself, the wife, and Gerta, his victim, came a new flood, which literally lifted her to her feet. She rose and walked, her head held high. "This is the sin of man against woman," she said. "The offense is against womanhood. Against motherhood. Against—the child."

She stopped.

The child. His child. That, too, he sacrificed and injured—doomed to degradation.

Mrs. Marroner came of stern New England stock. She was not a Calvinist, hardly even a Unitarian, but the iron of Calvinism was in her soul: of that grim faith which held that most people had to be damned "for the glory of God."

Generations of ancestors who both preached and practiced stood behind her; people whose lives had been sternly moulded to their highest moments of religious conviction. In sweeping bursts of feeling, they achieved "conviction," and afterward they lived and died according to that conviction.

When Mr. Marroner reached home a few weeks later, following his letters too soon to expect an answer to either, he saw no wife upon the pier, though he had cabled, and found the house closed darkly. He let himself in with his latch-key, and stole softly upstairs, to surprise his wife.

No wife was there.

He rang the bell. No servant answered it.

He turned up light after light, searched the house from top to bottom; it was utterly empty. The kitchen wore a clean, bald, unsympathetic aspect. He left it and slowly mounted the stairs, completely dazed. The whole house was clean, in perfect order, wholly vacant.

One thing he felt perfectly sure of—she knew.

Yet was he sure? He must not assume too much. She might have been ill. She might have died. He started to his feet. No, they would have cabled him. He sat down again.

For any such change, if she had wanted him to know, she would have written. Perhaps she had, and he, returning so suddenly, had missed the letter. The thought was some comfort. It must be so. He turned to the telephone and again hesitated. If she had found out—if she had gone—utterly gone, without a word—should he announce it himself to friends and family?

He walked the floor; he searched everywhere for some letter, some word of explanation. Again and again he went to the telephone—and always stopped. He could not bear to ask: "Do you know where my wife is?"

The harmonious, beautiful rooms reminded him in a dumb, helpless way of her—like the remote smile on the face of the dead. He put out the lights, could not bear the darkness, turned them all on again.

It was a long night—

In the morning he went early to the office. In the accumulated mail was no letter from her. No one seemed to know of anything unusual. A friend asked after his wife—"Pretty glad to see you, I guess?" He answered evasively.

About eleven a man came to see him: John Hill, her lawyer. Her cousin, too. Mr. Marroner had never liked him. He liked him less now, for Mr. Hill merely handed him a letter, remarked, "I was requested to deliver this to you personally," and departed, looking like a person who is called on to kill something offensive.

"I have gone. I will care for Gerta. Good-bye. Marion."

That was all. There was no date, no address, no postmark, nothing but that.

In his anxiety and distress, he had fairly forgotten Gerta and all that. Her name aroused in him a sense of rage. She had come between him and his wife. She had taken his wife from him. That was the way he felt.

At first he said nothing, did nothing, lived on alone in his house, taking meals where he chose. When people asked him about his wife, he said she was traveling—for her health. He would not have it in the newspapers. Then, as time passed, as no enlightenment came to him, he resolved not to bear it any longer, and employed detectives. They blamed him for not having put them on the track earlier, but set to work, urged to the utmost secrecy.

What to him had been so blank a wall of mystery seemed not to embarrass them in the least. They made careful inquiries as to her "past," found where she had studied, where taught, and on what lines; that she had some little money of her own, that her doctor was Josephine L. Bleet, M.D., and many other bits of information.

As a result of careful and prolonged work, they finally told him that she had resumed teaching under one of her old professors, lived quietly, and apparently kept boarders; giving him town, street, and number, as if it were a matter of no difficulty whatever.

He had returned in early spring. It was autumn before he found her.

A quiet college town in the hills, a broad, shady street, a pleasant house standing in its own lawn, with trees and flowers about it. He had the address in his hand, and the number showed clear on the white gate. He walked up the straight gravel path and rang the bell. An elderly servant opened the door.

"Does Mrs. Marroner live here?"

"No, sir."

"This is number twenty-eight?"

"Yes, sir."

"Who does live here?"

"Miss Wheeling, sir."

Ah! Her maiden name. They had told him, but he had forgotten.

He stepped inside. "I would like to see her," he said.

He was ushered into a still parlor, cool and sweet with the scent of flowers, the flowers she had always loved best. It almost brought tears to his eyes. All their years of happiness rose in his mind again—the exquisite beginnings; the days of eager longing before she was really his; the deep, still beauty of her love.

Surely she would forgive him—she must forgive him. He would humble himself; he would tell her of his honest remorse—his absolute determination to be a different man.

Through the wide doorway there came in to him two women. One like a tall Madonna, bearing a baby in her arms.

Marion, calm, steady, definitely impersonal, nothing but a clear pallor to hint of inner stress.

Gerta, holding the child as a bulwark, with a new intelligence in her face, and her blue, adoring eyes fixed on her friend—not upon him.

He looked from one to the other dumbly.

And the woman who had been his wife asked quietly:

"What have you to say to us?"

THE WIDOW'S MIGHT *

James had come on to the funeral, but his wife had not; she could not leave the children—that is what he said. She said, privately, to him, that she would not go. She never was willing to leave New York except for Europe or for summer vacations; and a trip to Denver in November—to attend a funeral—was not a possibility to her mind.

Ellen and Adelaide were both there: they felt it a duty—but neither of their husbands had come. Mr. Jennings could not leave his classes in Cambridge, and Mr. Oswald could not leave his business in Pittsburgh—that is what they said.

The last services were over. They had had a cold, melancholy lunch and were all to take the night train home again. Meanwhile, the lawyer was coming at four to read the will.

"It is only a formality. There can't be much left," said James.

"No," agreed Adelaide, "I suppose not."

"A long illness eats up everything," said Ellen, and sighed. Her husband had come to Colorado for his lungs years before and was still delicate.

"Well," said James rather abruptly, "what are we going to do with Mother?"

*"The Widow's Might" appeared in the January 1911 issue of The Forerunner, 3-7.

"Why, of course—" Ellen began, "we *could* take her. It would depend a good deal on how much property there is—I mean, on where she'd want to go. Edward's salary is more than needed now." Ellen's mental processes seemed a little mixed.

"She can come to me if she prefers, of course," said Adelaide. "But I don't think it would be very pleasant for her. Mother never did like Pittsburgh."

James looked from one to the other.

"Let me see—how old is Mother?"

"Oh she's all of fifty," answered Ellen, "and much broken, I think. It's been a long strain, you know." She turned plaintively to her brother. "I should think you could make her more comfortable than either of us, James—with your big house."

"I think a woman is always happier living with a son than with a daughter's husband," said Adelaide. "I've always thought so."

"That is often true," her brother admitted. "But it depends." He stopped, and the sisters exchanged glances. They knew upon what it depended.

"Perhaps if she stayed with me, you could—help some," suggested Ellen.

"Of course, of course, I could do that," he agreed with evident relief. "She might visit between you—take turns—and I could pay her board. About how much ought it to amount to? We might as well arrange everything now."

"Things cost awfully in these days," Ellen said with a crisscross of fine wrinkles on her pale forehead. "But of course it would be only just *what* it costs. I shouldn't want to *make* anything."

"It's work and care, Ellen, and you may as well admit it. You need all your strength—with those sickly children and Edward on your hands. When she comes to me, there need be no expense, James, except for clothes. I have room enough and Mr. Oswald will never notice the difference in the house bills—but he does hate to pay out money for clothes."

"Mother must be provided for properly," her son declared. "How much ought it to cost—a year—for clothes?"

"You know what your wife's cost," suggested Adelaide, with a flicker of a smile about her lips.

"Oh, *no*," said Ellen. "That's no criterion! Maude is in society, you see. Mother wouldn't *dream* of having so much."

James looked at her gratefully. "Board—and clothes—all told; what should you say, Ellen?"

Ellen scrabbled in her small black handbag for a piece of paper, and found none. James handed her an envelope and a fountain pen.

"Food—just plain food materials—costs all of four dollars a week now—for one person," said she. "And heat—and light—and extra service. I should think six a week would be the *least*, James. And for clothes and carfare and small expenses—I should say—well, three hundred dollars!"

"That would make over six hundred a year," said James slowly. "How about Oswald sharing that, Adelaide?"

Adelaide flushed. "I do not think he would be willing, James. Of course, if it were absolutely necessary—"

"He has money enough," said her brother.

"Yes, but he never seems to have any outside of his business—and he has his own parents to carry now. No—I can give her a home, but that's all."

"You see, you'd have none of the care and trouble, James," said Ellen. "We—the girls—are each willing to have her with us, while perhaps Maude wouldn't care to, but if you could just pay the money—"

"Maybe there's some left, after all," suggested Adelaide. "And this place ought to sell for something."

"This place" was a piece of rolling land within ten miles of Denver. It had a bit of river bottom, and ran up towards the foothills. From the house the view ran north and south along the precipitous ranks of the "Big Rockies" to westward. To the east lay the vast stretches of sloping plain.

"There ought to be at least six or eight thousand dollars from it, I should say," he concluded.

"Speaking of clothes," Adelaide rather irrelevantly suggested, "I see Mother didn't get any new black. She's always worn it as long as I can remember."

"Mother's a long time," said Ellen. "I wonder if she wants anything. I'll go up and see."

"No," said Adelaide. "She said she wanted to be let alone—

and rest. She said she'd be down by the time Mr. Frankland got here."

"She's bearing it pretty well," Ellen suggested, after a little silence.

"It's not like a broken heart," Adelaide explained. "Of course Father meant well—"

"He was a man who always did his duty," admitted Ellen. "But we none of us—loved him—very much."

"He is dead and buried," said James. "We can at least respect his memory."

"We've hardly seen Mother—under that black veil," Ellen went on. "It must have aged her. This long nursing."

"She had help toward the last—a man nurse," said Adelaide.

"Yes, but a long illness is an awful strain—and Mother never was good at nursing. She has surely done her duty," pursued Ellen.

"And now she's entitled to a rest," said James, rising and walking about the room. "I wonder how soon we can close up affairs here—and get rid of this place. There might be enough in it to give her almost a living—properly invested."

Ellen looked out across the dusty stretches of land.

"How I did hate to live here!" she said.

"So did I," said Adelaide.

"So did I," said James.

And they all smiled rather grimly.

"We don't any of us seem to be very—affectionate, about Mother," Adelaide presently admitted. "I don't know why it is—we never were an affectionate family, I guess."

"Nobody could be affectionate with Father," Ellen suggested timidly.

"And Mother—poor Mother! She's had an awful life."

"Mother has always done her duty," said James in a determined voice, "and so did Father, as he saw it. Now we'll do ours."

"Ah," exclaimed Ellen, jumping to her feet, "here comes the lawyer. I'll call Mother."

She ran quickly upstairs and tapped at her mother's door.

"Mother, oh Mother," she cried. "Mr. Frankland's come."

"I know it," came back a voice from within. "Tell him to go

ahead and read the will. I know what's in it. I'll be down in a few minutes."

Ellen went slowly back downstairs with the fine crisscross of wrinkles showing on her pale forehead again, and delivered her mother's message.

The other two glanced at each other hesitatingly, but Mr. Frankland spoke up briskly.

"Quite natural, of course, under the circumstances. Sorry I couldn't get to the funeral. A case on this morning."

The will was short. The estate was left to be divided among the children in four equal parts, two to the son and one each to the daughters after the mother's legal share had been deducted, if she were still living. In such case they were furthermore directed to provide for their mother while she lived. The estate, as described, consisted of the ranch, the large, rambling house on it, with all the furniture, stock, and implements, and some five thousand dollars in mining stocks.

"That is less than I had supposed," said James.

"This will was made ten years ago," Mr. Frankland explained. "I have done business for your father since that time. He kept his faculties to the end, and I think that you will find that the property has appreciated. Mrs. McPherson has taken excellent care of the ranch, I understand—and has had some boarders."

Both the sisters exchanged pained glances.

"There's an end to all that now," said James.

At this moment, the door opened and a tall black figure, cloaked and veiled, came into the room.

"I'm glad to hear you say that Mr. McPherson kept his faculties to the last, Mr. Frankland," said the widow. "It's true. I didn't come down to hear that old will. It's no good now."

They all turned in their chairs.

"Is there a later will, madam?" inquired the lawyer.

"Not that I know of. Mr. McPherson had no property when he died."

"No property! My dear lady—four years ago he certainly had some."

"Yes, but three years and a half ago he gave it all to me. Here are the deeds."

There they were, in very truth—formal and correct, and quite simple and clear—for deeds. James R. McPherson, Sr., had assuredly given to his wife the whole estate.

"You remember that was the panic year," she continued. "There was pressure from some of Mr. McPherson's creditors; he thought it would be safer so."

"Why—yes," remarked Mr. Frankland. "I do remember now his advising with me about it. But I thought the step unnecessary."

James cleared his throat.

"Well, Mother, this does complicate matters a little. We were hoping that we could settle up all the business this afternoon—with Mr. Frankland's help—and take you back with us."

"We can't be spared any longer, you see, Mother," said Ellen.

"Can't you deed it back again, Mother," Adelaide suggested, "to James, or to—all of us, so we can get away?"

"Why should I?"

"Now, Mother," Ellen put in persuasively, "we know how badly you feel, and you are nervous and tired, but I told you this morning when we came, that we expected to take you back with us. You know you've been packing—"

"Yes, I've been packing," replied the voice behind the veil.

"I dare say it was safer—to have the property in your name—technically," James admitted, "but now I think it would be the simplest way for you to make it over to me in a lump, and I will see that Father's wishes are carried out to the letter."

"Your father is dead," remarked the voice.

"Yes, Mother, we know—we know how you feel," Ellen ventured.

"I am alive," said Mrs. McPherson.

"Dear Mother, it's very trying to talk business to you at such a time. We all realize it," Adelaide explained with a touch of asperity. "But we told you we couldn't stay as soon as we got here."

"And the business has to be settled," James added conclusively.

"It is settled."

"Perhaps Mr. Frankland can make it clear to you," went on James with forced patience.

"I do not doubt that your mother understands perfectly,"

murmured the lawyer. "I have always found her a woman of remarkable intelligence."

"Thank you, Mr. Frankland. Possibly you may be able to make my children understand that this property—such as it is—is mine now."

"Why assuredly, assuredly, Mrs. McPherson. We all see that. But we assume, as a matter of course, that you will consider Mr. McPherson's wishes in regard to the disposition of the estate."

"I have considered Mr. McPherson's wishes for thirty years," she replied. "Now, I'll consider mine. I have done my duty since the day I married him. It is eleven thousand days—today." The last with sudden intensity.

"But madam, your children—"

"I have no children, Mr. Frankland. I have two daughters and a son. These two grown persons here, grown up, married, having children of their own—or ought to have—were my children. I did my duty by them, and they did their duty by me—and would yet, no doubt." The tone changed suddenly. "But they don't have to. I'm tired of duty."

The little group of listeners looked up, startled.

"You don't know how things have been going on here," the voice went on. "I didn't trouble you with my affairs. But I'll tell you now. When your father saw fit to make over the property to me—to save it—and when he knew that he hadn't many years to live, I took hold of things. I had to have a nurse for your father—and a doctor coming; the house was a sort of hospital, so I made it a little more so. I had half a dozen patients and nurses here—and made money by it. I ran the garden—kept cows—raised my own chickens—worked out-of-doors—slept out-of-doors. I'm a stronger woman today than I ever was in my life!"

She stood up, tall, strong, and straight, and drew a deep breath.

"Your father's property amounted to about eight thousand dollars when he died," she continued. "That would be two thousand dollars to James and one thousand dollars to each of the girls. That I'm willing to give you now—each of you—in your own name. But if my daughters will take my advice, they'd better let me send them the yearly income—in cash—to spend as they like. It is good for a woman to have some money of her own."

"I think you are right, Mother," said Adelaide.

"Yes indeed," murmured Ellen.

"Don't you need it yourself, Mother?" asked James, with a sudden feeling of tenderness for the stiff figure in black.

"No, James, I shall keep the ranch, you see. I have good reliable help. I've made two thousand dollars a year—clear—off it so far, and now I've rented it for that to a doctor friend of mine—woman doctor."

"I think you have done remarkably well, Mrs. McPherson—wonderfully well," said Mr. Frankland.

"And you'll have an income of two thousand dollars a year," said Adelaide incredulously.

"You'll come and live with me, won't you?" ventured Ellen.

"Thank you, my dear, I will not."

"You're more than welcome in my big house," said Adelaide.

"No thank you, my dear."

"I don't doubt Maude will be glad to have you," James rather hesitatingly offered.

"I do. I doubt it very much. No thank you, my dear."

"But what *are* you going to do?"

Ellen seemed genuinely concerned.

"I'm going to do what I never did before. I'm going to *live!*"

With a firm swift step, the tall figure moved to the windows and pulled up the lowered shades. The brilliant Colorado sunshine poured into the room. She threw off the long black veil.

"That's borrowed," she said. "I didn't want to hurt your feelings at the funeral."

She unbuttoned the long black cloak and dropped it at her feet, standing there in the full sunlight, a little flushed and smiling, dressed in a well-made traveling suit of dull mixed colors.

"If you want to know my plans, I'll tell you. I've got six thousand dollars of my own. I earned it in three years—off my little rancho-sanitarium. One thousand I have put in the savings bank—to bring me back from anywhere on earth, and to put me in an old lady's home if it is necessary. Here is an agreement with a cremation company. They'll import me, if necessary, and have me duly—expurgated—or they don't get the money. But

I've got five thousand dollars to play with, and I'm going to play."

Her daughters looked shocked.

"Why, Mother—"

"At your age—"

James drew down his upper lip and looked like his father.

"I knew you wouldn't any of you understand," she continued more quietly. "But it doesn't matter any more. Thirty years I've given you—and your father. Now I'll have thirty years of my own."

"Are you—are you sure you're—well, Mother?" Ellen urged with real anxiety.

Her mother laughed outright.

"Well, really well, never was better, have been doing business up to today—good medical testimony that. No question of my sanity, my dears! I want you to grasp the fact that your mother is a Real Person with some interests of her own and half a lifetime yet. The first twenty didn't count for much—I was growing up and couldn't help myself. The last thirty have been—hard. James perhaps realizes that more than you girls, but you all know it. Now, I'm free."

"Where *do* you mean to go, Mother?" James asked.

She looked around the little circle with a serene air of decision and replied.

"To New Zealand. I've always wanted to go there," she pursued. "Now I'm going. And to Australia—and Tasmania—and Madagascar—and Terra del Fuego. I shall be gone some time."

They separated that night—three going east, one west.

MR. PEEBLES' HEART*

He was lying on the sofa in the homely, bare little sitting room—an uncomfortable stiff sofa, too short, too sharply upcurved at the end, but still a sofa, whereon one could, at a pinch, sleep.

Thereon Mr. Peebles slept, this hot still afternoon; slept uneasily, snoring a little, and twitching now and then, as one in some obscure distress.

Mrs. Peebles had creaked down the front stairs and gone off on some superior errands of her own—with a good palm-leaf fan for a weapon, a silk umbrella for a defense.

"Why don't you come too, Joan?" she had urged her sister, as she dressed herself for departure.

"Why should I, Emma? It's much more comfortable at home. I'll keep Arthur company when he wakes up."

"Oh, Arthur! He'll go back to the store as soon as he's had his nap. And I'm sure Mrs. Older's paper'll be real interesting. If you're going to live here, you ought to take an interest in the club, seems to me."

"I'm going to live here as a doctor—not as a lady of leisure, Em. You go on—I'm contented."

*"Mr. Peebles' Heart" appeared in the September 1914 issue of The Forerunner, 225–229.

So Mrs. Emma Peebles sat in the circle of the Ellsworth Ladies' Home Club, and improved her mind, while Dr. J. R. Bascom softly descended to the sitting room in search of a book she had been reading.

There was Mr. Peebles, still uneasily asleep. She sat down quietly in a cane-seated rocker by the window and watched him awhile—first professionally, then with a deeper human interest.

Baldish, grayish, stoutish, with a face that wore a friendly smile for customers and showed grave, set lines that deepened about the corners of his mouth when there was no one to serve; very ordinary in dress, in carriage, in appearance was Arthur Peebles at fifty. He was not "the slave of love" of the Arab tale, but the slave of duty.

If ever a man had done his duty—as he saw it—he had done his, always.

His duty—as he saw it—was carrying women. First his mother, a comfortable competent person, who had run the farm after her husband's death, and added to their income by summer boarders until Arthur was old enough to "support her." Then she sold the old place and moved into the village to "make a home for Arthur," who incidentally provided a hired girl to perform the manual labor of that process.

He worked in the store. She sat on the piazza and chatted with her neighbors.

He took care of his mother until he was nearly thirty, when she left him finally; and then he installed another woman to make a home for him—also with the help of the hired girl. A pretty, careless, clinging little person he married, who had long made mute appeal to his strength and carefulness, and she had continued to cling uninterruptedly to this day.

Incidentally a sister had clung also. Both the daughters were married in due time, with sturdy young husbands to cling to in their turn; and now there remained only his wife to carry, a lighter load than he had ever known—at least numerically.

But either he was tired, very tired, or Mrs. Peebles' tendrils had grown tougher, tighter, more tenacious, with age. He did not complain of it. Never had it occurred to him in all these years that there was any other thing for a man to do than to carry whatsoever women came within range of lawful relationship.

Had Dr. Joan been—shall we say—carriageable—he would have cheerfully added her to the list, for he liked her extremely. She was different from any woman he had ever known, different from her sister as day from night, and, in lesser degree, from all the female inhabitants of Ellsworth.

She had left home at an early age, against her mother's will, absolutely run away; but when the whole countryside rocked with gossip and sought for the guilty man—it appeared that she had merely gone to college. She worked her way through, learning more, far more, than was taught in the curriculum, became a trained nurse, studied medicine, and had long since made good in her profession. There were even rumors that she must be "pretty well fixed" and about to "retire"; but others held that she must have failed, really, or she never would have come back home to settle.

Whatever the reason, she was there, a welcome visitor—a source of real pride to her sister, and of indefinable satisfaction to her brother-in-law. In her friendly atmosphere he felt a stirring of long unused powers; he remembered funny stories, and how to tell them; he felt a revival of interests he had thought quite outlived, early interests in the big world's movements.

"Of all unimpressive, unattractive, *good* little men—" she was thinking, as she watched, when one of his arms dropped off the slippery side of the sofa, the hand thumped on the floor, and he awoke and sat up hastily with an air of one caught off duty.

"Don't sit up as suddenly as that, Arthur, it's bad for your heart."

"Nothing the matter with my heart, is there?" he asked with his ready smile.

"I don't know—haven't examined it. Now—sit still—you know there's nobody in the store this afternoon—and if there is, Jake can attend to 'em."

"Where's Emma?"

"Oh, Emma's gone to her 'club' or something—wanted me to go, but I'd rather talk with you."

He looked pleased but incredulous, having a high opinion of that club, and a low one of himself.

"Look here," she pursued suddenly, after he had made himself comfortable with a drink from the swinging ice-pitcher, and another big cane rocker, "what would you like to do if you could?"

"Travel!" said Mr. Peebles, with equal suddenness. He saw her astonishment. "Yes, travel! I've always wanted to—since I was a kid. No use! We never could, you see. And now—even if we could—Emma hates it." He sighed resignedly.

"Do you like to keep store?" she asked sharply.

"*Like* it?" He smiled at her cheerfully, bravely, but with a queer blank hopeless background underneath. He shook his head gravely. "No, I do not, Joan. Not a little bit. But what of that?"

They were still for a little, and then she put another question. "What would you have chosen—for a profession—if you had been free to choose?"

His answer amazed her threefold: from its character, its sharp promptness, its deep feeling. It was in one word—"Music!"

"Music!" she repeated. "Music! Why I didn't know you played—or cared about it."

"When I was a youngster," he told her, his eyes looking far off through the vine-shaded window, "Father brought home a guitar—and said it was for the one that learned to play it first. He meant the girls of course. As a matter of fact I learned it first—but I didn't get it. That's all the music I ever had," he added. "And there's not much to listen to here, unless you count what's in church. I'd have a Victrola—but—" he laughed a little shamefacedly, "Emma says if I bring one into the house she'll smash it. She says they're worse than cats. Tastes differ, you know, Joan."

Again he smiled at her, a droll smile, a little pinched at the corners. "Well—I must be getting back to business."

She let him go, and turned her attention to her own business, with some seriousness.

"Emma," she proposed, a day or two later, "how would you like it if I should board here—live here, I mean, right along?"

"I should hope you would," her sister replied. "It would look nice to have you practicing in this town and not live with me— all the sister I've got."

"Do you think Arthur would like it?"

"Of course he would! Besides—even if he didn't—you're *my* sister—and this is my house. He put it in my name, long ago."

"I see," said Joan, "I see."

Then after a little—"Emma, are you contented?"

"Contented? Why, of course I am. It would be a sin not to be. The girls are well married—I'm happy about them both. This is a real comfortable house, and it runs itself—my Matilda is a jewel if ever there was one. And she doesn't mind company— likes to do for 'em. Yes—I've nothing to worry about."

"Your health's good—that I can see," her sister remarked, regarding with approval her clear complexion and bright eyes.

"Yes—I've nothing to complain about—that I know of," Emma admitted, but among her causes for thankfulness she did not even mention Arthur, nor seem to think of him till Dr. Joan seriously inquired her opinion as to his state of health.

"His health? Arthur's? Why he's always well. Never had a sick day in his life—except now and then he's had a kind of a breakdown," she added as an afterthought.

Dr. Joan Bascom made acquaintances in the little town, both professional and social. She entered upon her practice, taking it over from the failing hands of old Dr. Braithwaite, her first friend, and feeling very much at home in the old place. Her sister's house furnished two comfortable rooms downstairs, and a large bedroom above. "There's plenty of room now the girls are gone," they both assured her.

Then, safely ensconced and established, Dr. Joan began a secret campaign to alienate the affections of her brother-in-law. Not for herself—oh no! If ever in earlier years she had felt the need of someone to cling to, it was long, long ago. What she sought was to free him from the tentacles—without reentanglement.

She bought a noble Gramophone with a set of first-class records, told her sister smilingly that she didn't have to listen, and Emma would sit sulkily in the back room on the other side of the house, while her husband and sister enjoyed the music. She grew used to it in time, she said, and drew nearer, sitting on the porch perhaps; but Arthur had his long-denied pleasure in peace.

It seemed to stir him strangely. He would rise and walk, a new fire in his eyes, a new firmness about the patient mouth, and Dr. Joan fed the fire with talk and books and pictures, with study of maps and sailing lists and accounts of economical tours.

"I don't see what you two find so interesting in all that stuff about music and those composers," Emma would say. "I never did care for foreign parts—musicians are all foreigners, anyway."

Arthur never quarrelled with her; he only grew quiet and lost that interested sparkle of the eye when she discussed the subject.

Then one day, Mrs. Peebles being once more at her club, content and yet aspiring, Dr. Joan made bold attack upon her brother-in-law's principles.

"Arthur," she said, "have you confidence in me as a physician?"

"I have," he said briskly. "Rather consult you than any doctor I ever saw."

"Will you let me prescribe for you if I tell you you need it?"

"I sure will."

"Will you take the prescription?"

"Of course I'll take it—no matter how it tastes."

"Very well. I prescribe two years in Europe."

He stared at her, startled.

"I mean it. You're in a more serious condition than you think. I want you to cut clear—and travel. For two years."

He still stared at her. "But Emma—"

"Never mind about Emma. She owns the house. She's got enough money to clothe herself—and I'm paying enough board to keep everything going. Emma doesn't need you."

"But the store—"

"Sell the store."

"Sell it! That's easy said. Who'll buy it?"

"I will. Yes—I mean it. You give me easy terms and I'll take the store off your hands. It ought to be worth seven or eight thousand dollars, oughtn't it—stock and all?"

He assented, dumbly.

"Well, I'll buy it. You can live abroad for two years, on a couple of thousand, or twenty-five hundred—a man of your tastes. You know those accounts we've read—it can be done easily. Then you'll have five thousand or so to come back to—and can invest it in something better than that shop. Will you do it?"

He was full of protests, of impossibilities.

She met them firmly. "Nonsense! You can too. She doesn't need you, at all—she may later. No—the girls don't need you—and they may later. Now is your time—*now*. They say the Japanese sow their wild oats after they're fifty—suppose you do! You can't be so *very* wild on that much money, but you can spend a year in Germany—learn the language—go to the opera—take walking trips in the Tyrol—in Switzerland; see England, Scotland, Ireland, France, Belgium, Denmark—you can do a lot in two years."

He stared at her fascinated.

"Why not? Why not be your own man for once in your life—do what *you* want to—not what other people want you to?"

He murmured something as to "duty"—but she took him up sharply.

"If ever a man on earth has done his duty, Arthur Peebles, you have. You've taken care of your mother while she was perfectly able to take care of herself; of your sisters, long after they were; and of a wholly able-bodied wife. At present she does not need you the least bit in the world."

"Now that's pretty strong," he protested. "Emma'd miss me—I know she'd miss me—"

Dr. Bascom looked at him affectionately. "There couldn't a better thing happen to Emma—or to you, for that matter—than to have her miss you, real hard."

"I know she'd never consent to my going," he insisted, wistfully.

"That's the advantage of my interference," she replied serenely. "You surely have a right to choose your doctor, and your doctor is seriously concerned about your health and orders foreign travel—rest—change—and music."

"But Emma—"

"Now, Arthur Peebles, forget Emma for a while—I'll take care of her. And look here—let me tell you another thing—a change like this will do her good."

He stared at her, puzzled.

"I mean it. Having you away will give her a chance to stand up. Your letters—about those places—will interest her. She may want to go, sometime. Try it."

He wavered at this. Those who too patiently serve as props sometimes underrate the possibilities of the vine.

"Don't discuss it with her—that will make endless trouble. Fix up the papers for my taking over the store—I'll draw you a check, and you get the next boat for England, and make your plans from there. Here's a banking address that will take care of your letters and checks—"

The thing was done! Done before Emma had time to protest. Done, and she left gasping to upbraid her sister.

Joan was kind, patient, firm, and adamant.

"But how it *looks*, Joan—what will people think of me! To be left deserted—like this!"

"People will think according to what we tell them and to how you behave, Emma Peebles. If you simply say that Arthur was far from well and I advised him to take a foreign trip—and if you forget yourself for once, and show a little natural feeling for him—you'll find no trouble at all."

For her own sake, the selfish woman, made more so by her husband's unselfishness, accepted the position. Yes—Arthur had gone abroad for his health—Dr. Bascom was much worried about him—chance of a complete breakdown, she said. Wasn't it pretty sudden? Yes—the doctor hurried him off. He was in England—going to take a walking trip—she did not know when he'd be back. The store? He'd sold it.

Dr. Bascom engaged a competent manager who ran that store successfully, more so than had the unenterprising Mr. Peebles. She made it a good paying business, which he ultimately bought back and found no longer a burden.

But Emma was the principal change. With talk, with books, with Arthur's letters followed carefully on maps, with trips to see the girls, trips in which traveling lost its terrors, with the care of the house, and the boarder or two they took "for company," she so ploughed and harrowed that long-fallow field of Emma's mind that at last it began to show signs of fruitfulness.

Arthur went away leaving a stout, dull woman who clung to

him as if he was a necessary vehicle or beast of burden—and
thought scarcely more of his constant service.

He returned younger, stronger, thinner, an alert vigorous
man, with a mind enlarged, refreshed, and stimulated. He had
found himself.

And he found her, also, most agreeably changed, having developed not merely tentacles, but feet of her own to stand on.

When next the thirst for travel seized him, she thought she'd
go too, and proved unexpectedly pleasant as a companion.

But neither of them could ever wring from Dr. Bascom any
definite diagnosis of Mr. Peebles' threatening disease. "A dangerous enlargement of the heart" was all she would commit
herself to, and when he denied any such trouble now, she
gravely wagged her head and said it had "responded to treatment."

THE CRUX*

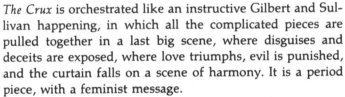

The Crux is orchestrated like an instructive Gilbert and Sullivan happening, in which all the complicated pieces are pulled together in a last big scene, where disguises and deceits are exposed, where love triumphs, evil is punished, and the curtain falls on a scene of harmony. It is a period piece, with a feminist message.

Dr. Jane Bellair, having long fled to Colorado to practice medicine, returns to the stultifying New England town of her youth and inspires an odd assortment of women to find a new home and a new life in the West. The whole town suffers, she says, from "an advanced stage of *arthritis deformans* of the soul." In the West not only can women vote, but they can more easily marry, and marry wisely, because the women, outnumbering the men, can do the choosing.

The fleeing contingent includes the heroine, Vivian Lane, age twenty-five, who has been too-patiently waiting for Morton Elder to return from the West. Vivian, yearning for a career as a kindergarten teacher, is denied an education by her parents, who insist she remain at home, supported by them, until she marries. Vivian's grandmother, Mrs. Pet-

*The Crux *appeared originally in Volume 2 of *The Forerunner (1910) and was published separately in 1911.

tigrew, a sprightly and spirited sixty-year-old, joyously joins the others to escape from the stereotyped view of "the aged" in which she is locked at home. Morton Elder's sister and aunt complete the group.

The women create their economic independence in Colorado by establishing a boardinghouse, which quickly attracts a variety of men and women of different ages, interests, and personalities. The recently created extended family also includes Dr. Richard Hale, a cantankerous, somewhat misogynistic, self-reliant, gentle, and good man, who one senses suffered deep disappointment and pain in his early years.

Complexities and confusions abound when Morton Elder suddenly appears, with the "rough good looks and fluent manner which easily find their way to the good will of many female hearts." He finds Vivian's tenderness and delicacy compelling, and he undergoes feelings of genuine remorse for his wasted years and profligate behavior, of which we have some hints in the frequent allusions to his coarse and reddened complexion. Vivian's uneasy feelings about her rediscovered lover are minimized by Adela St. Cloud, who, in the spirit of woman's noble duty, urges Vivian to devote her life to uplifting and improving the sinner.

The fundamental point of the story, the crux of it, is that Morton Elder has venereal disease, and innocent Vivian must be warned. In the excerpt below, a confrontation occurs as Jane Bellair, humanist, feminist, unbound by tradition, tries unsuccessfully to persuade decent, but traditional, Richard Hale to expose Morton. When he refuses, Dr. Bellair makes the disclosure, explaining as well her own tragic history.

Vivian does reject Morton, and she recovers very slowly from the loss of his attention and affection. But she learns that although "love has gone" and might never come again, her work—she has by this time established a kindergarten—gives her a sense of usefulness and independence, and therefore genuine pleasure. She is lonely for an intimate relationship, but she is not unhappy.

The story ends with a variety of happy couples—even

Grandma Pettigrew marries—the only exception being Adela St. Cloud, who does not change and therefore does not deserve. Richard Hale, who confesses that his misogyny was rooted in an adolescent infatuation with the shallow and cruel Adela, chastises himself for having made a solemn oath never to ask a woman to marry him. "You don't have to," Vivian assures him, defying this tradition as well.

D r. Bellair went to Dr. Hale's office and sat herself down solidly in the patient's chair.

"Dick," she said, "are you going to stand for this?"

"Stand for what, my esteemed but cryptic fellow-practitioner?" . . .

"All right, Dick—if you want it made perfectly clear to your understanding. Do you mean to let Morton Elder marry Vivian Lane?"

"What business is it of mine?" he demanded, more than brusquely—savagely.

"You know what he's got."

"I am a physician, not a detective. And I am not Miss Lane's father, brother, uncle, or guardian."

"Or lover," added Dr. Bellair, eyeing him quietly. She thought she saw a second's flicker of light in the deep gray eyes, a possible tightening of set lips. "Suppose you are not," she said, "nor even a humanitarian. You *are* a member of society. Do you mean to let a man whom you know has no right to marry, poison the life of that splendid girl?"

He was quite silent for a moment, but she could see the hand on the farther arm of his chair grip it till the nails were white.

"How do you know he—wishes to marry her?"

"If you were about like other people, you old hermit, you'd know it as well as anybody. I think they are on the verge of an engagement, if they aren't over it already. Once more, Dick, shall you do anything?"

"No," said he. Then, as she did not add a word, he rose and walked up and down the office in big strides, turning upon her at last.

"You know how I feel about this. It is a matter of honor—

professional honor. You women don't seem to know what the word means. I've told that good-for-nothing young wreck that he has no right to marry for years yet, if ever. That is all I can do. I will not betray the confidence of a patient."

"Not if he had smallpox, or scarlet fever, or the bubonic plague? Suppose a patient of yours had the leprosy, and wanted to marry your sister; would you betray his confidence?"

"I might kill my sister," he said, glaring at her. "I refuse to argue with you."

"Yes, I think you'd better refuse," she said, rising. "And you don't have to kill Vivian Lane, either. A man's honor always seems to want to kill a woman to satisfy it. I'm glad I haven't got the feeling. Well, Dick, I thought I'd give you a chance to come to your senses, a real good chance. But I won't leave you to the pangs of unavailing remorse, you poor old goose. That young syphilitic is no patient of mine." And she marched off to perform a difficult duty.

She was very fond of Vivian. The girl's unselfish sweetness of character and the depth of courage and power she perceived behind the sensitive, almost timid, exterior appealed to her. If she had had a daughter, perhaps she would have been like that. If she had had a daughter, would she not have thanked anyone who would try to save her from such a danger? From that worse than deadly peril, because of which she had no daughter. . . .

Dr. Bellair had asked Vivian to take a walk with her; and they sat together, resting, on a high lonely hill, a few miles out of town.

"It's a great pleasure to see this much of you, Dr. Bellair," said the girl, feeling really complimented.

"I'm afraid you won't think so, my dear, when you hear what I have to say—what I *have* to say."

The girl flushed a little. "Are you going to scold me about something? Have I done anything wrong?" Her eyes smiled bravely. "Go on, Doctor. I know it will be for my best good."

"It will indeed, dear child," said the doctor, so earnestly that Vivian felt a chill of apprehension.

"I am going to talk to you 'as man to man' as the story books say, as woman to woman. When I was your age I had been married three years."

Vivian was silent, but stole out a soft sympathetic hand and slipped it into the older woman's. She had heard of this early-made marriage, also early broken, with various dark comments to which she had paid no attention.

Dr. Bellair was Dr. Bellair, and she had a reverential affection for her.

There was a little silence. The doctor evidently found it hard to begin. "You love children, don't you, Vivian?"

The girl's eyes kindled, and a heavenly smile broke over her face. "Better than anything in the world," she said.

"Ever think about them?" asked her friend, her own face whitening as she spoke. "Think about their lovely little soft helplessness—when you hold them in your arms and have to do *everything* for them. . . ."

The girl's eyes were like stars. She was looking into the future; her breath came quickly; she sat quite still.

The doctor swallowed hard, and went on. . . .

"Then when they are grown, and sort of catch up, and you have those splendid young lives about you, intimate strong friends and tender lovers. And you feel as though you had indeed done something for the world." . . .

"Oh, Doctor! To care like that and not—!"

"Yes, my dear," said the doctor, quietly. "And not have any. Not be able to have any—ever."

Vivian caught her breath with pitying intensity, but her friend went on.

"Never be able to have a child, because I married a man who had gonorrhea. In place of happy love, lonely pain. In place of motherhood, disease. Misery and shame, child. Medicine and surgery, and never any possibility of any child for me."

The girl was pale with horror. "I—I didn't know—" She tried to say something, but the doctor burst out impatiently:

"No! You don't know. I didn't know. Girls aren't taught a word of what's before them till it's too late—not *then*, sometimes! Women lose every joy in life, every hope, every capacity for service or pleasure. They go down to their graves without anyone's telling them the cause of it all."

"That was why you—left him?" asked Vivian presently.

"Yes, I left him. When I found I could not be a mother, I determined to be a doctor, and save other women, if I could."

She said this with such slow, grave emphasis that Vivian turned a sudden startled face to her, and went white to the lips. . . .

"You must not marry Morton Elder. . . . I do not know whether he has gonorrhea or not; it takes a long microscopic analysis to be sure; but there is every practical assurance that he's had it, and I know he's had syphilis."

If Vivian could have turned paler, she would have, then.

"I've heard of—that," she said, shuddering.

"Yes, the other is newer to our knowledge, far commoner, and really more dangerous. They are two of the most terrible diseases known to us—highly contagious, and in the case of syphilis, hereditary. Nearly three-quarters of the men have one or the other, or both."

But Vivian was not listening. Her face was buried in her hands. She crouched low in agonized weeping. . . . She turned to the doctor, her lips quivering. "He *loves* me!" she said. "I—we—he says I am all that holds him up, that helps him to make a newer, better life. And he has changed so—I can see it! He says he has loved me, really, since he was seventeen!"

The older, sterner face did not relax.

"He told me he had—done wrong. He was honest about it. He said he wasn't—worthy."

"He isn't," said Dr. Bellair.

"But surely I owe some duty to him. He depends on me. And I have promised—"

The doctor grew grimmer. "Marriage is motherhood," she said. "That is its initial purpose. I suppose you might deliberately forgo motherhood, and undertake a sort of missionary relation to a man, but that is not marriage."

"He loves me," said the girl with gentle stubbornness. . . . Her eyes met those of her friend fairly. "And I love him!" she said.

"Will you tell that to your crippled children?" asked Dr. Bellair. "Will they understand it if they are idiots? Will they see it if they are blind? Will it satisfy you when they are dead?"

The girl shrank before her.

"You *shall* understand," said the doctor. "This is no case for idealism and exalted emotion. . . . Another result—of gonorrhea—is to have children born blind. Their eyes may be saved, with care. But it is not a motherly gift for one's babies—blindness. You may have years and years of suffering yourself—any or all of those diseases 'peculiar to women' as we used to call them! And we pitied the men who 'were so good to their invalid wives'! You may have any number of still-born children, year after year. And every little marred dead face would remind you that you allowed it! And they may be deformed and twisted, have all manner of terrible and loathsome afflictions, they and their children after them, if they have any. And many do! Dear girl, don't you see that's wicked?"

Vivian was silent, her two hands wrung together, her whole form shivering with emotion.

"Don't think that you are 'ruining his life,' " said the doctor kindly. "He ruined it long ago—poor boy!"

The girl turned quickly at the note of sympathy. . . .

"Even if it did break his heart, and yours—even if you both lived single, he because it is the only decent thing he can do now, you because of a misguided sense of devotion, that would be better than to commit this plain sin. Beware of a biological sin, my dear; for it there is no forgiveness."

WHAT
DIANTHA
DID *

Diantha Bell lives with her parents in California, her father having moved the family from New England after several business failures, only to repeat the pattern in a sunnier climate. Unwilling to acknowledge his ineptitude for business, or his wife's skill in that area, both husband and wife behave in dutiful ways, according to social custom, and both are unhappy in their jobs, he in business and she in the home. Diantha's fiancé, Ross Warden, forced to leave college when his father died, also does his duty as head of the family grocery business by supporting his mother and four healthy sisters. Only Diantha refuses to live by convention. She leaves home to launch a business career—scientific management of housework.

The dedication that opens the book appears below. It is followed by an excerpt that describes the unorthodox decision Diantha has reached and its dreadful impact on her family. The selection concludes with an astounding and ingenious presentation by Diantha to her father of a cost-accounting statement that dramatically demonstrates her financial contribution as a dutiful daughter to the age of

*What Diantha Did *originally appeared in Volume 1 of* The Forerunner, *from November 1909 through October 1910. It was published separately in 1912.*

twenty-one, when she declares her independence and leaves.

A good deal transpires in the lives of Ross Warden and Diantha Bell before the period introduced by the second excerpt. Diantha learns the skills of housekeeping by apprenticing herself to a private family as a housekeeper. She then organizes a business of cooked food delivery and housecleaning. She rounds up the servant girls of the wealthy community, Orchardina, to which she has moved, and houses them in a Union House, where they have community and privacy, and where they form a House Workers' Union. While the servant girls are out during the day cleaning homes and handling the food-delivery service, Diantha uses the Union House for a meeting place, a businessmen's restaurant, and a community cafeteria. She also operates a catering service for picnics and parties. In the evening the young women use the rooms for dancing, lectures, dining, and dormitories. Diantha hopes to instill a sense of their own worth in these women and a respect for the value of their labor, but the profits ultimately are Diantha's alone and her business is privately, not collectively, owned. Despite Gilman's commitment to socialist principles, which is illustrated dramatically in her utopian fiction, she does not envision any enterprise under capitalism other than a privately owned one.

Diantha demonstrates what genuine filial love means when she entices her mother to join her in her work. Mrs. Bell is revitalized when she discards the tedious life of the private housekeeper to engage her skills in the business world. Even Diantha's father grudgingly joins them and is finally freed from the humiliation of more failures. In the meantime, Ross Warden, with some prompting and unknown support from others, has sold his grocery store and established a ranch, complete with an experimental laboratory filled with guinea pigs.

In the second excerpt, which I have called "The Struggle," the two young people confront each other with their enormously differing views. Eventually Ross is persuaded that the only way to succeed with Diantha is to accept her career, and so they marry. By this time Diantha is running a hotel complex financed by her wealthy patron. Circumstances require that Diantha live, alone at first and later with her children, at the hotel, and commute to the ranch, an arrangement not altogether satisfactory, but the best that is possible given their aspirations. In the final excerpt, Diantha finally achieves genuine happiness when her husband learns to value her work and respect her commitment to it.

We are left with two overriding messages, one public and one personal. Diantha's career goal is clearly stated by her: " . . . to get 'housework' on a business basis, that's all; and prove, *prove*, PROVE what a good business it is." Gilman had long argued that just as men no longer build their own houses or make their own shoes, so should women no longer be expected to clean their own houses or cook their own food. The work in the home, she insisted, should be subjected to the same specialization and division of labor as that done outside it.

For the personal theme, Gilman refers the reader to a poem of hers that ends with these lines:

Your door, O long imprisoned,
Is locked inside!

Dedication

With earnest love and a warm wish to help; with the highest respect for her great work and the desire to see it done more easily, pleasantly, scientifically, economically, hygienically, and beautifully; with the hope that she may have a happier life, a larger income, better health, and full success in living; this book is affectionately dedicated to
THE HOUSEWIFE

The Beginning—The Problem

In the dead quiet of the afternoon, Diantha and her mother sat there sewing. . . .

"What *do* you do it for anyway, Mother? I always hated this job—and you don't seem to like it."

"They wear almost twice as long, child, you know. The middle gets worn and the edges don't. Now they're reversed. As to liking it—" She gave a little smile, a smile that was too tired to be sarcastic, but which certainly did not indicate pleasure.

"What kind of work do you like best—really?" her daughter inquired suddenly, after a silent moment or two.

"Why—I don't know," said her mother. "I never thought of it. I never tried any but teaching. I didn't like that. Neither did your Aunt Esther, but she's still teaching."

"Didn't you like any of it?" pursued Diantha.

"I liked arithmetic best. I always liked arithmetic when I went to school—used to stand highest in that."

"And what part of housework do you like best?" the girl persisted.

Mrs. Bell smiled again, wanly. "Seems to me sometimes as if I couldn't tell what part I like least!" she answered. Then with sudden heat: "Oh, my child! Don't you marry till Ross can afford at least one servant for you!"

Diantha put her small, strong hands behind her head and leaned back in her chair. "We'll have to wait some time for that, I fancy," she said. . . . "Now sit still for once, Mother dear; read or lie down. Don't stir till supper's ready."

And from pantry to table she stepped, swiftly and lightly, setting out what was needed, greased her pans and set them before her, and proceeded to make biscuit.

Her mother watched her admiringly. "How easy you do it!" she said. "I never could make bread without getting flour all over me. You don't spill a speck!"

Diantha smiled. "I ought to do it easily by this time. Father's got to have hot bread for supper—or thinks he has!—and I've made it every night when I was at home for these ten years back."

"I guess you have," said Mrs. Bell proudly. "You were only eleven when you made your first batch. I can remember just as well! I had one of my bad headaches that night—and it did seem as if I couldn't sit up! But your father has to have his biscuit whether or no. And you said, 'Now, Mother, you lie right still on that sofa and let me do it! I can!' And you could. You did!

They were better'n mine that first time—and your father praised 'em—and you've been at it ever since."

"Yes," said Diantha, with a deeper note of feeling that her mother caught, "I've been at it ever since."

"Except when you were teaching school," pursued her mother. . . .

"I've got something to tell you presently, Mother." . . .

"I do hope you and Ross haven't quarrelled."

"No, indeed we haven't, Mother. Ross is splendid. Only—"

"Only what, Diantha?"

"Only he's so tied up!" said the girl, brushing every chip from the hearth. "He's perfectly helpless there, with that mother of his—and those four sisters."

"Ross is a good son," said Mrs. Bell, "and a good brother. I never saw a better. He's certainly doing his duty. Now if his father'd lived, you two could have got married by this time maybe, though you're too young yet."

Diantha washed and put away the dishes she had used, saw that the pantry was in its usual delicate order, and proceeded to set the table, with light steps and no clatter of dishes.

"I'm twenty-one," she said.

"Yes, you're twenty-one," her mother allowed. "It doesn't seem possible, but you are. My first baby!" She looked at her proudly.

"If Ross has to wait for all those girls to marry—and to pay his father's debts—I'll be old enough," said Diantha grimly.

Her mother watched her quick, assured movements with admiration, and listened with keen sympathy. "I know it's hard, dear child. You've only been engaged six months—and it looks as if it might be some years before Ross'll be able to marry. He's got an awful load for a boy to carry alone."

"I should say he had!" Diantha burst forth. "Five helpless women!—or three women and two girls. Though Cora's as old as I was when I began to teach. And not one of them will lift a finger to earn her own living."

"They weren't brought up that way," said Mrs. Bell. "Their mother doesn't approve of it. She thinks the home is the place for a woman, and so does Ross—and so do I," she added rather faintly.

Diantha put her pan of white puff-balls into the oven, sliced a quantity of smoked beef in thin shavings, and made white sauce for it, talking the while as if those acts were automatic. "I don't agree with Mrs. Warden on that point, nor with Ross, nor with you, Mother," she said. "What I have to tell you is this: I'm going away from home—to work."

Mrs. Bell stopped rocking, stopped fanning, and regarded her daughter with wide, frightened eyes.

"Why, Diantha!" she said. "Why, Diantha! You wouldn't leave your mother!"

Diantha drew a deep breath and stood for a moment looking at the feeble little woman in the chair. Then she went to her, knelt down, and hugged her close—close.

"It's not because I don't love you, Mother. It's because I do. And it's not because I don't love Ross either—it's because I *do*. I want to take care of you, Mother, and make life easier for you as long as you live. I want to help him—to help carry that awful load—and I'm going—to—do—it!"

She stood up hastily, for a step sounded on the back porch. It was only her sister, who hurried in, put a dish on the table, kissed her mother, and took another rocking-chair.

"I just ran in," said she, "to bring those berries. . . . Why, Mother! What's the matter? You're crying!" . . .

"You might as well know now as later," said her sister. "I have decided to leave home, that's all."

"To leave home!" Mrs. Peters sat up straight and stared at her. "To leave home—and Mother!"

"Well?" said Diantha, while the tears rose and ran over from her mother's eyes. "Well, why not? You left home—and mother—before you were eighteen."

"That's different!" said her sister sharply. "I left to be married—to have a home of my own. And besides, I haven't gone far! I can see Mother every day."

"That's one reason I can go now better than later on," Diantha said. "You are close-by in case of any trouble."

"What on earth are you going for? Ross isn't ready to marry yet, is he?"

"No—nor likely to be for years. That's another reason I'm going."

"But what *for*, for goodness' sake?"

"To earn money—for one thing."

"Can't you earn money enough by teaching?" the mother broke in eagerly. "I know you haven't got the same place this fall—but you can get another easy enough."

Diantha shook her head. "No, Mother, I've had enough of that. I've taught for four years. I don't like it, I don't do it well, and it exhausts me horribly. And I should never get beyond a thousand or fifteen hundred dollars a year if I taught for a lifetime."

"Well, I declare!" said her sister. "What do you *expect* to get? I should think fifteen hundred dollars a year was enough for any woman!"

Diantha peered into the oven and turned her biscuit pan around.

"And you're meaning to leave home just to make money, are you?"

"Why not?" said Diantha firmly. "Henderson did—when he was eighteen. None of you blamed him."

"I don't see what that has to do with it," her mother ventured. "Henderson's a boy, and boys have got to go, of course. A mother expects that. But a girl—why, Diantha! How can I get along without you! With my health!"

"I should think you'd be ashamed of yourself to think of such a thing!" said young Mrs. Peters.

A slow step sounded outside, and an elderly man, tall, slouching, carelessly dressed, entered, stumbling a little over the rag-mat at the door. . . .

"A man should be master in his own household," Mr. Bell proclaimed, raising a dripping face from the basin and looking around for the towel—which his wife handed him.

"You won't have much household to be master of presently," said Mrs. Peters provokingly. "Half of it's going to leave."

Mr. Bell came out of his towel and looked from one to the other for some explanation of this attempted joke. "What nonsense are you talking?" he demanded. . . .

Diantha set the plateful on the table, puffy, brown, and crisply crusted. "Supper's ready," she said. "Do sit down, Mother," and she held the chair for her. "Minnie's quite right, Father, though I meant not to tell you till you'd had supper. I am going away to work."

Mr. Bell regarded his daughter with a stern, slow stare, not so much surprised as annoyed by an untimely jesting. He ate a hot biscuit in two . . . mouthfuls, and put more sugar in his large cup of tea. "You've got your mother worked up with your non-sense," said he. "What are you talking about, anyway?"

Diantha met his eyes unflinchingly. . . . Mr. Bell ate until he was satisfied, and betook himself to a comfortable chair by the lamp, where he unfolded the small local paper and lit his pipe.

"When you've got through with the dishes, Diantha," he said coldly, "I'll hear about this proposition of yours." . . .

Her mother was patiently darning large socks with many holes—a kind of work she especially disliked. "You'll have to get some new socks, Father," she ventured. "These are pretty well gone."

"Oh, they'll do for a while yet," he replied, not looking at them. "I like your embroidery, my dear."

That pleased her. She did not like to embroider, but she did like to be praised. . . .

Finally Mr. Bell laid down his finished paper and his emptied pipe and said: "Now, then, out with it." . . .

"I have decided to leave home and to go to work," [Diantha] said.

"Don't you have work enough to do at home?" he inquired, with the same air of quizzical superiority which had always an-noyed her so intensely, even as a little child.

She would cut short this form of discussion. "I am going away to earn my living. I have given up school-teaching—I don't like it, and there isn't money enough in it. I have plans—which will speak for themselves later."

"So," said Mr. Bell. "Plans all made, eh? I suppose you've considered your mother in these plans?"

"I have," said his daughter. "It is largely on her account that I'm going."

"You think it'll be good for your mother's health to lose your assistance, do you?"

"I know she'll miss me; but I haven't left the work on her shoulders. I am going to pay for a girl—to do the work I've done. It won't cost you any more, Father; and you'll save some—for she'll do the washing too. You didn't object to Henderson's going away—at eighteen. You didn't object to Minnie's going away—at seventeen. Why should you object to my going—at twenty-one?"

"I haven't objected—so far," replied her father. "Have your plans also allowed for the affection and duty you owe your parents?"

"I have done my duty—as well as I know how," she answered. "Now I am twenty-one, and self-supporting—and have a right to go."

"Oh, yes. You have a right—a legal right—if that's what you base your idea of a child's duty on! And while you're talking of rights—how about a parent's rights? How about common gratitude? How about what you owe to me—for all the care and pains and cost it's been to bring you up? A child's a rather expensive investment these days."

Diantha flushed. She had expected this, and yet it struck her like a blow. It was not the first time she had heard it—this claim of filial obligation.

"I have considered that position, Father. I know you feel that way—you've often made me feel it. So I've been at some pains to work it out—on a money basis. Here is an account—as full as I could make it." She handed him a paper covered with neat figures. The totals read as follows:

Miss Diantha Bell,
    To Mr. Henderson R. Bell, Dr.

To medical and dental expenses	$ 110.00
To school expenses	76.00
To clothing, in full	1,130.00
To board and lodging at $3.00 a week	2,184.00
To incidentals	100.00
	$3,600.00

He studied the various items carefully, stroking his beard, half in anger, half in unavoidable amusement. Perhaps there was a tender feeling, too, as he remembered that doctor's bill—the first he had ever paid, with the other, when she had scarlet fever; and saw the exact price of the high chair which had served all three of the children, but of which she magnanimously shouldered the whole expense.

The clothing total was so large that it made him whistle—he knew he had never spent $1,130.00 on one girl's clothes. But the items explained it:

Materials, three years at an average of $10 a year............ $ 30.00
Five years averaging $20 each year......................... 100.00
Five years averaging $30 each year......................... 150.00
Five years averaging $50 each year......................... 250.00

$530.00

The rest was "Mother's labor," averaging twenty full days a year at $2 a day, $40 a year. For fifteen years, $600. Mother's labor—on one child's clothes—footing up to $600. It looked strange to see cash value attached to that unfailing source of family comfort and advantage.

Board and lodging was put low, at $3 per week, but the items had a footnote as to house rent in the country and food raised on the farm. Yes, he guessed that was a full rate for the plain food and bare little bedroom she had always had.

"It's what Aunt Esther paid the winter she was here," said Diantha.

Circuses—three .... $ 1.50
Share in melodeon 50.00
(Yes, she was one of five to use and enjoy it.)

Music lessons.. $30.00

And quite a large margin left here called "Miscellaneous," which he smiled to observe made just an even figure, and suspected she had put it in for that purpose as well as from generosity.

"This board account looks kind of funny," he said, "only fourteen years of it!"

"I didn't take table-board—nor a room—the first year—nor much the second. I've allowed one dollar a week for that, and two dollars for the third—that takes out two, you see. Then it's a hundred and fifty-six dollars a year till I was fourteen and earned board and wages, two more years at a hundred and fifty-six dollars—and I've paid since I was seventeen, you know."

"Well—I guess you did—I guess you did." He grinned genially. "Yes," he continued slowly, "guess that's a fair enough account. 'Cording to this you owe me thirty-six hundred dollars, young woman! I didn't think it cost that much to raise a girl."

"I know it," said she. "But here's the other side."

It was the other side. He had never once thought of such a side to the case. This account was as clear and honest as the first and full of exasperating detail. She laid before him the second sheet of figures and watched while he read, explaining hurriedly—

"It was a clear expense for ten years—not counting help with the babies. Then I began to do housework regularly—when I was ten or eleven, two hours a day; three when I was twelve and thirteen—real work you'd have to pay for, and I've only put it at ten cents an hour. Then mother was sick the year I was fourteen, and I did it all but the washing—all a servant would have done for five dollars a week. Ever since then I have done three hours a day outside of school, full-grown work now, at twenty cents an hour. That's what we have to pay here, you know."

Thus it mounted up:

Mr. Henderson R. Bell,
    To Miss Diantha Bell, Dr.
For labor and services—
    Two years, two hours a day at 10¢ an hour.............. $ 146.00
    Two years, three hours a day at 10¢ an hour 219.00
    One year, full wages at $5 a week 260.00
    Six years and a half, three hours a day at 20¢.......... 1,423.50
                                                             _____
                                                             $2,048.50

Mr. Bell meditated carefully on these figures. To think of that child's labor footing up to two thousand dollars and over! It was lucky a man had a wife and daughters to do this work, or he could never support a family.

Then came her school-teaching years. She had always been a fine scholar, and he had felt very proud of his girl when she got a good school position in her eighteenth year.

California salaries were higher than Eastern ones, and times had changed, too; the years he taught school, he remembered, the salary was only $300—and he was a man. This girl got $600, next year $700, $800, $900—why, it made $3,000 she had earned in four years! Astonishing! Out of this she had a balance in the bank of $550. He was pleased to see that she had been so saving. And her clothing account—little enough, he admitted, for four years and six months, $300. All incidentals for the whole time, $50—this, with her balance, made just $900. That left $2,100.

"Twenty-one hundred dollars unaccounted for, young lady!— besides this little nest egg in the bank—I'd no idea you were so wealthy. What have you done with all that?"

"Given it to you, Father," said she quietly, and handed him the third sheet of figures.

Board and lodging at $4 a week for four years and a half made $936, that he could realize; but "cash advanced" $1,164 more— he could not believe it. That time her mother was so sick, and Diantha had paid both the doctor and the nurse—yes—he had been much cramped that year—and nurses come high. For Henderson Jr.'s expenses to San Francisco, and again for Henderson when he was out of a job. Mr. Bell remembered the boy's writing for the money, and his not having it, and Mrs. Bell saying she could arrange with Diantha.

Arrange! And the girl had kept this niggardly account of it! For Minnie's trip to the Yosemite—and what was this?—for his raisin experiment—for the new horse they simply had to have, for the drying apparatus that year he lost so much in apricots— and for the spraying materials—yes, he could not deny the items, and they covered that $1,164 exactly.

Then came the deadly balance of the account between them.

Her labor	$2,047.00
Her board	936.00
Her "cash advanced"	1,164.00
	$4,147.00
His expense for her	3,600.00
Due her from him	$ 547.00

Diantha revolved her pencil between firm palms, and looked at him rather quizzically while her mother rocked and darned and wiped away an occasional tear. She almost wished she had not kept accounts so well.

Mr. Bell pushed the papers away and started to his feet.

"This is the most shameful piece of calculation I ever saw in my life," said he. "I never heard of such a thing! You go and count up in cold dollars the work that every decent girl does for her family and is glad to! I wonder you haven't charged your mother for nursing her?"

"You notice I haven't," said Diantha coldly.

"And to think," said he, gripping the back of a chair, "to think that a girl who can earn nine hundred dollars a year teaching school, and stay at home and do her duty by her family besides, should plan to desert her mother outright—now she's old and sick! Of course I can't stop you. You're of age, and children nowadays have no sense of natural obligation after they're grown up. You can go, of course, and disgrace the family as you propose—but you needn't expect to have me consent to it or approve of it—or of you. It's a shameful thing—and you are an unnatural daughter—that's all I've got to say!"

Mr. Bell took his hat and went out—a conclusive form of punctuation much used by men in discussions of this sort.

The Middle—The Struggle

[Several months have passed. Diantha Bell, having mastered domestic housekeeping skills as an apprentice in a private home, now manages a successful business. Weary of waiting for her to return to him, Ross Warden, secretly aided by a wealthy fan of Diantha's, sells his hated grocery store and establishes the ranch and laboratory for which he has long yearned.]

"I shall turn over the store at once. It won't take long to move and settle; there's enough money over to do that. And the ranch pays, Diantha! It really *pays*, and will carry us all. How long will it take you to get out of this?"

She raised her head.

"Get out of—what?" she faltered.

"Why, the whole abominable business you're so deep in here. Thank God, there's no shadow of need for it any more!"

The girl's face went white, but he could not see it. She would not believe him.

"Why, dear," she said, "if your ranch is as near as that, it would be perfectly easy for me to come in to the business—with a car. I can afford a car soon."

"But I tell you there's no longer any need," said he. "Don't you understand? This is a paying fruit ranch, with land rented to advantage, and a competent manager right there running it. It has simply changed owners. I'm the owner now! There's two or three thousand a year to be made on it—has been made on it! There is a home for my people—a home for us! Oh, my beloved girl! My darling! My own sweetheart! Surely—*surely* you won't refuse me now!"

Diantha's head swam dizzily.

"But, Ross," she urged, "you don't understand! I've built up a good business here—a real, successful business. Mother is in it; Father's to come down; there is a big patronage! It grows. I *can't* give it up!"

"Not for me? Not when I can offer you a home at last? Not when I show you that there is no longer any need of your earning money?" he said hotly.

"But, dear—dear!" she protested. "It isn't for the money; it is the work I want to do—it is my work! You are so happy now that you can do your work—at last! This is mine!"

When he spoke again his voice was low and stern.

"Do you mean that you love—your 'work'—better than you love me?"

"No! It isn't that! That's not fair!" cried the girl. "Do you love *your* work better than *you* love me? Of course not! You love *both*. So do I. Can't you see? Why should I have to give up anything?"

"You do not have to," he said patiently. "I cannot compel you to marry me. But now, when at last—after these awful years—I can really offer you a home—you refuse!"

"I have not refused," she said slowly.

"Ah, dearest! And you will not! You will marry me?"

"I will marry you, Ross!"

"And when? When, dearest?"

"As soon as you are ready."

"But—can you drop this at once?"

"I shall not drop it."

Her voice was low, very low, but clear and steady.

He rose to his feet with a muffled exclamation, and walked the length of the piazza and back.

"Do you realize that you are saying no to me, Diantha?"

"You are mistaken, dear. I have said that I will marry you whenever you choose. But it is you who are saying, 'I will not marry a woman with a business.' "

"This is foolishness!" he said sharply. "No man—that is a man—would marry a woman and let her run a business."

"You are mistaken," she answered. "One of the finest men I ever knew has asked me to marry him—and keep on with my work!"

"Why didn't you take him up?"

"Because I didn't love him." She stopped, a sob in her voice, and he caught her in his arms again.

It was late indeed when he went away, walking swiftly with black rebellion in his heart, and Diantha dragged herself to bed.

She was stunned, deadened, exhausted; torn with a desire to run after him and give up—give up anything to hold his love. But something, partly reason and partly pride, kept saying within her: "I have not refused him; he has refused me!" . . .

The End—The Resolution

Ross Warden did his best. . . . He had been brought to see that Diantha had a right to do this if she would, and that he had no right to prevent her; but he did not like it any the better.

When she rolled away in her little car in the bright, sweet mornings, a light went out of the day for him. He wanted her there, in the home—his home—his wife—even when he was not in it himself. And in this particular case it was harder than for most men, because he was in the house a good deal, in his study, with no better company than a polite Chinaman some distance off.

It was by no means easy for Diantha, either. To leave him tugged at her heartstrings as it did at his; and if he had to struggle with inherited feelings and conditions, still more was she beset with an unexpected uprising of sentiments and desires she had never dreamed of feeling.

With marriage, love, happiness, came an overwhelming instinct of service—personal service. She wanted to wait on him, loved to do it, regarded Wang Fu with positive jealousy when he brought in the coffee and Ross praised it. She had a sense of treason, of neglected duty, as she left the flower-crowned cottage day by day.

But she left it, she plunged into her work, she schooled herself religiously.

"Shame on you!" she berated herself. "Now—*now* that you've got everything on earth—to weaken! You could stand unhappiness; can't you stand happiness?" And she strove with herself, and kept on with her work.

After all, the happiness was presently diluted by the pressure of this blank wall between them. She came home, eager, loving, delighted to be with him again. He received her with no complaint or criticism, but always an unspoken, perhaps imagined, sense of protest. She was full of loving enthusiasm about his work, and he would dilate upon his harassed guinea-pigs and their development with high satisfaction.

But he never could bring himself to ask about her labors with any genuine approval; she was keenly sensitive to his dislike for the subject, and so it was ignored between them, or treated by him in a vein of humor with which he strove to cover his real feeling. . . .

Within a year of her marriage Diantha was at the head of this pleasing Center of Housekeeping. She kept the hotel itself so that it was a joy to all its patrons; she kept the little houses homes of pure delight for those who were so fortunate as to hold them; and she kept up her "c. f. d." [cooked food delivery] business till it grew so large she had to have quite a fleet of delivery-wagons.

Orchardina basked and prospered; its citizens found their homes happier and less expensive than ever before, and its citizenesses began to wake up and to do things worthwhile.

Two years, and there was a small Ross Warden born.

She loved it, nursed it, and ran her business at long range for six months. But then she brought nurse and child to the hotel with her, placed them in the cool, airy nursery in the garden, and varied her busy day with still hours by herself—the baby in her arms.

Back together they came before supper, and found unbroken joy and peace in the quiet of home; but always in the background was the current of Ross's unspoken disapproval.

Three years, four years.

There were three babies now; Diantha was a splendid woman of thirty, handsome and strong, pre-eminently successful—and yet, there were times when she found it in her heart to envy the most ordinary people who loved and quarrelled and made up in the little outlying ranch-houses along the road; they had nothing between them, at least. . . .

Ross had prospered in his work. It may be that the element of dissatisfaction in his married life spurred him on, while the unusual opportunities of his ranch allowed free effort. . . .

Diantha sat in friendly talk with Mrs. Weatherstone [her wealthy friend and patron] one quiet day, and admitted that she had had no cause for complaint.

"And yet—?" said her friend.

Young Mrs. Warden smiled. "There's no keeping anything from you, is there? Yes—you're right. I'm not quite satisfied. I suppose I ought not to care—but, you see, I love him so! I want him to *approve* of me—not just put up with it, and bear it! I want him to *feel* with me—to care. It is awful to know that all this big life of mine is just a mistake to him—that he condemns it in his heart." . . .

In her heart of hearts she was not wholly happy.

Then one night came by the last mail a thick letter from Ross— thicker than usual. She opened it in her room alone, their room—to which they had come so joyously five years ago.

He told her of his journeyings, his lectures, his controversies and triumphs rather briefly—and then:

My darling, I have learned something at last, on my travels, which will interest you, I fancy, more than the potential speed of all the guinea-pigs in the world, and its transmissibility.

From what I hear about you in foreign lands, I have at last begun to grasp the nature and importance of your work.

As a man of science I must accept any truth when it is once clearly seen; and, though I've been a long time about it, I do see at last what brave, strong, valuable work you have been doing for the world. Doing it scientifically, too. Your figures are quoted, your records studied, your example followed. You have established certain truths in the business of living which are of importance to the race. As a student I recognize and appreciate your work. As man to man I'm proud of you—tremendously proud of you. As your husband! Ah! my love! I am coming back to you—coming soon, coming with my whole heart, yours! Just wait, my darling, till I get back to you!

Your Lover and Husband

Diantha held the letter close, with hands that shook a little. She kissed it—kissed it hard, over and over—not improving its appearance as a piece of polite correspondence.

Then she gave way to an overmastering burst of feeling, and knelt down by the wide bed, burying her face there, the letter still held fast. It was an odd prayer, if any human ear had heard it.

"Thank you!" was all she said, with long, deep sobbing sighs between. "Thank you!—Oh—thank you!"

BENIGNA MACHIAVELLI*

Benigna Machiavelli is a handbook on survival in the modern world for a girl-woman. The excerpts below are drawn from bits and pieces of the original twelve installments and so represent an abbreviated version of the entire story. Benigna grows as the story grows, not only in her wisdom and maturity, but chronologically as well. In the complete version the story opens with a flashback of Benigna's infancy and early childhood, and then moves into the present tense with Benigna as a young girl. By the middle of the full story she is eighteen, and at the end she has reached her twenty-first birthday, completed the first stage of her life, and is ready to marry.

The education of Benigna Machiavelli is a study in deception. She learns to withhold her real self from others, while subjecting her character and behavior to an unrelenting discipline, imposed by herself and known only to herself. It is an invention within an invention. Benigna lives in her private world, which is itself Gilman's fictionalized recreation of the kind of environment she would have liked

*Benigna Machiavelli *was published in Volume 5 of* The Forerunner *(1914) and was never published separately.*

in her own early life. Benigna's power over her life is what Charlotte would have chosen: a sweet sister, not a teasing brother; a loving mother who, despite her passivity, can be inspired to seek and find autonomy; a mean father who is sent away, not one who runs away; a gentle lover who wants her but whom she refuses; time and opportunity to engage her skills in the business world while she is young and fresh; and union with a man who permits her to keep her name, and thus her identity. At the age of twenty-one, Benigna triumphs over a variety of inner and outer obstacles that it took Charlotte Gilman many more years to conquer, if she ever did.

Benigna's father is a genuine villain, all the more vicious for being commonplace and unrecognized. He probably thought himself a good man, Benigna muses; the Ten Commandments do not forbid a person from being tedious, ungenerous, tyrannical, and verbally abusive. People "can be as brutal to each other's minds" as to their bodies, observes Benigna, and she lived with a father who torments his family. His nasty character is worsened by his alcoholism, which is also not detected outside the family circle. His is ultimately the cruelest deception. Benigna's mother, in the name of patience, self-sacrifice, and duty, submits to her husband's persecutions and lacks even the sense to manipulate him, as Benigna has learned to do. "Mother has a regular talent for suffering," she says, with a touch of contempt.

Benigna in her fantasy makes her father lovable but in her reality she sends him away. Perhaps Gilman dealt with her own absent father by creating a fictional father-in-residence who is so "conspicuously unpleasant" that he must be sent away by a daughter. Benigna's mother, the embodiment of the "virtuous woman," has much in common with Gilman's mother, who continued to "love" her rejecting and ungiving husband, while withholding affection from her children. Benigna's period of wandering, in which she accumulates experience and worldliness, compares in important ways with the years of exile to which Gilman subjected herself after her divorce and during which she published the book that made her famous. As Benigna returns home to marry her cousin, so too, did her creator return from her self-imposed banishment to marry hers.

I learned a lot, when I was a child, from novels and stories; even fairy stories have some point to them—the good ones. The thing that impressed me most forcibly was this: that the villains always went to work with their brains and accomplished something. To be sure they were "foiled" in the end, but that was by some special interposition of Providence, not by any equal exertion of intellect on the part of the good people. The heroes and heroines and middle ones were mostly very stupid. If bad things happened, they practiced patience, endurance, resignation, and similar virtues; if good things happened, they practiced modesty and magnanimity and virtues like that, but it never seemed to occur to any of them to make things move their way. Whatever the villains planned for them to do, they did, like sheep. The same old combinations of circumstances would be worked off on them in book after book—and they always tumbled! . . .

And it seemed to me, even as a very little child, that what we wanted was good people with brains, not just negative, passive, good people, but positive, active ones, who gave their minds to it.

"A good villain! That's what we need!" said I to myself. "Why don't they write about them? Aren't there any?"

I never found any in all my beloved story books, or in real life. And gradually, I made up my mind to be one!

My sister, Peggy, was older than I, over a year. She was a dear good child, and people liked her. They liked her before they liked me, because she was so pretty. And I saw that because so many people liked Peggy they did nice things for her, so I made up my mind to be liked too. I couldn't be as pretty, but then people like other things; it wasn't hard to find out how to please them.

At first I got into trouble more than Peggy did, from being more enterprising, and I got her in too, sometimes. But I never got into the same trouble twice. You can learn things even from being naughty. Indeed, I found that you learn, by being naughty, the things you have to practice to be good. You learn what not to do—and how not to.

Mother used to make the loveliest gingersnaps, and keep them in a tight tin box in the sideboard, and we were forbidden to touch them, of course. But when I got them out, Peggy would eat some, naturally. One day Mother caught us, very crumby and sticky-fingered, and smelling of ginger and molasses.

"What have my little girls been doing?" asked Mother.

We protested that we'd been doing nothing. Then Mother led us to a mirror and pointed out our crumby, sticky little mouths and hands. Peggy, being six, was wise enough not to attempt concealment.

"We've been—eating—gingersnaps," she owned.

"That is a good little girl, to confess it," said Mother.

And then Peggy, encouraged, added: "And I wouldn't have done it, Mama, truly, but Ben took 'em out and gave me some."

"Oh, but that is naughty—to tell tales of little sister: Mama must punish you both."

We were promptly put to bed, to meditate on our sins, and I meditated to some purpose. "Crumbs" was one subject of my study. "When you eat anything that you shouldn't, you should always be sure to wash your face and hands." "Confess" was another. I thought about this most earnestly.

"Mama," I asked, when she was kissing us good-night, "what is 'confess'?"

And she took advantage of the occasion to explain the nature and virtue of confession at some length.

"Is it confession if I tell you I—Mama!—I broke a kitty yesterday— 'tepped on it and broke it!" I cried, eager to partake of the new virtue. But Mother was suspicious—as we hadn't any kitty at the time—and explained to me the evil nature of lying, as well as the value of confession and repentance.

Then I made a plan.

A few days after, Mother being in the kitchen, I again helped myself to gingersnaps and even induced Peggy to partake, explaining to her that we could wash our faces and hands and nobody would ever know. This we did, and went unsuspected, but later on, I "confessed" with great freedom and fervor, but carefully said nothing at all about Peggy's part of the misdemeanor. Under questioning, that damsel was made to admit her share in the offense, and this time I had great credit—both for confessing and for not telling tales; indeed Peggy got all the punishment for once, for Mother said she was older than I and more to blame. . . .

The most awful thing in my world at that time was the behavior of Father, especially to Mother. Of course I didn't know then what it was all about, but I could hear how he talked and scolded till Mother would break down and cry, and then he would be severe with us too.

One of the strongest impressions of all my very early childhood is that of being waked out of my first sleep one night by one of these quarrels. I sat up, big-eyed and frightened, in my crib—it was like an awful dream. Father came home just drunk enough to be ugly—of course I didn't know that then—and he was saying fierce loud things to Mother, and Mother was crying. . . .

She was crying so she couldn't answer, and he grabbed her by the arm, and she cried out, and I was so scared I fell out of bed. I was too frightened to cry, and they were both frightened because I lay so still, and Mother ran and Father ran and they picked me up and felt of my arms and collar-bones, and put arnica on my forehead, and comforted me when I did cry at last, and I went to sleep holding a hand of each, and Father humming, "The Land o' the Leal."

Afterward I thought and thought about it, marveling at the sudden stop to that quarrel. And next time I saw Father being disagreeable to Mother I created a diversion by tipping over a small worktable. But to my surprise Father spanked me and even Mother was cross, and I was sent to bed prematurely.

I could hear them still quarreling, while Mother picked up the spools and things—he told her she didn't know how to bring up children—I remember that because I resented it so, even then.

So I meditated on the success of falling out of bed that time, and the failure of tipping over the work basket.

"It isn't the noise," I said to myself. "It was being scared. They thought I was hurt—dead maybe! That's it!" And the next time they had a real quarrel I fell downstairs—just as bumpy as I could and crying awfully. That worked all right. They ran and picked me up and got the arnica; but Father was still cross—he went away and slammed the door pretty soon; and I think Mother must have had her suspicions, for I didn't hear any more real quarrels for some years. . . .

My grandfather was Scotch; Andrew MacAvelly was his name, and Father was named after him. Mother was a Quaker from Pennsylvania, Benigna Chesterton, and I was named after her. But Grandpa MacAvelly's wife was an Italian woman—this is the most important part of it—a splendid, big, handsome Italian woman, and a lineal descendant of the famous Machiavelli family.

That's where I come in. I'm a Machiavelli, and proud of it. The Scotch name I have to wear outside, like a sort of raincoat, but my real name I always feel is Machiavelli, Benigna Machiavelli. I mean never to marry and change it. . . .

I was about ten when I found out what was the matter with my father; yes, I was ten the June before, and this was in the winter some time, because the cars were heated. I remember how hot the seat was under me, and my feet seemed too big for my rubbers. The cars were full; it was a rainy night, and I was squeezed up against Mother, and a man was squeezed up against me. He was pretty red in the face and was disputing incessantly, first with one passenger and then another.

"Mama," I whispered, "is it polite to talk loud in the car?"

"Sh!" said she, looking frightened. "No, dear, it isn't—but keep still—don't notice him!"

I couldn't help noticing, however, he made so much disturbance, and he smelled so, too. Presently he began to harangue a stern-looking woman with a short skirt and a man's soft hat, and she promptly replied: "Better be quiet, my man, else we shall think you're drunk."

He was still for a minute, looking rather redder, and then said: "Why did you think I'm drunk, madam?"

"Because I can smell the whiskey on your breath," she answered, quite confidentially. "And because you talk too much. Just keep still and the others may not notice it."

He kept still, and so did I, but I was thinking hard. I knew the smell—I had often noticed it when I kissed Father; and I knew the color, and I knew the talk, but I had never known what it came from before. . . .

I had read about that Spartan boy with the fox gnawing his vitals, and envied him his grit even while I disbelieved the story. Also the Spartan spear story—training the boys to use extra big ones, so that the real spear, to the man's hand, should seem "as a feather." And the savages, too, with their awful ordeals—the things they used to do to the boys when they were admitted among the men.

The Ordeal theory always appealed to me very strongly, and, while I had no fox to gnaw my vitals, I used to practice with mosquitoes. I'd keep perfectly still and let 'em suck and sting and swell up with my blood, visibly. They were easier to kill afterward, too. Once I let a bee sting me, but that was worse; it hurt so I plastered mud on it pretty quick. And when Mother put our winter flannels on us too soon, which she always did, I used to play it was a hair shirt.

So when Father was horrid to me I would say to myself: "This is an Ordeal." And I'd stand it. I had to stand it, you see, any-way, but by taking it as an Ordeal it became glorious. And not only glorious, but useful. I was astonished to find, from those mosquitoes and things, that a pain isn't such an awful thing if you just take it as if you wanted it. And when Father rebuked me, and was so sarcastic and tedious, even while it really hurt, and the tears ran down my cheeks, I would be thinking inside: "How foolish it is to keep on talking after you've really made your point."

If you have an active mind, a real active mind that likes to work, there is profitable experience in most everything.

School was in some ways a better place to learn things than at home. I don't mean the study in the schoolbooks—a little of that goes a long way—but the things you can learn about peo-ple, and how to manage them. At first school seems very im-pressive, so big and busy, so many children, so many rules. But you get used to it.

I remember once, when I was about eight, sitting there with my lesson all learned, and thinking. It was a reading lesson, and I never did see the sense in those. Why, if you could read you could read—and that was all there was to it. I always read the reader through as soon as I got it, and 'twasn't half so nice as a real book, anyway.

The others were studying their lessons, however, and the big room was very still, all but the dull buzz children make when they are studying. I sat there and wondered why we had to maintain that oppressive silence. "Suppose we talked out loud," I thought. "What would happen? Suppose I did? I'm going to— just to see."

Then I cast about in my infant mind for the shortest word I knew, and all at once, across the dull murmur of the quiet schoolroom, rose a clear young voice saying, "It!"

The teacher was much astonished, for I was usually a model pupil. "Who said that word?" she demanded.

"I did," said I. She called me up to the desk and put her arm around me.

"Why did you do that?" she asked.

"I wanted to see what would happen," I answered.

And I found out. Nothing happened. She gave me a mild reprimand—told me not to do it again, which was needless; I wasn't going to. I'd found out what I wanted to know.

It is easy to please a teacher, and you don't have to be very smart either. You only have to be "good"—that is, keep the rules. . . .

Teachers are easy—and there's only one of 'em. The children—they are harder.

But I kept my eyes open. I noticed who were the favorites, and why; who were the ones they didn't like, and why; and of those whys which of the good ones I could adopt and which of the bad ones avoid. As to studying, if you know your lessons pretty well, that pleases teacher. If you know 'em too well, then the children don't like it. The girl they disliked most was at the very head. Teacher didn't like her, either—I could see that, for all she got the best marks. But if you know your lessons well enough to be able to help the others some; well enough to keep up but not well enough to get too far ahead—that pleases everybody. It's easier, too, and more amusing. I was quick enough at lessons, but I found time to sharpen pencils for ever so many girls and to do lots of things beside.

With the children—just playing—I found that the thing they liked best of all was somebody who said, "Let's do this," and "Let's play that." So I used to think up things to do, and learn games on purpose—and make 'em up. . . .

Some things you can do easily. Others are harder. Some you can't seem to do at all. I found my hardest things at home. That is, there was one hard thing, big and troublesome. I couldn't seem to manage it at all—I mean Father. . . .

I gave my mind to the subject of Peggy from the first. Why was she prettier than I was? That I used to wonder when I wasn't five. But I admired her prettiness with all my heart, and loved her dearly. She was sweet-tempered and docile and popular, not like other pretty sisters I read about in story books, and we grew up very close together. . . .

But as I got older—and I did get older far faster than she did—my respect for her as older sister began to dwindle, and instead of looking up to her for her age and her good looks, I began to look down on her a little, because she wasn't as strong as I was intellectually. And then I got over that and began to see that for patience and sweetness and being a darling she was far superior to me. How one does change as one grows older! . . .

When I was very little I took advantage of her sometimes, like that about the gingersnaps, but not afterward. As a matter of fact, when she did once in a while get into trouble, I could help her out and did, gladly. She was nicer than any other girl's sister I knew.

Then there was Mother—dear, blessed Mother! She was just all goodness. Such an unselfish sweet person I never saw, nor one so anxious to do what was right at any cost—even Father admitted that, when he had to.

But Mother, for all her goodness, was just like the good people in the story books—she hadn't enough sense. It did seem sometimes, as if she hadn't what Alison [the housekeeper] called "common wit," at least about Father. With us children she was wonderful, a real educator, but with him it seemed as if her duty and unselfishness absolutely blinded her.

And I suppose, much as I love Mother, I have to admit, if this is going to be what they used to call "a veracious chronicle," that even goodness—without sense—is sometimes wearying. . . .

Anyway we had to see and hear all dear Mother's patient, futile efforts to keep that father of ours good-natured. I suppose nobody really could have done it, but as early as eight or nine years old I used to think of things to say—and to *not* say—that I really do feel would have been wiser.

I've heard Mother ask him for money—when she had to, just *had* to—to buy thread to sew our clothes with. And he'd argue about it, and want to see her accounts. Poor Mother! Just to ask for her account book was enough to make her cry almost. She had no head for figures, and he had. He had everything as clear as could be in his mind, and kept insisting on her keeping her expenses like that, and she really could not do it, though she tried. It wasn't, I can see now, that he *meant* to hurt her so much, but, oh dear! it was so hard on Mother!

I believe—this means now that I know so much more about life—I believe that people can be as brutal to each other's minds as they used to be in old times to their bodies. They can lash and burn and torture; they can cramp young brains as the Chinese do young feet; they can imprison and load with chains and starve and rack—all without its showing outside or anybody's blaming them.

And I've seen Mother wince when Father spoke to her just as if it was a whip; and set her teeth and turn white and hold her hands tight, other times; and pray, pray dreadfully, for strength to bear it, to be patient, to do her duty, to love, honor, and obey—of course she never dreamed I was under the bed. . . .

To get away from all this and think things into shape—make everything all right in my mind—was a great relief, as you can well imagine. So I used to lie there nights and arrange it all in my mind—what I'd do if I had my wishes. I would be perfectly beautiful, of course, and oh, so wise and good! Mother should grow so well and happy and have all the lovely soft clothes she wanted—gray and lavender and pale rose and pearl, the colors she liked best. And she should have money, all the money she wanted, and we would refurnish the house from top to bottom—I had heard her wish for new furniture. . . .

For Father I was never sure what to do. Mostly I changed him, changed him so that he was hardly recognizable, but so that we could love him. I always did want to love Father, but couldn't. Peggy did, though, I really believe.

But all that was only thinking. Daytimes I had to manage, if I could. . . . He was the Master and Owner and Governor. He "commanded and forbade and released prisoners and remitted the customs taxes" like the sultans in the stories, only mostly he imprisoned and put the taxes on.

Father had severe ideas of discipline and how children should be "trained." People act as if children were performing dogs, or horses, or something that has to be "broken." Mother felt very differently. She had studied to be a kindergartner before Father married her; she really cared about children and making them happy. But Father scorned "all these morbid modern follies of child-culture" and used to take pleasure in ridiculing and abusing Mother's ideas. He wouldn't let us go to a kindergarten, but he couldn't help Mother's teaching us in the nursery in that wise way, so we really had some advantage of it. . . .

As I grew up I noticed more and more how horrid Father was to Mother, and one of the problems I set myself to work out was how to—well how to mitigate him. I couldn't stop him—I couldn't take Mother away, or Peggy. But there are always ways. I'd say to myself: "Now suppose he was a Giant or an Ogre—and had us—what could I do to outwit him?" Or "Suppose he was an Enemy—and had us in prison—or enslaved— what could I do for Mother and Peggy?" Opposition was out of the question—or Conquest—or Escape. Wives and children can't escape, it appears. I tried to think that out, but gave it up.

Once I went to Mr. Cutter about it. In George MacDonald's books the minister does such wonderful things in families, always. Mr. Cutter was very kind, but he didn't seem to appreciate the point of view at all.

"My dear little girl," he said to me, "a child has no right to criticize her parents. You read too many story books with that active brain of yours. Your business is to study your lessons and obey your parents. You are getting morbid, my dear."

You see, he didn't know. When he called, Father was polite enough; and I dare say he was to strangers generally; and as to his treatment of us—well, I guess I didn't make it clear. People didn't know he drank either; and they thought he was a "good family man" because he stayed at home evenings. And as he didn't beat us till we screamed, nobody knew what we suffered.

If children realized their strength, we could not manage them as we do. Perhaps it is just as well, for most children seem to have so little sense. Sometimes I feel as if I would like to start a Revolution among children; but then when I see how foolish they are, it is discouraging.

For instance, every child has to suffer from the clothes put on to it. The more loving and careful mothers are, the more under-flannels and overcoats and rubbers they pile on to the children. Such thick cloth, too!

Why, you'll see poor, fat, toddling things in coats of stiff, heavy stuff, thicker than their fingers—so stiff and heavy that the poor child cannot bend its arms! How would a grown person like to wear a coat stiffer and thicker than a door-mat, so that they stood there in a barrel, a hot wooly barrel, with arms that wouldn't shut? Well, the parents pile on what they see fit, and the children have to put up with it.

I didn't.

If they put on more clothes than I wanted, I practiced passive resistance—simply sat down and stayed there.

"Please take it off!" I said. "*Please* take it off. *Please* take it *off!*" And I wouldn't move till they did. They could carry me, but that was tiresome. You can punish a child, of course, but if the child is willing—quite polite, but determined—you can't punish them forever.

"You were the most stubborn baby!" Mother used to say. "I'm so glad you are more reasonable now, Benigna."

I am. She does not dream—dear Mother!—how very reasonable I am.

But most children certainly are not.

My efforts were quite a good deal interfered with by having to conceal my real character. That makes life more interesting, but more complicated, too. . . .

I began to keep two diaries. There was the little one I started when I was a child of eight. Anybody could read that. It was in my little desk. I'm keeping it up, too—and it's about ten years now; but for the last six I've kept another that nobody ever saw. It was lots of fun hiding it.

The little one has facts in it. It is really very handy sometimes as a family record book, when they dispute about the day they started the furnace last year, or the date of the big snowstorm.

I used always to sit down after supper and write in it, and Father would make caustic remarks, and Mother defend me, and dear Peggy come and kiss me and say she thought keeping a diary was real nice—she wished she could remember to do it.

Then in the precious minutes when I was alone, or when I was supposed to be writing something else in school, I would put down what I really thought and felt, and hide it—like a spy with plans of the Enemy's Fortifications.

If you have enormous interesting plans to carry out and are leading not only a double but almost a triple life, you *have* to have a way to free your mind.

Then I began this, a sort of story of my life, and when it is up to now I mean to destroy my second diary altogether.

The reason I want to write it—this, I mean—is partly self-consciousness, I suppose. I'm quite old enough to see that. But what of it? If you *are* big, you *have* to know it—there's no use pretending not to, to yourself, of all persons.

There have been infant prodigies before now, in music, or arithmetic, or things like that. I was an infant prodigy in common sense, that's all; just plain intelligence, with, of course, that splendid Machiavellian streak thrown in.

I have a big, clear, definite Purpose now, a great long one, stretching through life.

I mean to help people—all sorts of people, in all sorts of ways—*without their knowing it!* This is not philanthropy—not at all. Anybody can get rich, and give money to poor people. I don't mean that. There are plenty of rich people who need help, the kind I mean. Children with horrid parents, parents with horrid children, wives with horrid husbands, husbands with horrid wives, all kinds of workers who ought to have different work—who need encouragement and to be set in the right surroundings—good people to be nice to, and bad people to get even with. I do particularly love to get even with people, like a Corsican. . . .

The one thing that I feel I have to thank Father for is that he played checkers and chess so well, and was willing to play with me.

I nearly spoiled it when I began to beat him. Mad! You never saw anybody so mad. He just couldn't stand it. Then he said he wouldn't play at all, and I was horrified. . . .

"Just one more, Father!" I begged him. "For revenge, you know."

Well—he beat that one. And he beat most of the time after that, keeping one ahead always, sometimes two, sometimes three, but with me always near enough to make him a little anxious. Meanwhile I gained and gained. I could see my checkmates farther and farther ahead, and just at the proper moment I would make a misplay. I'd give him a pawn and learn to play just as well; a bishop, and work harder; a knight, and still keep up; a queen, and then get his. I played games within games, all splendid practice, and yet Father beat the most, and was satisfied.

He bragged of me, too, and sometimes had me play a game with friends of his; he liked me to beat them. So we got on very well, with proper care on my part.

And I began to see for myself in my own practice, that it isn't the winning that matters; it's the game; it's learning how to play. . . .

Then there was typewriting, of course. Father had one, but refused to let me touch it. He certainly was not a helpful parent—unless by calling out ingenuity.

It was perfectly absurd that I should have to fuss and scheme and go out of the house to learn, when that stood there all day, idle. So I made up my mind that I had a perfect right to use it—and began. . . .

He caught me at last—came home early one day, and, of course, he made an awful fuss. But I was quiet and gentle and polite—just stood there and let him tear up my sheet of paper and scold. I didn't say a thing—not a thing, except those mild stave-off remarks you *have* to make. You see, when a parent is angry, he scolds—or she, if it is some other girl's parent. And scolding is silly, always silly. I noticed that almost in infancy.

"What do you mean by doing so and so?" they shout—as if the child had deep-laid intentions. (As a matter of fact, I had, very often, but most children don't—not they.)

"How many times must I tell you not to do that?" they demand furiously. And I always felt like making an estimate, saying: "Eight," at a venture, or "Fifteen." But if you try to reply to a plain question, they call it "impertinence." Then they call names in a caustic way, complain of the trouble you make;

sometimes I've really heard them say: "I'm sure I don't know what to do with you," in a fierce voice, using their own failure as a club. Of course, the child might say politely: "I'm sorry for that," or "Too bad," but they'd only catch it worse. But you have to say "Yes," and "No," and "I'm sorry," or "I won't do it again." If you say absolutely nothing it makes them more and more enraged. "Do you hear me?" they demand, knowing that you can't help it. "What have you to say for yourself?" or "Answer me this minute!" they yell.

Being scolded is like surf bathing—you have to know when to duck and when to jump. I was very skillful, Father scolded so much.

Well, I wriggled through this scolding safely. When he got to a certain point I put my handkerchief to my eyes and ran out of the room. You mustn't do that too soon or you get called back and have to take it worse, but after a while you can—when you see that they can't think of much more to say. . . .

He scolded quite a good deal, but I have noticed this: if you have really *done* a thing—if it is accomplished—then even a scolding person can't think of so much to say. Besides, what they say does not matter—the thing is done. . . .

As I look back at the things I did when I was twelve, they seem foolish enough. One does not know much at twelve—even a girl. And boys! How they do behave! . . .

The girls who were most popular with boys at that age were the dressy ones, pretty, and what I called foolish. But the boys liked them so, that was plain. . . .

So I studied the matter. First I looked at the most successful ones as I knew them in real life. They were awfully foolish girls, as a rule. Some of them didn't seem to know what they were doing at all. You might as well praise honey for drawing flies. It didn't seem worthwhile to me.

Then I looked at the smart ones, those you read about in history, or in fiction, that had this wonderful power. Mary, Queen of Scots, had it—and much good it did her, poor thing. Helen of Troy had it. Cleopatra had it. No end of prominent women had it—but what did they do with it—and how did they come out in the end?

What I can't understand is how people can read history, or

fiction, for that matter, and not learn anything. This attraction of theirs is really like the honey—they only succeed in being eaten, after all. For another thing, all their wonderful power is so short-lived. It is only young ones who have it, apparently. And surely anyone knows youth doesn't last forever. . . .

Any child knows it's going to grow up—if it knows anything. Any girl knows she's going to be a woman. Any woman knows she's going to be an old woman—if she doesn't die sooner.

But do we *do* anything about it? Not we. We all act as if time stopped by about day after tomorrow. Well, I am planning to live a long time, ninety or a hundred years, maybe, and I want to have fun *all* the time—not just between fifteen and thirty—or even forty.

So I concluded I'd rather miss that one kind of power and try for others that would keep. . . .

[Benigna visits her grandfather on his farm but is soon called home because her mother is sick.]

Dr. Bronson was worried, I could see that. He had known Mother so long, and he seemed really interested.

"She must go away," he told Father. "She needs a change—and rest—perfect rest."

She did; even I could see that. But she didn't go; just sat around, pale and weak, and tired-looking, and I ran the house. . . .

The doctor told her she must have a separate room and sleep more—but she never dared mention it but once—Father was furious.

"He'll interfere between a man and his wife, will he!" he said. "We'll have a doctor who knows the laws of decency better than that!" And Mother dropped the subject. She couldn't bear to think of losing Dr. Bronson.

When Father scolded at Mother, which was often, I could hear in my attic because there was a stove-pipe hole that was used to warm the place when they had stoves. It was covered now with a piece of tin, but tin doesn't shut out sound much.

Besides, I fixed it so it would turn—just took out a nail or two and moved it sideways. I never could see why people are so fierce about listening. It doesn't say in the Bible: "Thou shalt not listen"—I looked, with a concordance. And there's no law against it. You have to find out things somehow—especially if you're handicapped by not telling lies. . . .

When Mother was fairly well again—as well as she ever was, poor dear—I began to worry about Peggy.

Peggy was about as sweet and nice a child as ever was, but Father thwarted her so she just had to do something. She had an idea she wanted to go to college, but he set his foot down hard on that. College was no place for a woman—no daughter of his should be seen in such a place—and so on. So she had to give up that ambition. An ambition is a great deal of company, wholesome too, I think.

Next she set her heart on music. They said she had a voice—somebody encouraged her, and she quite blossomed out again, and wanted to take lessons and even go abroad—maybe!

That idea fared no better than the other. He said he had no money to waste on such foolishness, that the place for girls was at home, that a wife need not be an opera singer—all sorts of things like that. She could sing ballads to him in the evenings quite well enough, he said—no more was necessary.

Well, Peggy took to novel reading. I didn't wonder. If you can't do things yourself, you have to get interested in other people's doing them.

And then Father must needs cut off the novels—as far as he could. She did read some—surreptitiously—but they were no longer a real resource.

So of course I wasn't surprised when she began to take an interest in boys. . . .

I don't think Mother would have minded his treatment of her so much—she had a regular talent for suffering—if he had been fair to us children, or if he had been more—well, generally decent.

I don't mean that Father was an immoral man—no, indeed. He didn't even drink in the melodramatic way and "come reeling, rolling home"; he sat quietly at home and drank, and got uglier and uglier in his temper. He didn't beat Mother with a club, nor jump on her like the British workman, but he would make her listen by the hour to those interminable arguments of his till I have heard her sob and shake for half the night afterward—while he snored.

[So Benigna tricks her father into leaving the family and returning to Scotland. She succeeds by appealing to his vulnerable qualities: passion for Scotland, desire for easy money, and lack of commitment to wife and children. And he takes off.]

You needn't imagine that I let Father go off without having some sort of provision in my mind for Mother. I had been studying Mother all my life, more or less, and had a theory as to what would make her happiest.

It's particularly hard to understand your own parents—they stand so close to you and they are always there; it is like living on the side of a mountain—you can't see it.

Of course you love them, at first anyway, and admire them, and all that; and then if they turn out to be conspicuously unpleasant, like Father, you have to struggle with your bringing up to recognize it.

Of course I know the commandment "Honor thy father and mother"—as a means to longevity—but my goodness! If your father drinks, and isn't any earthly use, and abuses your mother—can you honor that? I couldn't, and I'm willing to die sooner, if that's the consequence.

Then again, if once you begin to criticize and blame a parent, it is hard to do them justice—they are so near. The child—the little thing that has looked up to the big thing for so long—all its life—cannot easily see around a parent's faults when it first recognizes them, cannot make allowances and be patient. If I'd been thirty or forty, I might have been more patient with Father, maybe—but I would have assisted his departure just the same; it was the best thing possible under the circumstances.

The great difficulty with Mother was her patient discouragement. I couldn't seem to get her ambitious for anything.

"My life is over," she used to say patiently. "I must not complain. You girls have your lives before you. You will go on and marry and be happy, I hope, and I will live in your happiness. A mother's life is in her children."

Now I loved Mother enough—I'm sure of that; but I wasn't at all contented with this prospect of her just living around in my happiness and Peggy's all the rest of her life. If it was just metaphorical—why, that would be a very slim sort of diet for her;

and if it meant practically to live in our houses after we were married—that didn't seem to be fair to any of us. I've seen it done, lots of times.

When one gets to be a genuine, well-established grandma—cap and glasses and soft shoes—it is all right; there's no other right place for a real helpless, amiable grandma.But for an able-bodied, middle-aged woman to try to be a professional grandma at forty or fifty—it doesn't fully employ her faculties.

Here was my dear little mother, only forty years old—young, for a man, and by no means aged for a woman. Living in a daughter's happiness—even two daughters' happiness—is not a sufficient occupation for a middle-aged woman. Sometimes, being still active and having no other field of interest, they mess up the daughter's happiness a good deal—I've seen that done too.

So I used to sit and look at dear Mother with those noncommittal eyes of mine (I was always proud of my eyes; they were so inexpressive; they didn't give me away) and wonder how I could get her roused up to see that she ought to have ten—twenty—thirty years of satisfying life before her, with lots of happiness of her own, to use and give away. She thought it was all over with her life on account of Father—but what sort of a life did she have with him?

I had a secret conviction that there was a stretch before her which she would find much pleasanter than what lay behind. So I had planned out a career for Mother.

Our assets were the house, and Mother's motherliness. Of course, the obvious thing was boarders. . . .

Father had written home a few times—not often—and I had read his letters. What if it is a prison offense? It doesn't say anything against it in the Bible. Anyhow, it seemed to me right; and what I think is right I mean to do, law or no law. These laws people make, they unmake as fast as they make 'em; always having new ones and altering old ones, or repealing them. And they don't even pretend to have a revelation or anything. Besides, some are made on purpose by rich men, and the lawmakers paid to do it—I've read about that. . . .

There was one thing I never thought of—that was anybody's falling in love with me.

It was that nice Robert Aylesworth—just the dearest boy, he was—I was as fond of him as could be, but as for marrying him—oh, never!

Of course I did not mean to marry at all—I'd seen enough of it. Besides—how could I marry, and be Benigna Machiavelli!

I was planning for such a number of things to do in life—one after the other. Most people seem to me to spend their lives in coops. The boys run into an office and the girls run into a house, headlong, and there they sit, as long as they live, in coops.

I wanted Adventures—and I meant to have them. . . .

[Benigna is determined to wander for a year or more to see how life works and to learn how to run things. In preparation, she makes a chart of her life, "a good deal like an ancient map—chopped off short with 'unexplored region,' or 'circling unknown sea,' but it was good enough as far as it went." It begins this way.]

"Twenty-one," I said. "Shall be in a couple of months. Healthy and strong.

"Present capacities:

"A. Housekeeping, managing, purchasing.

"B. Cooking, catering, serving.

"C. Sewing, designing, dressmaking.

"D. Stenography and typewriting.

"Education: ordinary.

"Special talents: self-control; understanding people; knowing how to manage them.

"Purposes in life:

"A. To grow. To be as big as I can—in every sort of way.

"B. To use my powers to straighten things as far as I can."

I was very certain about A, completely clear indeed, and determined; B was sort of misty. So far, I had just done little things that came up, and there always seemed to be something that needed fixing.

"Now then," I wrote down, "how can I grow the most and the fastest in the next five years—or six—or seven?"

You see, I had not made up my mind *inflexibly* not to marry; I just didn't mean to if I could help it, and certainly not till I had done a lot of other things first. So I planned for five years, definitely. Twenty-six is quite young enough to "settle down," as they call it.

"I'll get a job in an office, just for a starter," I said. "Get an idea of real business methods."

"Here is a lifetime," I said solemnly. "I'll lay it out as if I was not to marry—that's safest. And the other end is the place to plan from.

"Age. What do I want to have about me—and behind me—when I'm old?"

Then I'd sit back in my rocker and look out at the big trees and soft changing shadows on the grass, and *think*, think hard, about Age.

There were plenty of old people to think about; I knew a lot of 'em, mostly as grandmas and grandpas.

Health was the main thing. To keep well always so as to be pink and straight and cheerful at seventy—that was certainly common sense. . . .

Then, besides health, any old person has to have some money. If they haven't, they're just poor relations, and are put upon.

Of course the old men generally do, but the old women generally don't. A grandpa is a person to be considered on account of what he may give you—before or after; but a grandma is only to be considered according to whether you love her or not, apparently.

"I shall have my own money, and enough of it," I determined, "married or single. And I shall have a home—a home of my own—not just somebody else's home that I keep house in. . . ."

Health—money—home—what next?

Friends! Now that is the most important of all, almost. Friends are the richest kind of riches. I've noticed old folks mourn because of the "dropping off of their friends"—their "old friends." One would think that friends were strictly limited to one crop, like brothers and sisters. I mean to plant mine in succession, like green peas and sweet corn, so I'll always have ripe ones.

Health—money—home—friends. How about family? That I wouldn't plan for. If it came, it would come—I was planning for life without it—so's to be on the safe side. There's a certain definite proportion of unmarried women—funny that girls never plan accordingly!

What next? What *kind* of an old woman did I want to be? Here was where that big A, "To grow," came in. I wanted above all things to be—a *worthy* person. To be a plus and not a minus. Not to spend my days wanting things and hanging on to people, and being hurt or pleased or disappointed by the things they did. I wanted to be a *wise* person—wise and able. One that other folks would come to for advice and help, and not be disappointed. Sort of, "Oh, we'll ask Benigna Machiavelli—she'll tell us!"

Of course I knew amiable old ladies, and awfully nice ones, but they didn't know much about Life—only about recipes and patterns and their special notions about babies.

Now my idea was to enlarge my circle of experience as widely as possible, and to keep on enlarging it.

So I meditated very deeply, on how much could be put into that five years, and more, if I had more free time to use in the same way. . . .

Oh! Oh!! Oh!!! How splendid I did feel when I set out for Chicago, all by myself, just twenty-one that very week.

I went to one of those young-woman homes at first—that was for experience. And I got it. While sampling, I went to one after another, all I could get into, in Chicago, and learned and learned and learned.

One notebook is about those "Homes." I got acquainted with girls there, lots of them, and that was specially useful. All I'd found out with my school friends was corroborated here. . . .

At the office I learned some things, and gained what I wanted—speed and precision in my work, and some knowledge of business habits and manners. At the end of a month I changed. My five years was all too short to waste much time on these preliminaries.

Then things began to move. I kept my house address at the cheapest of the homes, and started in on a career of industry of the most varied character. . . .

Plain of dress and quiet of manner, with my serious face and steady eyes, I got jobs without very much difficulty. . . .

I joined Unions—and was discharged for it. I went to Settlement Clubs and Classes and learned a lot. Then it seemed a good chance to start in on the child question, and after helping a bit, gratuitously, in the Settlement Nursery, I got a regular place in one.

That was meat and drink to me. I had always liked babies, but not—well, not to lose my heart entirely to just one. This roomful appealed to me very much. The head nurse was an extremely capable one, and taught me a great deal. I put in a month in this kind of nursery work, and then thought I'd increase my experience in that line.

By the good offices of the Settlement people I got a sort of assistant nursemaid place in a rich family, and had all I wanted of that in a fortnight. But I made the acquaintance of a very good lady's maid there, who became cheerfully confidential and told me about her various places, mistresses, and duties.

I answered advertisements and got a maid's place, at low wages, stating that I had worked in other lines before; and then I began to learn new things, very fast.

Why do not people realize that you cannot know life if you stay always on one level? Why, the average woman knows only her own kind of people. She may travel around the world, and never learn as much as she would in traveling *up and down a bit*— in her own city.

I had been associating with office-girls, shop-girls, factory-girls, and nurse-girls. Now I did not associate—in the ordinary sense—with rich ladies; but I had to learn about them—I couldn't help it.

With my hair depressingly low and plain, with the regulation dress of my "class," and with the manners of the same, which I studied and practiced with joy, I don't believe Mother would have known me—at the first look.

As to make-up—I began to find out about that even as a lady's maid—and was ready to try for the position with an actress.

Long before that first year was up, I had some practical inside knowledge of nine trades, and a week-to-week trial of a dozen more. I had been a waitress in a cheap restaurant, a chambermaid in a hotel, a sales-girl, a cap-maker, a necktie-maker, a skirt worker, a box-maker, a typist and stenographer, and a nurse—besides a lot of mere investigating experiments. . . .

In considering all the things that happened in these first stirring years of my life, and examining the separate bits of biography I was always preparing—I have pieced together some of them in this account—I see how absurd it is for novelists to try to "end" a story. There is no end to anybody's story, until they are dead, and some people think that is only the beginning. . . .

That boarder business suited Mother even better than I hoped it would. It was not only that she liked it, but that it strengthened her. I'd really never thought of that side of it much, I was so used to dear Mother's being down-trodden and discouraged.

After all, it wasn't so much Father as an outside force that kept Mother down—it was mostly her ideas of duty. She thought she had to submit and obey and all that; she was bound by her own notions.

There's a lot of philosophy there—I can see it. And then there was habit. If you are always being hectored and looked down on, and never have the chance to do anything worthwhile, it does get on your nerves—makes you think you're no good.

And now everything was different. Mother had room to exercise her faculties; that strengthened her. She found she was really earning money—this grew very slowly into her realization. . . .

It was just beautiful to see her whole outlook widen and brighten and grow firmer, as it were. . . .

As to me, I had met several men since I left Robert. One or two of them had been sincerely attracted to me, so I got kind of used to the pressure—I couldn't fall in love with them all, you see. And quite a number had manifested that sort of devotion which makes any cool-headed woman discount the whole lot; it is at once so selfish and so *impersonal*.

It's no compliment; far from it! You being a Female, a Young Unattached Female, and they being Males (of any age, attached or at large), the proper thing is for them to make advances. Also the proper thing for the girl is to make retreats—according to the conventions. In which case they continue to come on.

But I followed different tactics.

I got my first scare in a Chicago workshop—on the stairs leading to it, that is. Rather dark and narrow stairs and the foreman coming up as I went down. He took right hold of me and kissed me before I could stop him, but he repented all the way down—back down and head first.

It washed off, all right, and I got another job—didn't go back there, even for my wages. But I was somewhat alarmed as well as angry, and determined to provide against that sort of thing as well as the slower kind.

There was a fine woman doctor I used to see at the Settlement, and I went to her.

"Doctor," I said, "I am a young woman, working for my living. I find that some men are disagreeable and some dangerous. Will you give me some very clear advice, both as to the nature and the extent of the danger, and the best methods of self-protection?"

She tilted back in her office chair and looked me over. "You are certainly a very cool young woman," she said.

"Why not?" I answered. "If I was traveling in the jungles of Hindustan, I'd want to know all about the snakes and tigers: how to avoid them; how to fight them; how to treat injuries. It appears that we girls are in another kind of jungle, and some of us have never even heard that the cobra is dangerous. I know better than that, but I want to know more. I want some straight practical knowledge, anatomical and psychological."

"You shall have it," she said. And she gave me books and pamphlets to read—quite a number of them.

I learned a lot. Out of the lot there are . . . two bits of information which ought to prove useful to damsels in distress.

For extreme cases, is "the womanly art of self-defense." A girl is not a mouse and a man is not an elephant.

Of course, if one is overwhelmed by numbers, that's another story, or if one is stunned with an unexpected blow; but when just one man tries to "make love" offensively to a girl who doesn't want him to, she need not run, nor shriek, nor faint.

Stand steady, cold, quiet, with a steely eye; and if he is not checked by that psychological wall—if he comes too close—kick, kick hard and accurately. This is "unladylike," but not so regrettable as being mishandled. . . .

We were all sitting about in the pleasant parlor one evening—the family. . . . As it happened, the rest of the boarders were all off somewhere or in their rooms, or over in the other house, so it was just us. . . .

Then all at once there was a great scuffling and stamping on the steps; the front door opened, letting a fine, cold blast swing our curtains, and making the fire flash up—and in walked Father!

There was another man, still stamping in the hall, but that didn't count.

Father! He had come back!

We all started up and stood staring. Mother had her hand to her heart and couldn't seem to speak.

"'Tis a fine welcome you are giving me," he said presently, for we were all literally too much astonished to speak. . . .

"You are welcome home, Andrew," she said. "We were startled—not expecting you. But you are welcome."

She kissed him, sweetly enough, and turned to the others.

"This is Robert Aylesworth, that I wrote you of, our son that is to be; and this is my friend—my sister—Mary Windsor."

[Robert Aylesworth, having been rejected by Benigna, has promptly fallen in love with Peggy, her sister, who cheerfully accepts his offer of marriage.]

Father was stiffly polite.

"Aye!" he said. "I heard of this son and came to look him over. And I have heard of you too, madam." He bowed to her. "I have brought another new relation home with me—come in, laddie."

And there came in from the hall, blushing with shyness, yet bravely cordial, a tall, lean, high-colored young Scotchman.

"Kiss your cousins, my lad!" cried Father, slapping him on the back. "Make him welcome, girls—'tis your own bloodkin, Home MacAvelly, of Homeburn."

We got out a jolly little supper for them and sat about talking for a while.

Miss Windsor went to her room and Robert to his; the young cousin was shown to another. We girls were sent to bed, and there was no one in the big, bright parlor by the red fire but Mother and Father.

I couldn't stand it. I'm a good creeper, and I crept downstairs again—the back stairs—and in through the kitchen and dining-room to the closed parlor doors. A table knife wedged them open softly and the fine new hangings were a further shield.

I wasn't going to have my lifework upset, maybe, and not know about it. . . .

I fancy he was a trifle awed by the new Something about Mother—not only her air of prosperity and beauty, but a different mental attitude. She was no longer merely something of *his*; she was her own.

But he gathered himself together and began to lay down the law. Doubtless he had rehearsed it to himself many times on the voyage over, or in those cold stone-built chambers on the other side.

He had come back now; he saw his way to making a good living (Father always saw his way, but seldom got to it), and all this boardinghouse experiment must stop at once. . . .

Then Mother spoke. I could see the pink curve of her cheek, and her fine shapely hand lying quietly on the arm of her chair.

"Andrew," she said, "I am glad that you bring the matter up at once, so that we have a clear understanding to begin with. I enjoy keeping boarders. I find it a successful and fairly lucrative business and I intend to keep on with it."

He blustered. Someway the ground was new; he could not drop into his old, superior tone at once. He spoke of the rights of a man in his own house.

"You forget, Andrew," she answered mildly, "that the house is mine. It is perfectly legal and proper for me to run this business if I choose—and I do choose."

He talked of her duty to him.

"I have done my duty to you, as I saw it, for many a long year; I have loved and served you and submitted to all your opinions. Now I shall still love you. You are my husband and the father of my children—but I have opinions of my own now, Andrew. I think that this is right to do—and I shall do it."

It wasn't easy for her, and yet, to my astonishment, it wasn't half as hard as I should have thought. I suppose if she had stood up to him like that in the beginning, things never would have been so hard.

"Let us not quarrel on the night of your homecoming, Andrew," she said in that dear, gentle voice of hers. "You are my loved husband and I am your wife. But you come home to a somewhat different woman from the poor thing you left. I truly think, my dear, that you will be happier with me now than you were then."

And that is precisely what happened. . . .

And then I began to think about that new cousin. What a nice name—Home. I'd read about the Homes in Scotch history and knew we were connected.

He was just the type of man I liked—tall, sinewy, active but quiet, able to sit still or to jump quick—and far.

He had nice eyes, steady, keen, gray-blue eyes, that looked right into one. Good, thick, sturdy hair, red-brown, vigorous, fine hair.

Home MacAvelly!

All at once I stopped still in my tracks, and stood seized by an idea—MacAvelly! His name was MacAvelly, too! And I had thought I never could!

UNPUNISHED*

In her last substantial piece of fiction, and her only detective novel, *Unpunished*, Gilman deals with the hideously villainous male authority figure not by persuasion or confrontation or flight, as she has in earlier works, but by killing him off, in a variety of ways: gun, rope, blunt instrument, and poison. Wade Vaughn is an extreme and grotesque version of all the run-of-the-mill tyrant-father figures in Gilman's other fiction. Like the others, he too deceives: he presents himself to the public as a benevolent and caring patron of a badly crippled woman and two defenseless children. In the privacy of his home—the place where the sadistic action always occurs—he is the tormentor of the helpless and a vicious blackmailer of those who entrusted their secrets to him as their attorney. Vaughn betrays all decency.

In the excerpt below, from Chapter VII, "The Record," Jacqueline Warner describes the family's history and present circumstance: As a result of an automobile accident which killed her husband and the husband of her sister,

---

*Unpunished *is in the Charlotte Perkins Gilman collection of The Schlesinger Library, Radcliffe College.*

Iris, both women, with their young children, were taken in by Vaughn, who married one and drove her to suicide, while tormenting the other, who remains for lack of alternative.

Unpunished opens with the discovery of Vaughn's murder. A husband-and-wife detective team, Bess and Jim Hunt, are the vehicles through whom the mystery unfolds. Initially only Bess Hunt asserts the right of the helpless and tormented to seek vengeance by murder. By the time the story is over and the full complexity is unraveled, the reader, too, presumably, is convinced that all the people who thought they were killing Vaughn, and the one who actually did, Jacqueline Warner, are morally innocent. After all, the law not only did not protect her and her children, it kept them firmly in Vaughn's grasp. Her freedom and safety had to come from her own actions. In the case of this evil and powerful man, salvation for others came through his death. Only then could the loving members of that distorted family, Jacqueline and her now-adult children, leave the hated home to create a new and genuinely nurturing one. The innocent are rewarded with love and marriage. Iris and Hal, the first-cousin children, marry. Jacqueline Warner, at the age of forty-five, undergoes surgery to restore her beauty, and then she marries Ross Akers, who is also freed from the horror of blackmail by Vaughn's death. It is a customary Gilman happy ending, but it is achieved through murder, and the legacy of *Unpunished* is an uncharacteristic ghoulishness and bitterness.

Chapter VII. The Record

10:30 A.M. July 11th, 1921. My name is Jacqueline Warner. I am thirty-one years old. Here I sit in my wheel chair, with my crippled feet and my twisted face, helpless, and completely in the power of Wade Vaughn, my brother-in-law. We are living in the old house. I have the room that was Mother's once, and afterward Father's, and I have found his small typewriter and a lot of paper, in the window seat. Wade doesn't know about it.

And today I have found Father's wall-safe, a secret panel thing, quite secure. So I am going to write an account of this man and what he has done to us. It will be well hidden there, and some day I will tell Hal how to open it. If I die here, he can read this and see why I stood it. . . .

We can't get out. He's got us in a trap. I'm helpless to earn a living for myself and two children, helpless and hideous. And it could be cured, Dr. Akers tells me, my feet and my face too—almost, with this wonderful facial surgery they use now—but that would cost money, and Wade has it all. When I asked to have it done, humiliated myself and begged, urged that if I were straightened out I could earn enough to pay him back, he said I was sufficiently useful to him as I was, and more likely to stay! Like the Chinese women. . . .

And there he sits in my father's chair at the table, at my father's desk in the study, drinking my father's old whiskey, master of the house, and of all the money—and of us. . . .

That means my boy Hal, my sister's daughter Iris, and my poor self. For their sakes I must keep my head, keep up their spirits, hold on and bear it till Hal's through college if possible—if nothing happens to Iris meanwhile.

After Hal has his education we can clear out, even if we lose all our pitiful inheritance, starve together if need be, but be free of him.

I have hunted and hunted, hoping that Father might have made another will before he died, but I can't find a word. What I have found is this little wall-safe with some money, $500 plus $14.70 in a purse, and this I'm going to keep hidden, so that if we have to go quickly we could live on it for a while.

Now that I have a safe hiding place, I'm going to make a record of what he has done to us—partly because it may be legally useful, if ever he is brought to justice, but mainly as a "release" as they call it now, to get it off my mind. I'll tell Hal, but I won't worry Iris, dear child. She is far happier in not knowing about him.

Now to begin at the beginning of our troubles, being born! There were two sisters of us, Iris, who is dead, and I. We loved each other dearly, and were so happy together that we could put up with Father's queernesses. He was a peculiar man, strict, domineering, with antiquated notions about the education of girls, and particularly as to obedience. We were trained to mind like whipped dogs.

Poor Mother couldn't stand it; she died when we were little children. I can just remember how pale and thin she looked that last time I saw her, and how frightened. She held us both tight in her arms, especially little Iris, and she told me, in a whisper, her eyes on the door for fear Father would come in, to be good to my sister, to take care of her—to love her—love her—love her! I guess she died for lack of love, poor Mother. Iris didn't need to be told; she loved everybody, even Father.

I didn't. I was a stubborn rebellious little thing, but soon found out it was no use rebelling against him while I was a child. He had us educated at home, governesses, tutors, and so on, an excellent education, but no freedom and no companionship or society. It's no wonder we were so devoted to each other. He was afraid of the influence of "the modern girl," and he did his best to bring us up fifty years behind the times. Still, he could not keep out all books and papers—we could read!

I wanted to go to college, but I might as well have asked for a trip to the moon. I wanted desperately to be an actress, but that I knew better than to mention. We could study at home, in lines he thought suitable, and we did, mostly languages.

We lived here in this old house which had belonged to Father's family for generations. It's built up all about us now, but there is still quite a garden, for Brooklyn. It is on the corner of Field and Grove streets; the names show what the place was like when first built on.

I was about nineteen and Iris near eighteen when Wade Vaughn came into the picture. We never knew much about Father's business, something to do with real estate, I think. He was considered rich, and had quite a few lawsuits. Mr. Vaughn was a very successful lawyer, a youngish man, about thirty I guess—he seemed old to us. He was inclined to be stout, even then; he had a thick red mouth and small hard eyes. We despised him.

But Father seemed to like him immensely, had him at the house all the time. He had won some difficult case for him, I believe, and was retained as a sort of general adviser. He agreed with Father in all his opinions, flattered and pleased him, and he tried very hard to make up to us girls, but we couldn't bear him. Pretty soon he wanted to marry Iris—my little sister!

He went to Father first, which delighted him of course; he quite approved. But when Wade proposed, she refused him. Poor little blue-eyed child—she had a shivering dislike of him, used to say he made her feel creepy. No wonder!

Then Father issued his ultimatum, gave her his direct command that she must marry Wade Vaughn. I don't suppose Iris had ever disobeyed him in her life, nor I since I was six. And I doubt if she could have held out against him even at eighteen but for one thing—in spite of all the restrictions with which she was surrounded, she had managed to fall in love.

The man was our new minister, Sydney Booth, very young for the position, but already a noted preacher. I think Father suspected him somewhat, his pastoral calls were rather frequent, but our chaperone-housekeeper liked him and I fancy she did not mention all of them. At any rate Iris had lost her heart to him completely, and it gave her strength to resist Wade Vaughn.

I helped, of course. I told her she was legally of age now and had a right to marry whom she pleased, and that it was wrong, dead wrong, to marry a man she didn't love at all. So we took our fate in our hands and ran away. I shall never forget the splendid feeling of being free! We were heroically willing to starve by inches, but vowed we would never go back.

Iris was saved any real privation because Sydney promptly married her. He tried his pious best to make friends with Father and reconcile him to us, but when Father was angry an enraged rhinoceros would have been more easily appeased. He vowed he would never see either of us again, and that we should not touch a cent of his money—he was most insulting to Sydney about that, called him a pious fraud, a fortune hunter, talked about priests and women. When Sydney came back from that meeting and told us about it, he was far too angry for a Christian, let alone a minister. However, he and Iris were very happy, and little Iris was born, almost as lovely as her mother she grew to be.

Meanwhile I had my troubles, but I did manage to get on the

stage, and there I met Haldane Warner, an English actor, and married him. He was a fine actor and finer man—in many ways. Our baby was born before Iris, my boy Hal. He is about perfect.

Before I go on with the dreadful part of this story, I want to thankfully acknowledge nine years of considerable happiness. That is more than some people ever have. Sydney, Iris said, was an angel; they did seem perfectly happy together. I had my wonderful boy, and my chosen profession, and experience.

It was Hal's tenth birthday, and all of us were celebrating by a long drive in Sydney's big car. I never knew what caused the accident. Only the children escaped unhurt. Haldane and Sydney were killed. Iris was so utterly overcome by shock as almost to lose her mind, and I was a senseless, hideous cripple. . . . There was no one who could describe what happened, only my Hal told of a big car coming fast—it must have gone away fast too!

My father was notified. He had said he would never see us again, so he sent Wade Vaughn to attend to the wreckage. He took us all to his house. I had concussion of the brain besides my other injuries and was unconscious for many days.

When I first came to myself there was Iris by my side, so delighted to have me know her that she was almost like herself again. There was my boy struggling not to cry for joy because his mother was awake, and little Iris, who did cry and clung to us both. Of course I was weak and queer, and was just beginning to ask what had happened when Wade Vaughn sauntered in.

He stood there and looked at me and smiled. I didn't know then how my face looked, that it was hurt so dreadfully. He has a wide slow tight smile, like a Roman emperor who has devised a new method of torture and is trying it on his pet enemy.

"We must not excite her, Iris," he said. "It will delay her recovery. You may be quite easy in your mind, Jacqueline. There was an automobile accident. The children are unhurt, as you see, but Mr. Warner and Mr. Booth were both killed, and you are considerably cut up. But I have married Iris and will take care of all of you so you need not worry."

My recovery *was* delayed, by many weeks of varying delirium. Whenever I did remember that dreadful announcement scene I thought it was part of the vague horrors I was drowned in. But there came a time when I felt that my mind was really my own again. . . .

There sat Iris at my bed, with a book in her lap but not reading. Her eyes were fixed unseeingly, her sweet mouth quivered now and then, and big slow tears ran down one at a time. I watched her silently for a moment, and then that scene came back and I knew it was true. But this time I did not go off. I thought, "Here is my sister. If this awful thing is true, she needs me more than ever. I must keep steady."

So I made a little movement, and when she turned I was smiling quietly up at her. Then she was in my arms, crying and trying not to for my sake. I held her and soothed her, told her not to worry, that I was going to get well and would take care of her, and she was comforted a little.

As days passed, I gradually got hold of the facts. Hal told me what he could remember of the accident, and of their coming to this house, and that Vaughn had really married Aunt Iris.

"How soon?" I asked him, and he said, "Right away—that is in a week or two, I guess."

It was. Within a fortnight. Of course she wasn't responsible. Her mind was blank with irregular patches of memory, all unrelated. She was always such a loving dependent little thing. He told her anything he wanted to, that for my sake and the children's sake and to please her father she should marry him. When she had a moment's memory of Sydney he told her that he had been dead for a long time and that now her duty was to the children and her poor crippled sister, that if she married him he would keep me and take care of me. I got it out of her bit by bit, never hinting at any blame. He took her to the city hall, got the license, they were married by the mayor, and Iris no more responsible than a baby. He explained to people that he did it in order to take care of her, and got credit for devoted affection and benevolence. That is the kind of a man Wade Vaughn is. It was a long while before I was clear-headed enough to get it all straight, and fully realize our position. My poor head had been so battered it was almost fatal. But for the children I wish it had been. . . .

Iris did not know at all what she had done, nor realize her loss. She was long in that vague crushed condition and sometimes talked as if Sydney was still alive.

So I lay there and faced the facts. The fact of my disfigurement and cripplement was a large one. When at last I got hold of a mirror it was a shock. The windshield, I suppose; I was on the front seat. My sight was not affected, but what a pair of eyes! The worst one I wear a patch over when not alone. And a big red shrunken scar on one cheek that pulls up the mouth in half a grin.

No woman likes to be hideous, nor man either, I suppose. There I was, pretty well cut off from any hope of independence. At least it seemed so at first. There was my boy. The important thing for him was a decent home and an education. There were no near relations on the English side. As to my loss—my injury, my profession—I shut that door inside, shut it hard on hopelessness.

Here was my darling sister who had been my care since I was a mere child myself. Never had she needed me as she did now. If she was to live, to recover her mind, to be a mother to little Iris, I must stay with her and be strong and wise. I thought it all out and saw that I must, as the older novelists used to say, "dissemble," and keep friends with Vaughn.

One day when I was fairly well, first sitting up in my chair, he strolled in and proceeded to make the position clear to me in his own thorough way.

"I know you don't like me, Jacqueline, never did. But that does not interfere with my pleasure in keeping you here. I can talk freely to you, you are more intelligent than Iris, even when she is quite herself."

I kept still, listening. My expression did not matter.

"It is sadly evident that you are in no shape to earn a decent living for yourself and your boy, even if you wished to leave your sister. She, being my wife, I shall of course take care of, and her child—Sydney Booth's child." At this he smiled a little, that wide slow smile, and I saw he was watching my hands, that were gripping so tightly on the arms of my chair.

"Now I am also prepared to take care of you and your child, on terms, Jacqueline, on terms. I have brought you a copy of your father's will. You may keep it awhile and study it, so you can see how little you can have to look forward to in that direction. A very determined man, your father. He left it with me in case of accident—you may not have heard that he has gone abroad?"

I had not. How should I?

"He made a previous will, soon after you and your sister so offended him by your disobedience, leaving some of his property to me and some to various charities. But after I married Iris, and assumed the care of you and your son, I represented to him that he ought at least to contribute to the support and education of his grandchildren. This is the result.

"I don't wish you to feel under any coercion, my dear Jacqueline. You are perfectly free to take your boy and leave if you prefer. Or you may write to any of your friends and see if they are willing to undertake your support—a rather unattractive cripple, and a small boy, with a devoted brother-in-law quite willing to keep you both."

I was still keeping quiet. It was deadly clear that there was no way out, at present.

"Now if you remain, I have no doubt that you will be extremely useful in the house. Iris, I regret to say, is frequently not quite herself, as you have probably remarked. So I shall ask you to take the care of the house off her hands; you are, I believe, quite competent for work of that sort. The terms I spoke of are merely like those made by your father in that will, and apply to you and the boy. Merely obedience. Think it over, my dear sister, think it over."

He went off and left me with that iniquitous will; and I did think it over.

MOVING
THE
MOUNTAIN *

Gilman dramatized her vision of an ideal social order in her utopian novels, the first of which is *Moving the Mountain*. It appeared in 1911 and is set in the United States in 1940. It seems that the American people elected socialism and not the Republican ticket in 1920. In the following twenty years society moved beyond socialism to a New Religion, called Living and Life, in a world in which the profit motive has been eliminated and social, not individual, goals are sought.

John Robertson, lost in Tibet thirty years before, in 1910, is found by his sister, Nellie, now a college president, and brought to what is for him a strange country, a new social-ist-humanist world which is revealed to us through his skeptical perception.

Unlike many utopian fantasies of the late nineteenth and early twentieth centuries, the most famous being Edward Bellamy's *Looking Backward*, Gilman's society is new and wonderful essentially because the people, not the technology, are changed. Her world is brought about by "no other change than a change in mind, the mere awakening of peo-

---

*Moving the Mountain *appeared originally in Volume 2 of* The Forerunner *(1911) and was published separately later that same year.*

ple, especially the women, to existing possibilities." The transformation is in new ideas, and that occurs with the realization by half the adult world of their enormous, but unacknowledged, powers. Women learn that civilization was created by constructive industry, not warfare and aggression, and that it was women who domesticated animals, developed agriculture, and shaped the nurturing cultures that flowed from the rearing of children, always and in all societies a woman's occupation. By the time of universal suffrage, women, having been made "rich by the experience of the first trials," use their organizational and political skills to lead the struggle for a new order. "We make a different kind of people now" is a refrain that John Robertson hears over and over, a counterpoint to his repeated assertion that "You can't alter human nature."

All sorts of Gilman's ideas are played with in dramatic form: the central role of child-rearing as a key to the creation of a new kind of person; the collective nature of life, which paradoxically enables one's true individualism to flower; the decentralization of society into recognizable and manageable communities and neighborhoods; women's new role in selective breeding as the force in evolutionary progress—just as men have for eons molded women to their choosing by not marrying those who did not conform to their notions of femininity, now women select from competing males, as is the case in most other species.

A sense of the new social relations and industrial structure can be gleaned from the few pages excerpted below. John Robertson is dining with his newly found family: his sister, Nellie Robertson; her husband, Owen Montrose; and their children, Hallie Robertson and Jerrold Montrose.

The book ends on a characteristically happy note. John Robertson, growing homesick for noise, foul smells, and tense, unhappy people, returns to visit his relatives who refuse to share in the new society and choose to live in the old way: Uncle Jake, Aunt Dorcas, and their now middle-aged daughter, Cousin Drusilla. At first John feels the comfort of shared experience, illustrating how difficult it is for us to change because we seek the familiar, even if the familiar is bad. But soon John shrinks from the narrowness and alienation of their life. He proposes to Drusilla, his first cousin, and the two misfits rejoin the larger society to live happily thereafter.

They called me to supper. "Most of us have our heartiest meal in the middle of the day," my sister said. "The average man, O Victim of Copious Instruction," added my brother-in-law, "does his work in the morning: the two hours that he has to, or the four that he usually puts in. Eight to twelve, or nine to one—that is the working day for everybody. Then home, rest, a bath maybe, and then—allow me to help you to some of our Improvements!"

I was hungry, and this simple meal looked and smelled most appetizing. There was in particular a large shining covered dish, which, being opened, gave forth so savory a steam as fairly to make my mouth water. A crisp and toothsome bread was by my plate; a hot drink, which they laughingly refused to name, proved most agreeable; a suave, cool salad followed; fruits, some of which were new to me, and most delicate little cakes, closed the meal.

They would not tell me a thing, only saying, "Have some more!" and I did. . . .

"What is this undeniably easy-to-take concoction you have stuffed me with?"

"My esteemed new brother," Owen answered, "we have been considering your case in conclave assembled, and we think it is wiser to feed you for a while and demand by all the rites of hospitality that you eat what is set before you and ask no questions for conscience' sake. . . ."

"I will now produce information," began Hallie, "my office being that of Food Inspector."

"Her main purpose in bringing you here, Uncle, was to give you food and then talk about it," said Jerrold solemnly. Hallie only made a face at him, and went on:

"We have a magnificent system of production and distribution," she explained, "with a decreasing use of animal foods."

"Was this a vegetarian meal?" I asked in a hollow voice.

"Mostly; but you shall have meat when you want it—better meat than you used to get, too." . . .

So my fair niece, looking like any other charming girl in a pretty evening frock, began to expound her specialty. Her mother begged to interrupt for the moment. "Let me recall to him things as they were—which you hardly know, you happy child. Don't forget, John, that when we were young we did not know what good food was."

I started to protest, but she shook her finger at me.

"No, we didn't, my dear boy. We knew 'what we liked,' as the people said at the picture show; but that did not make it good— good in itself or good for us. The world was ill-fed. Most of the food was below par; a good deal was injurious, some absolutely poison. People sold poison for food in 1910, don't forget that! You may remember the row that was beginning to be made about it."

I admitted recalling something of the sort, though it had not particularly interested me at the time.

"Well, that row went on—and gained in force. The women woke up."

"If you have said that once since we met, my dear sister, you've said it forty times. I wish you would make a parenthesis in these food discussions and tell me how, when, and why the women woke up." . . .

"Some women were waking up tremendously before you left, John Robertson, only I dare say you never noticed it. They just kept on, faster and faster, till they all did—about all. There are some Dodos left, even yet, but they don't count—discredited grandmothers!"

"And, being awake?" I gently suggested.

"And, being awake, they—" She paused for an instant, seeking an expression, and Jerrold's smooth bass voice put in, "They saw their duty and they did it."

"Exactly," his mother agreed, with a proudly loving glance at him. "That's just what they did! And in regard to the food business, they recognized at last that it was their duty to feed the world—and that it was miserably done! So they took hold."

"Now, Mother, this is my specialty," Hallie interposed.

"When a person can only talk about one thing, why oppose them?" murmured Jerrold. But she quite ignored him, and reopened her discussion.

"We—that is, most of the women and some of the men—began to seriously study the food question, both from a hygienic and an economic standpoint. I can't tell you that thirty years' work in a minute, Uncle John, but here's the way we manage it now: We have learned very definitely what people ought not to eat, and it is not only a punishable, but a punished offense to sell improper food stuffs."

"How are the people to know?" I ventured.

"The people are not required to know everything. All the food is watched and tested by specialists; what goes into the market is good—all of it."

"By impeccable angelic specialists—like my niece?"

She shook her head at me. "If they were not, the purchaser would spot them at once. You see, our food supply is not at the mercy of the millions of ignorant housewives any more. Food is bought and prepared by people who know how—and they have all the means—and knowledge—for expert tests."

"And if the purchaser too was humanly fallible?"

She cast a pitying glance at me, and her father took the floor for a moment.

"You see, John, in the old time the dealers were mostly poor, and sold cheap and bad stuff to make a little money. The buyers were mostly poor, and had to buy the cheap and nasty stuff. Even large manufacturers were under pressure, and had to cheat to make a profit—or thought they had to. Then when we got to inspectors and such like, they were under the harrow, too, and were by no means impeccable. Our big change is this: Nobody is poor now."

"I hear you say that," I answered, "but I can't seem to get it through my head. Have you really divided all the property?"

"John Robertson, I'm ashamed of you!" cried Nellie. "Even in 1910 people knew better than that—people who knew anything!"

"That wasn't necessary," said Owen, "nor desirable. What we have done is this: First, we have raised the productive capacity of the population; second, we have secured their right to our natural resources; third, we have learned to administer business without waste. The wealth of the world grows enormously. It is not what you call 'equally distributed,' but everyone has enough. There is no economic danger any more; there is economic peace."

"And economic freedom?" asked I sharply.

"And economic freedom. People choose the work they like best, and work—freely, more than they have to."

I pondered on this. "Ah, but they *have to*—labor is compulsory."

Owen grinned. "Yes, labor is compulsory—always was. It is compulsory on everyone now. We used to have two sets who wouldn't work—paupers and the idle rich; no such classes left—all busy."

"But, the freedom of the individual—" I persisted.

"Come, come, brother; society always played hob with the freedom of the individual whenever it saw fit. It killed, imprisoned, fined; it had compulsory laws and regulations; it required people to wear clothes and furnished no clothes for them to wear. If society has a right to take human life, why has it not a right to improve it? No, my dear man," continued Owen (he was evidently launched on *his* specialty now), "society is not somebody else domineering over us! Society is us—taking care of ourselves."

I took no exception to this, and he began again. "Society, in our young days, was in a state of auto-intoxication. It generated its own poisons, and absorbed them in peaceful, slow suicide. To think—it seems impossible now—to *think* of allowing anybody to sell bad food!"

"That wasn't the only bad thing they sold," I suggested. . . .

"You never were sure of getting *anything* pure," he said scornfully, "no matter what you paid for it. How we submitted to such rank outrage for so long I cannot imagine! This was taken up very definitely some twenty years ago, by the women mostly."

"Aha—when the women woke up!" I cried.

"Yes, just that. It is true that their being mostly mere housewives and seamstresses was a handicap in some ways; but it was a direct advantage in others. They were almost all consumers, you see, not producers. They were not so much influenced by considerations of the profits of the manufacturer as they were by the direct loss to their own pockets and health. Yes," he smiled reminiscently, "there were some pretty warm years while this thing was thrashed out. One of the most successful lines of attack was in the New Food system, though. . . ."

"You see, Uncle, it's one thing to restrain and prevent and punish—and another thing to substitute improvements. . . .

"The first company began about 1912 or '13, I think. Just some women with a real business sense, and enough capital. They wisely concluded that a block of apartments was the natural field for their services; and that professional women were their natural patrons."

"The unprofessional women—or professional wives, as you might call them— had only their housewifery to preserve their self-respect, you see," put in Owen. "If they didn't do housekeeping for a living, what—in the name of decency—did they do?"

"This was called the Home Service Company," said Hallie. "(I will talk, Mother!) They built some unusually attractive apartments, planned by women, to please women; this block was one of the finest designs of their architects—women, too, by the way."

"Who had waked up," murmured Jerrold, unnoticed.

"It was frankly advertised as specially designed for professional women. They looked at it, liked it, and moved in: teachers, largely doctors, lawyers, dressmakers—women who worked."

"Sort of a nunnery?" I asked.

"My dear brother, do you imagine that all working women were orphan spinsters, even in your day?" cried Nellie. "The self-supporting women of that time generally had other people to support, too. Lots of them were married; many were widows with children; even the single ones had brothers and sisters to take care of."

"They rushed in, anyhow," said Hallie. "The place was beautiful and built for enjoyment. There was a nice garden in the middle . . . very charming and attractive. There were arrangements on the top floor for nurseries and child-gardens; and the roof was for children all day; evenings the grown-ups had it. Great care was taken by the management in letting this part to the best professionals in child culture.

"There were big rooms, too, for meetings and parties; places for billiards and bowling and swimming—it was planned for real human enjoyment, like a summer hotel."

"But I thought you said this place was for women," I incautiously ventured.

"Oh, Uncle John! And has it never occurred to you that women like to amuse themselves? Or that professional women have men relatives and men friends? There were plenty of men in the building, and plenty more to visit it. They were shown how nice it was, you see. But the chief card was the food and service. This company engaged, at high wages, first-class houseworkers, and the residents paid for them by the hour; and they had a food service which was beyond the dreams of—of— homes, or boardinghouses."

"Your professional women must have been millionaires," I mildly suggested.

"You think so because you do not understand the food business, Uncle John; nobody did in those days. We were so used to the criminal waste of individual housekeeping, with its pitifully low standards, and to monotonous low-grade restaurant meals, with their waste and extortion, that it never occurred to us to estimate the amount of profit there really was in the business. These far-seeing women were pioneers—but not for long! Dozens are claiming first place now, just as the early 'Women's Clubs' used to.

"They established in that block a meal service that was a wonder for excellence, and for cheapness, too; and people began to learn."

I was impressed, but not convinced, and she saw it.

"Look here, Uncle John, I hate to use figures on a helpless listener, but you drive me to it."

Then she reached for the bookcase and produced her evidence, sparingly, but with effect. She showed me that the difference between the expense of hiring separate service and the same number of people patronizing a service company was sufficient to reduce expenses to the patrons and leave a handsome payment for the company.

Owen looked on, interpreting to my ignorance.

"You never kept house, old man," he said, "nor thought much about it, I expect; but you can figure this out for yourself easily enough. Here were a hundred families, equal to, say, five hundred persons. They hired a hundred cooks, of course, paid them something like six dollars a week—call it five on an average. There's five hundred dollars a week, just for cooks—twenty-six thousand dollars a year!

"Now, as a matter of fact (our learned daughter tells us this), ten cooks are plenty for five hundred persons—at the same price would cost thirteen hundred dollars a year!"

"Ten are plenty, and to spare," said Hallie, "but we pay them handsomely. One chef at three thousand dollars; two next-bests at two thousand dollars each, four thousand; two at one thousand dollars apiece, two thousand; five at eight hundred dollars, four thousand. That's thirteen thousand—half what we paid before, and the difference in service between a kitchen maid and a scientific artist."

"Fifty per cent saved on wages, and five hundred per cent added to skill," Owen continued. "And you can go right on and add ninety per cent saving in fuel, ninety per cent in plant, fifty per cent in utensils, and—how much is it, Hallie, in materials?"

Hallie looked very important.

"Even when they first started, when food was shamefully expensive and required all manner of tests and examinations, the saving was all of sixty per cent. Now it is fully eighty per cent."

"That makes a good deal all told, Uncle John," Jerrold quietly remarked, handing me a bit of paper. "You see, it does leave a margin of profit."

I looked rather helplessly at the figures, also at Hallie.

"It is a shame, Uncle, to hurry you so, but the sooner you get these little matters clear in your head, the better. We have these great food furnishing companies, now, all over the country; and they have market gardens and dairies, and so on, of their own. There is a Food Bureau in every city, and a National Food Bureau, with international relations. The best scientific knowledge is used to study food values, to improve old materials and develop new ones; there's a tremendous gain."

"But—do the people swallow things as directed by the government?" I protested. "Is there no chance to go and buy what you want to eat when you want it?"

They rose to their feet with one accord. Jerrold seized me by the hand.

"Come on, Uncle!" he cried. "Now is as good a time as any. You shall see our food department—come to scoff and remain to prey—if you like."

The elevator took us down, and I was led unresistingly among their shining modernities.

"Here is the source of supply," said Owen, showing where the basement supply room connected with a clean, airy subway under the glass-paved sidewalk. "Ice we make, drinking water we distill, fuel is wired to us; but the food stuffs are brought this way. Come down early enough and you would find these arteries of the city flowing steadily with—"

"Milk and honey," put in Jerrold.

"With the milk train, the meat train, the vegetable train, and so on."

"Ordered beforehand?" I asked.

"Ordered beforehand. Up to midnight you may send down word as to the kind of mushrooms you prefer—and no extra charge. During the day you can still order, but there's a trifle more expense—not much. But most of us are more than content to have our managers cater for us. From the home outfit you may choose at any time. There are lists upstairs, and here is the array."

There were but few officials in this part of the great establishment at this hour, but we were politely shown about by a scholarly looking man in white linen, who had been reading as we entered. They took me between rows of glass cases, standing as books do in the library, and showed me the day's baking; the year's preserves; the fragrant, colorful shelves of such fruit and vegetables as were not fresh-picked from day to day.

"We don't get today's strawberries till the local ones are ripe," Jerrold told us. "These are yesterday's, and pretty good yet."

"Excuse me, but those have just come in," said the white-linen person. "This morning's picking, from Maryland."

I tasted them with warm approval. There was a fascinating display of cakes and cookies, some old favorites, some of a new but attractive aspect; and in glass-doored separate ice-chambers, meats, fish, milk, and butter.

"Can people come in here and get what they want, though?" I inquired triumphantly.

"They can, and occasionally they do. But what it will take you some time to realize, John," my sister explained, "is the different attitude of people towards their food. We are all not only well fed—sufficiently fed—but so wisely fed that we seldom think of wanting anything further. When we do we can order from upstairs, come down to the eating room and order, send to the big depots if it is some rare thing, or even come in like this. To the regular purchasers it is practically free."

"And how if you are a stranger—a man in the street?"

"In every city in our land you may go into any eating house and find food as good—and cheap—as this," said Hallie, triumphantly.

HERLAND *

Home and husbands are profoundly altered in *Moving the Mountain*. In Gilman's gently playful utopian world of women, *Herland*, they are eliminated altogether—that is, until three American men stumble into its midst. In the community of sisterhood, these women embody a whole range of attributes men rarely believe women can have. They are powerful, agile, inventive, assertive, courageous. They shape their world with a social consciousness and a degree of humanity the men find astonishing. These three "typical" American men of 1915 are: Terry, wealthy, exploitative womanizer; Jeff, sentimental poet; and Van, the narrator, a man of reason, a sociologist. They initially meet and then learn to love, each in a different way, three typical Herlanders: Alima, Celis, and Ellador.

The story of *Herland* is the journey of the men, a journey that involves not physical movement, but developing consciousness. Like the earlier utopian novel, it is a story of conversion. And it is a witty and wisely satiric story. With ingenuous innocence, the women expose the ludicrous, but

Herland was serialized in Volume 6 of The Forerunner (1915) and was published separately for the first time in 1978 by Pantheon Books.

deeply cherished, beliefs and behavior of contemporary society. With grace and skill, qualities often lacking in ideologues of all persuasions, Gilman mischievously makes her case.

In *Herland*, the men find themselves for the first time viewed as sex objects, as potential fathers, for these women have no other concept of sexuality than that associated with parenting. Gilman's notion of a sex object is uniquely hers. It goes like this. Cow and bull, mare and stallion, are different sexes, but they are of the same species, and the qualities they share as members of the same species are more important than the differences they have. But among humans the female depends on the male for economic survival. Man is woman's economic environment and so the sex distinction is exaggerated. Indeed, the use of sex distinction, she says, is the way most females make a living. Thus, women are oversexed.

Take the difference, for example, between a wild cow and a milk cow. The wild cow is a female and produces adequate milk for her young. Otherwise she is essentially bovine. She is light, agile, and strong. She runs, jumps, and fights as does the male of the species. But humans have developed artficially the cow's capacity for producing milk. "She has become a walking milk machine," Gilman wrote in *Women and Economics*. The milk cow is oversexed. Physically women also belong to a species that is active and vigorous. But they have been so bred to sex activity that we can actually speak of a "feminine hand" or a "feminine foot," while we never refer to a "feminine paw" or a "feminine hoof." But the hand and the foot are not secondary sex characteristics, except insofar as men prize women for their smallness and feebleness. Such sex distinctions occur only in the human species, but they do not exist in Herland. When the men arrive, they are seen as potential fathers, as well as humans, and so they become sex objects, which makes them very uncomfortable.

In the opening scene, "The Expectation," excerpted below, the three men are musing about what this woman's world, about which they have heard, might be like. In "The

Arrival," the second excerpt, they land their plane and with astonishment examine the beautiful country, convinced that the signs of civilization presuppose the presence of men. Suddenly the inhabitants, all women, appear, and the confrontation that ensues begins the men's education.

In the final excerpt called "The Conversion," the reader gets a glimmer of the metamorphosis Van has undergone. The book concludes with the return of two of the men to America. Jeff, blithesomely happy, chooses to remain. Terry, demanding his husbandly right by leaping on his unwilling bride, is found guilty of antisocial behavior and expelled from the community. Van and Ellador decide to leave too, to embark on a visit to Van's world, she with joyful anticipation of the wonderful experiences to come, he with growing unease.

The Expectation

Jeff was a tender soul. I think he thought that country—if there was one—was just blossoming with roses and babies and canaries and tidies, and all that sort of thing.

And Terry, in his secret heart, had visions of a sort of sublimated summer resort—just Girls and Girls and Girls—and that he was going to be—well, Terry was popular among women even when there were other men around, and it's not to be wondered at that he had pleasant dreams of what might happen. I could see it in his eyes as he lay there, looking at the long blue rollers slipping by, and fingering that impressive moustache of his.

But I thought—then—that I could form a far clearer idea of what was before us than either of them.

"You're all off, boys," I insisted. "If there is such a place—and there does seem some foundation for believing it—you'll find it's built on a sort of matriarchal principle, that's all. The men have a separate cult of their own, less socially developed than the women, and make them an annual visit—a sort of wedding call. This is a condition known to have existed—here's just a survival. They've got some peculiarly isolated valley or table-land up there, and their primeval customs have survived. That's all there is to it."

"How about the boys?" Jeff asked.

"Oh, the men take them away as soon as they are five or six, you see."

"And how about this danger theory all our guides were so sure of?"

"Danger enough, Terry, and we'll have to be mighty careful. Women of that stage of culture are quite able to defend themselves and have no welcome for unseasonable visitors."

We talked and talked.

And with all my airs of sociological superiority I was no nearer than any of them.

It was funny though, in the light of what we did find, those extremely clear ideas of ours as to what a country of women would be like. It was no use to tell ourselves and one another that all this was idle speculation. We were idle and we did speculate, on the ocean voyage and the river voyage, too.

"Admitting the improbability," we'd begin solemnly, and then launch out again.

"They would fight among themselves," Terry insisted. "Women always do. We mustn't look to find any sort of order and organization."

"You're dead wrong," Jeff told him. "It will be like a nunnery under an abbess—a peaceful, harmonious sisterhood."

I snorted derision at this idea.

"Nuns, indeed! Your peaceful sisterhoods were all celibate, Jeff, and under vows of obedience. These are just women, and mothers, and where there's motherhood you don't find sisterhood—not much." . . .

The Arrival

So we sailed low, crossing back and forth, quartering the country as we went, and studying it. We saw—I can't remember now how much of this we noted then and how much was supplemented by our later knowledge, but we could not help seeing this much, even on that excited day—a land in a state of perfect cultivation, where even the forests looked as if they were cared for; a land that looked like an enormous park, only that it was even more evidently an enormous garden.

"I don't see any cattle," I suggested, but Terry was silent. We were approaching a village.

I confess that we paid small attention to the clean, well-built roads, to the attractive architecture, to the ordered beauty of the little town. We had our glasses out; even Terry, setting his machine for a spiral glide, clapped the binoculars to his eyes.

They heard our whirring screw. They ran out of the houses— they gathered in from the fields, swift-running light figures, crowds of them. We stared and stared until it was almost too late to catch the levers, sweep off and rise again; and then we held our peace for a long run upward.

"Gosh!" said Terry, after a while.

"Only women there—and children," Jeff urged excitedly.

"But they look—why, this is a *civilized* country!" I protested. "There must be men." . . .

[*Having landed the plane, the three men disembark to begin their exploration. They come upon an extraordinarily beautiful town. There is no noise, no dirt, no smoke, no movement—no sign that their arrival was noticed.*]

And then, turning a corner, we came into a broad paved space and saw before us a band of women standing close together in even order, evidently waiting for us.

We stopped a moment, and looked back. The street behind was closed by another band, marching steadily, shoulder to shoulder. We went on—there seemed no other way to do—and presently found ourselves quite surrounded by this close-massed multitude, women, all of them, but—

They were not young. They were not old. They were not, in the girl sense, beautiful; they were not in the least ferocious; and yet, as I looked from face to face, calm, grave, wise, wholly unafraid, evidently assured and determined, I had the funniest feeling—a feeling that I traced back and back in memory until I caught up with it at last. It was that sense of being hopelessly in the wrong that I had so often felt in early youth when my short legs' utmost effort failed to overcome the fact that I was late to school.

Jeff felt it too; I could see he did. We felt like small boys, very small boys, caught doing mischief in some gracious lady's house. But Terry showed no such consciousness. I saw his quick eyes darting here and there, estimating numbers, measuring distances, judging chances of escape. He examined the close ranks about us, reaching back far on every side, and murmured softly to me, "Every one of 'em over forty as I'm a sinner."

Yet they were not old women. Each was in the full bloom of rosy health, erect, serene, standing sure-footed and light as any pugilist. They had no weapons, and we had, but we had no wish to shoot. . . .

In all our discussions and speculations we had always unconsciously assumed that the women, whatever else they might be, would be young. Most men do think that way, I fancy.

"Woman" in the abstract is young, and we assume, charming. As they get older they pass off the stage, somehow, into private ownership mostly, or out of it altogether. But these good ladies were very much on the stage, and yet any of them might have been a grandmother.

We looked for nervousness—there was none.

For terror, perhaps—there was none.

For uneasiness, for curiosity, for excitement—and all we saw was what might have been a vigilance committee of women doctors, as cool as cucumbers, and evidently meaning to take us to task for being there.

Six of them stepped forward now, one on either side of each of us and indicated that we were to go with them. We thought best to accede, at first anyway, and marched along, one of these close at each elbow, and the others in close masses before, behind, on both sides. . . .

The Conversion

[*The men are each assigned a teacher, an older woman who introduces each to the language of Herland as well as to the nature of the collective life in that society. The three Herlanders are as eager to learn about the outside world as they are to explain their own, and frequently ask guileless, but astute, questions.*]

As I learned more and more to appreciate what these women had accomplished, the less proud I was of what we, with all our manhood, had done.

You see, they had had no wars. They had had no kings, and no priests, and no aristocracies. They were sisters, and as they grew, they grew together—not by competition, but by united action.

We tried to put in a good word for competition, and they were keenly interested. Indeed we soon found, from their earnest questions of us, that they were prepared to believe our world must be better than theirs. They were not sure; they wanted to know; but there was no such arrogance about them as might have been expected.

We rather spread ourselves, telling of the advantages of competition: how it developed fine qualities; that without it there would be "no stimulus to industry." Terry was very strong on that point.

"No stimulus to industry," they repeated, with that puzzled look we had learned to know so well. "*Stimulus? To Industry?* But don't you *like* to work?"

"No man would work unless he had to," Terry declared.

"Oh, no *man!* You mean that is one of your sex distinctions?"

"No, indeed!" he said hastily. "No one, I mean, man or woman, would work without incentive. Competition is the—the motor power, you see."

"It is not with us," they explained gently, "so it is hard for us to understand. Do you mean, for instance, that with you no mother would work for her children without the stimulus of competition?"

No, he admitted that he did not mean that. Mothers, he supposed, would of course work for their children in the home; but the world's work was different—that had to be done by men, and required the competitive element.

All our teachers were eagerly interested.

"We want so much to know—you have the whole world to tell us of, and we have only our little land! And there are two of you—the two sexes—to love and help one another. It must be a rich and wonderful world. Tell us—what is the work of the world, that men do—which we have not here?"

"Oh, everything," Terry said grandly. "The men do everything, with us." He squared his broad shoulders and lifted his chest. "We do not allow our women to work. Women are loved—idolized—honored—kept in the home to care for the children."

"What is 'the home'?" asked Somel a little wistfully.

But Zava begged: "Tell me first, do *no* women work, really?"

"Why, yes," Terry admitted. "Some have to, of the poorer sort."

"About how many—in your country?"

"About seven or eight million," said Jeff. . . .

[*As months pass, each of the three men responds quite differently to Herland life. Jeff is completely uncritical in his total and immediate acceptance of the new world. Van only slowly is persuaded that this woman's world is more humane and more joyful than his own. Terry, restless and angry, makes no concessions to what he sees as the challenge to his superior manhood. He tries to persuade his Herland wife to indulge in the pleasures of sexual love, but he cannot long accept her gentle refusal. Pushed beyond the limits of his male pride, he demands by force his husbandly prerogative, only to be humiliated as she and her friends overpower him. He is convicted of anti-social behavior and given the most serious sentence possible in Herland: exile.*]

Terry was under guard now, all the time, known as unsafe, convicted of what was to them an unpardonable sin.

He laughed at their chill horror. "Parcel of old maids!" he called them. "They're all old maids—children or not. They don't know the first thing about Sex."

When Terry said *Sex*, sex with a very large *S*, he meant the male sex, naturally: its special values, its profound conviction of being "the life force," its cheerful ignoring of the true life process, and its interpretation of the other sex solely from its own point of view.

I had learned to see these thing very differently since living with Ellador; and as for Jeff, he was so thoroughly Herlandized that he wasn't fair to Terry, who fretted sharply in his new restraint. . . .

We had quite easily come to accept the Herland life as normal, because it was normal—none of us make any outcry over mere health and peace and happy industry. And the abnormal, to which we are all so sadly well acclimated, [Ellador] had never seen.

The two things she cared most to hear about, and wanted most to see, were these: the beautiful relation of marriage and the lovely women who were mothers and nothing else; beyond these, her keen active mind hungered eagerly for the world life. . . .

In missing men, we three visitors had naturally missed the larger part of life, and had unconsciously assumed that they must miss it too. It took me a long time to realize—Terry never did realize—how little it meant to them. When we say *men, man, manly, manhood,* and all the other masculine derivatives, we have in the background of our minds a huge, vague, crowded picture of the world and all its activities. To grow up and "be a man," to "act like a man"—the meaning and connotation is wide indeed. That vast background is full of marching columns of men, of changing lines of men, of long processions of men; of men steering their ships into new seas, exploring unknown mountains, breaking horses, herding cattle, ploughing and sowing, and reaping, toiling at the forge and furnace, digging in the mine, building roads and bridges and high cathedrals, managing great businesses, teaching in all the colleges, preaching in all the churches; of men everywhere, doing everything—"the world."

And when we say *women,* we think *female*—the sex.

But to these women, in the unbroken sweep of this two-thousand-year-old feminine civilization, the word *woman* called up all that big background, so far as they had gone in social development; and the word *man* meant to them only *male*—the sex. . . .

They had no faintest approach to such a thing in their minds, knowing nothing of the custom of marital indulgence among us. To them the one high purpose of motherhood had been for so long the governing law of life, and the contribution of the father, though known to them, so distinctly another method to the same end, that they could not, with all their effort, get the point of view of the male creature whose desires quite ignore parentage and seek only for what we euphoniously term "the joys of love."

When I tried to tell Ellador that women too felt so, with us, she drew away from me, and tried to grasp intellectually what she could in no way sympathize with.

"You mean—that with you—love between man and woman expresses itself in that way—without regard to motherhood? To parentage, I mean," she added carefully.

"Yes, surely. It is love we think of—the deep sweet love between two. Of course we want children, and children come—but that is not what we think about."

"But—but—it seems so against nature!" she said. "None of the creatures we know do that. Do other animals—in your country?"

"We are not animals!" I replied with some sharpness. "At least we are something more—something higher. This is a far nobler and more beautiful relation, as I have explained before. Your view seems to us rather—shall I say, practical?Prosaic? Merely a means to an end! With us—oh, my dear girl—cannot you see? Cannot you feel? It is the last, sweetest, highest consummation of mutual love." . . .

"Be patient with me, dear," she urged sweetly. "I know it is hard for you. And I begin to see—a little—how Terry was so driven to crime."

"Oh, come, that's a pretty hard word for it. After all, Alima was his wife, you know," I urged, feeling at the moment a sudden burst of sympathy for poor Terry. For a man of his temperament—and habits—it must have been an unbearable situation.

But Ellador, for all her wide intellectual grasp, and the broad sympathy in which their religion trained them, could not make allowance for such—to her—sacrilegious brutality. . . .

Well—it was hard. He was madly in love with Alima, really—more so than he had ever been before, and their tempestuous courtship, quarrels, and reconciliations had fanned the flame. And then when he sought by that supreme conquest which seems so natural a thing to that type of man, to force her to love him as her master—to have the sturdy athletic furious woman rise up and master him—she and her friends—it was no wonder he raged.

Come to think of it, I do not recall a similar case in all history or fiction. Women have killed themselves rather than submit to outrage; they have killed the outrager; they have escaped; or they have submitted—sometimes seeming to get on very well with the victor afterward. . . .

"She kicked me," confided the embittered prisoner—he had to talk to someone. "I was doubled up with the pain, of course, and she jumped on me and yelled. . . . She's as strong as a horse. And of course a man's helpless when you hit him like that. No woman with a shade of decency—"

I had to grin at that, and even Terry did, sourly. He wasn't given to reasoning, but it did strike him that an assault like his rather waived considerations of decency. . . .

WITH HER IN OURLAND *

With Her in Ourland, the sequel to *Herland*, follows Ellador and Van as they travel the world, observing, analyzing, and talking, endlessly talking. Unlike *Herland*, in which Gilman's ideas are played out dramatically, *Ourland* is a series of loosely connected dialogues, in which Ellador's disarming questions and impressions cause Van, and the reader, to be shaken from the outrageous but unexamined notions that many of us hold deeply and defend vigorously.

It is not the style alone that makes reading *Ourland* difficult today. While revealing the absurd ideas that others uphold, Gilman unwittingly betrays her own. However extraordinary her humane and constructive vision is in general, she shares many odious attitudes upheld by the intellectual community of a hundred years ago. In some of her published writing, in *Ourland* in particular, and in her private correspondence, she expresses beliefs that are anti-Semitic, chauvinist, and racist. Although such sentiments dominated the intellectual circles of the country, and although Gilman represents the least outlandish wing in

*With Her in Ourland *was published in the final volume, Volume 7, of* The Forerunner *(1916) and never appeared separately.*

those circles, still her ideas are dreadful and they seriously mar her contribution as a social analyst and theorist.

The excerpts below were *not* chosen to expose Gilman's vulnerabilities but to highlight her exposure of others'.

[Ellador is distressed to discover that a world war has erupted.]

"We have always had war," Terry explained. "Ever since the world began—at least as far as history goes, we have had war. It is human nature."

"Human?" asked Ellador.

"Yes," he said, "human. Bad as it is, it is evidently human nature to do it. Nations advance, the race is improved by fighting. It is the law of nature." . . .

"Yes," he repeated, "you will have to accept life as it is. To make war is human activity."

"Are some of the soldiers women?" she inquired.

"Women! Of course not! They are men—strong, brave men. Once in a while some abnormal woman becomes a soldier, I believe, and in Dahomey—that's in Africa—one of the black tribes has women soldiers. But speaking generally it is men—of course."

"Then why do you call it 'human nature'?" she persisted. "If it was human, wouldn't they both do it?"

So he tried to explain that it was a human necessity, but it was done by the men because they could do it—and the women couldn't.

"The women are just as indispensable—in their way. They give us the children—you know—men cannot do that."

To hear Terry talk you would think he had never left home.

Ellador listened to him with her grave gentle smile. She always seemed to understand not only what one said, but all the background of sentiment and habit behind.

"Do you call bearing children 'human nature'?" she asked him.

"It's woman nature," he answered. "It's her work."

"Then why do you not call fighting 'man nature'—instead of 'human'?"

Terry's conclusion of an argument with Ellador was the simple one of going somewhere else. . . .

[Van, too, confronts Ellador's logical mind.]

The one special and predominant distinction given to her studies by her supreme femininity was what gave me the most numerous, and I may say, unpleasant surprises. In my world studies I had always assumed that humanity did thus and so, but she was continually shearing through the tangled facts with her sharp distinction that this and this phenomenon was due to masculinity alone.

"But Ellador," I protested, "why do you say—'the male Scandinavians continually indulged in piracy,' and 'the male Spaniards practiced terrible cruelties,' and so on? It sounds so—invidious—as if you were trying to make out a case against men."

"Why, I wouldn't do that for anything!" she protested. "I'm only trying to understand the facts. You don't mind when I say 'the male Phoenicians made great progress in navigation,' or 'the male Greeks developed great intelligence,' do you?"

"That's different," I answered. "They did do those things."

"Didn't they do the others, too?"

"Well—yes—they did them, of course; but why rub it in that they were exclusively males?"

"But weren't they, dear? Really? Did the Norse women raid the coasts of England and France? Did the Spanish women cross the ocean and torture the poor Aztecs?"

"They would have if they could!" I protested.

"So would the Phoenician women and Grecian women in the other cases—wouldn't they?"

I hesitated.

[Ellador is unprepared for the waste, corruption, and poverty she finds in the United States]

"I had warning that Europe was at war, and had read about it a little. It was like going into a—a slaughter-house, for the first time.

"Then all I learned in my studies in Europe prepared me to find what I did find in Asia—Asia was in some ways better than I had been told—in some ways worse. But here! Oh, Van!" That look of gray anguish had settled on her face again. She seized my arms, held me fast, searched my face as if I was withholding something. Big slow tears welled over and dropped. "This is the top of the tree, Van; this is the last young nation, beginning over again in a New World—a New World! Here was everything to make life richly happy—everything. And you had all the dreadful record of the past to guide you, to teach you at least what not to do. You had courage; you had independence; you had intelligence, education, opportunity. And such splendid principles to start with—such high ideals. And then all kinds of people coming! Oh, surely, surely, surely this should be the Crown of the World!

"Why, Van—Europe was like a man with—with delirium tremens. Asia was like something gnarled and twisted with hopeless age. But America is a Splendid Child . . . with . . ." She covered her face with her hands.

I couldn't stand this. I was an American, and she was my wife. I took her in my arms.

"Look here, you blessed Herlander," I said, "I'm not going to have my country wiped off the map in disgrace. You must remember that all judgment is comparative. You cannot compare any other country with your country for two reasons: first your long isolation; and second that miraculous manlessness of yours." . . .

"Here you are [she replied], a democracy—free—the power in the hands of the people. You let that group of conservatives saddle you with a constitution which has so interfered with free action that you've forgotten you had it. In this ridiculous helplessness—like poor old Gulliver—bound by the Lilliputians—you have sat open-eyed, not moving a finger, and allowed individuals—mere private persons—to help themselves to the biggest, richest, best things in the country. You know what is thought of a housekeeper who lets dishonest servants run the house with waste and robbery, or of a king who is openly preyed upon by extortionate parasites—what can we think of a Democracy, a huge, strong, young Democracy, allowing itself to become infested with such parasites as these? Talk of bloodsuckers! You have your oil-suckers and coal-suckers, water-suckers and wood-suckers, railroad-suckers and farm-suckers—

this splendid young country is crawling with them, and has not the intelligence, the energy, to shake them off."

"But most of us do not believe in Socialism, you see," I protested.

"You believe in it altogether too much," she replied flatly. "You seem to think that every step toward decent economic health and development has been appropriated by Socialism, and that you cannot do one thing toward economic freedom and progress unless you become Socialists!" . . .

She spoke most encouragingly, most approvingly, of the special efforts we were making in small groups or as individuals to socialize various industries and functions, but with far more fervor of the great "movements."

"The biggest of all, and closest related, are your women's movement and labor movement. Both seem to be swiftly growing stronger. The most inclusive forward-looking system is Socialism, of course. What a splendid vision of immediate possibilities that is. I cannot accustom myself to your not seeing it at once. Of course, the reason is plain: Your minds are full of your ancient mistakes, too; not so much racial and religious, as in beliefs of economic absurdities. It is so funny!"

[Van is surprised at Ellador's critical attitude toward the women she meets in America. She explains her point of view.]

"Put yourself in my place for a moment, Van. Suppose in Herland we had a lot of—subject men. Blame us all you want for doing it, but look at the men. Little creatures, undersized and generally feeble. Cowardly and not ashamed of it. Kept for sex purposes only or as servants, or both, usually both. I confess I'm asking something difficult of your imagination, but try to think of Herland women, each with a soft man she kept to cook for her, to wait upon her, and to—'love' when she pleased. Ignorant men mostly. Poor men, almost all, having to ask their owners for money and tell what they wanted for it. Some of them utterly degraded creatures, kept in houses for common use—as women are kept here. Some of them quite gay and happy—pet men, with pet names and presents showered upon them. Most of them contented, piously accepting kitchen work as their duty, living by the religion and laws and customs the women made.

Some of them left out and made fun of for being left—not owned at all—and envying those who were! Allow for a surprising percentage of mutual love and happiness, even under these conditions, but also for ghastly depths of misery and a general low level of mere submission to the inevitable. Then in this state of degradation fancy these men for the most part quite content to make monkeys of themselves by wearing the most ridiculous clothes. Fancy them, men, with men's bodies, though enfeebled, wearing open work lace underclothing, with little ribbons all strung through it; wearing dresses never twice alike and almost always foolish; wearing hats—" she fixed me with a steady eye in which a growing laughter twinkled—"wearing such hats as your women wear!"

At this I threw up my hands. "I can't!" I said. "It's all off. I followed you with increasing difficulty, even through the lace and baby ribbon, but I stop there. Men wear such hats! Men! I tell you it is unthinkable!"

"Unthinkable for such men?"

"Such men are unthinkable, really—contemptible, skulking, cowardly spaniels! They would deserve all they got."

"Why aren't you blaming the women of Herland for treating them so, Van?"

"Oh!" said I, and "Yes," said I, "I begin to see, my dear Herlander, why you're down on the women."

"Good," she agreed. "It's all true, what you say about the men, nothing could be blacker than that story. But the women, Van, the women! They are not dead! They are here, and in your country they have plenty of chance to grow. How can they bear their position, Van? How can they stand it another day? Don't they know they are *Women*?"

"No," said I slowly. "They think they are—women."

We both laughed rather sadly.

Presently she said, "We have to take the facts as we find them. Emotion does not help us any. It's no use being horrified at a—hermit crab—that's the way he is. This is the woman man made—how is she going to get over it?"

"You don't forget the ones who have gotten over it, do you? And all the splendid work they are doing?"

"I'm afraid I did for a moment," she admitted. "Besides—so

much of their effort is along side lines, and some of it in precisely the wrong direction."

"What would you have them do?"

"What would you have those inconceivable men of Herland do?" she countered. "What would you say to them—to rouse them?"

"I'd try to make them realize that they were *men*," I said. "That's the first thing."

"Exactly. And if the smooth, plump, crazily dressed creatures answered, 'A true man is always glad to be supported by the woman he loves,' what would you say to that?"

"I should try to make him realize what the world really was," I answered slowly, "and to see what was a man's place in it."

"And if he answered you—a hundred million strong—'A man's place is in the home!'—what would you say then?"

"It would be pretty hard to say anything—if men were like that."

"Yes, and it is pretty hard to say anything when women are like that—it doesn't reach them."

"But there is the whole women's movement—surely they are changing, improving."

[Ellador acknowledges that great change is occurring, primarily because so many women are leaving their homes to seek work in the larger community.]

"It would be inconceivable that they should have been so unutterably degraded for so long and not shown the results of it, the limitations. Instead of blaming them I should have been rejoicing at the wonderful speed with which they have surged forward as fast as any door was opened, even a crack. I have been looking at what might be called the unconscious as apart from the conscious women's movement, and it comforts me much."

"Just what do you mean?"

"I mean the women's clubs, here in this country especially, and largest of all the economic changes—the immense numbers who are at work."

"Didn't they always work? The poor ones, that is?"

"Oh yes, at home. I mean human work."

"Wage earning?"

"That, incidentally, as a descriptive term; but it would be a different grade of work, even without that."

"So I've heard people say, some people. But what is there superior in doing some fractional monotonous little job like bookkeeping, for instance, as compared with the management and performance of all the intimate tasks in a household?"

I was so solemn about this that she took me seriously, at least for a moment.

"It isn't the difference between a bookkeeper and a housekeeper that must be considered; it is the difference between an organized business world that needs bookkeeping and an unorganized world of separate families with no higher work than to eat, sleep, and keep alive."

[Van's love for Ellador has changed and grown.]

Her face had changed, somewhat, in our two years of travel and study; there was a sadness in it, such as it never wore in Herland, such as I had never seen in anyone while there; and for all her quiet courtesy, her gentle patience, her scientific interest and loving kindness, there was a lonely look about her, as of some albatross in a poultry yard.

To me she was even more tender and delicately sympathetic than in our first young happiness. She seemed to be infinitely sorry for me, though carefully refraining from expressing it. Our common experiences, our studying and seeing so much together, had drawn us very close, and for my own part I had a curious sense of growing detachedness from the conditions about me and an overwhelming attachment to her which transcended every other tie. It seemed as if my love for her as a human being, such love as a brother, a sister, a friend might feel, was now so much greater than my love of her as a woman, my woman, that I could not miss that fulfillment much while so contented in the larger relation.

I thought of the many cases I had known where the situation was absolutely reversed, where a man loved a woman solely because of sex desire, without ever knowing her nature as a person, without even wanting to.

I was very happy with Ellador.

[Ellador too has enlarged her universe.]

"At first I thought of men just as males—a Herlander would, you know. Now I know that men are people, too, just as much as women are; and it is as one person to another that I feel this big love for you, Van. You are so nice to live with. You are such good company. I never get tired of you. I like to play with you, and to work with you. I admire and enjoy the way you do things. And when we sit down quietly, near together—it makes me so happy, Van!"